D0114516

Queen Victoria's Maharajah
DULEEP SINGH
1838–93

BY

MICHAEL ALEXANDER

AND

SUSHILA ANAND

TAPLINGER PUBLISHING COMPANY

NEW YORK

First published in the United States in 1980 by
TAPLINGER PUBLISHING CO., INC.
New York, New York
Copyright © 1980 by Michael Alexander
and Sushila Anand
All rights reserved. Printed in Great Britain.
Library of Congress Catalog Card Number: 79–5426
ISBN 0–8008–6567–7

Contents

Illustrations

vii

Illustrations Nos. 10, 11, 12, 13, 14, 15, 16, 19, 22, 23, 24, 25, 26, 27, and 29 are reproduced by gracious permission of Her Majesty The Queen.

The authors and publishers are most grateful to all of the copyright holders for permission to reproduce the pictures.

Acknowledgements

THE extensive and most interesting material from the Royal Archives is reproduced by gracious permission of Her Majesty The Queen.

Sincere acknowledgement is also due to Sir Robin Mackworth-Young and his staff at the Royal Archives at Windsor Castle, in particular to Miss Jane Langton, MVO.

The authors would also like to thank the following for various forms of assistance: Nazir Ahmad; Dr Mulk Raj Anand; Bruce Anderson; Pamela, Lady Aylesford; Anne Baker; Oliver Baxter; Professor James R. Casada; Arabella Churchill; Ronald Eden; C.M. Farrer; Mark Girouard; Michael Goedhuis; John Gore; Richard Hall; the Hon. Sir John Henniker-Major; the Marquess of Hertford; the staff of the India Office Library; the Earl of Iveagh; Dr Ahmad Nabi Khan; the Earl of Leven; Edith Broun-Lindsay; Anthony Lort-Phillips; R.P. McDouall; the Marquess of Normanby; Michael Riviere; A.K. Robertson; Dolly Sahiar; K.S. Thapar and Ben Weinreb.

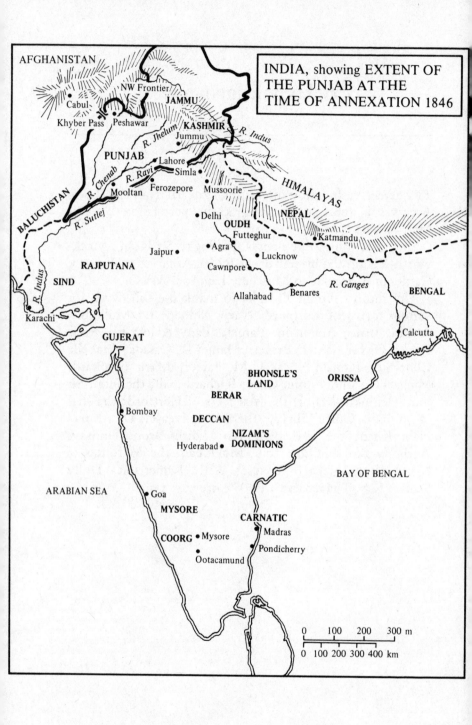

INDIA, showing EXTENT OF
THE PUNJAB AT THE
TIME OF ANNEXATION 1846

CHAPTER I

The Punjab Annexed

A T the beginning of the nineteenth century, the Honourable East India Company, by a combination of commercial acumen and military opportunism, was master of most of India. Among the remaining independent states, the Punjab was the most strategic of its territorial aspirations. India, it was feared, might be invaded through the arid passes of the North-West Frontier: Alexander the Great had moved that way into the 'Land of the Five Rivers' two thousand years earlier; the Mughals had followed to conquer the subcontinent, Afghans and Persians had plundered the fertile plains; there had been alarmist talk that Napoleon with Russian help, planned to follow in the footsteps of Alexander; and now Russia was again threatening to advance her empire step by step in that direction through the independent khanates of Central Asia. Both for commercial exploitation and the security of the subcontinent the company wanted control of the Punjab. Runjit Singh, the great Sikh warrior who had consolidated the kingdom from the disunited clans of his caste and made himself their maharajah, wanted his power endorsed and his territory extended.

Runjit Singh, 'Lion of the Punjab', was wary enough to know that the British were unlikely to be beaten in battle, but he thought himself wise enough to outwit them politically. In 1831, on what was described as another Field of Cloth of Gold, he made a treaty of friendship with the company which he hoped would allow him to pursue his ambitions unopposed. To the British, this diminutive tyrant, pockmarked and blind in one eye, was a man to be admired and he in his turn admired them, especially their military discipline which he sought to instil in his own army with the help of European officers. Runjit Singh stuck to his treaty of friendship – there was co-operation in an expedition to Afghanistan; there was resignation at British infiltration of his territory south of the Sutlej; there was tolerance at their occupation of the Sind he coveted himself. At least he acquired Jammu, Kashmir and Peshawar. Still trusting in the two-edged alliance, he seemed content to amass treasure and debauch his remaining days.

Duleep Singh,* the hero of this story, was the last of the four 'acknowledged' sons of Runjit Singh. He was born on 4 September 1838, at a time when the great man was unlikely to have been able to father a child for, apart from a preference for the company of beautiful boys, he had had two strokes and was partially paralysed; in addition, an indulgence in laudanum, brandy fortified with powdered pearls, and fat quails stuffed with spices, had wrought havoc with his liver.

Duleep Singh's mother was Jindan Kour, daughter of a palace doorkeeper, a woman of considerable character and influence in the royal household. Adopted by Runjit Singh at an early age, her ready wit and lack of sexual inhibitions had made her well qualified to organize the more outlandish entertainments of the court. It was said that the ageing Maharajah took perverse pleasure in her amours even to the extent of encouraging her lovemaking with his current favourite, formerly a *bhishti* or water-carrier in the palace courtyards. On the birth of a boy, Runjit Singh was amused to accept the flattering pretence that the child was his; by officially recognizing him as such he made more certain the continuance of his dynasty.

Runjit Singh died the following summer and was duly burned, along with a number of his self-sacrificing women-

---

* The spelling of Duleep Singh varies throughout the text. The authors have used that version by which the Maharajah was christened and which he used in signature.

folk, on a sandalwood pyre by the Ganges. While he lived, his personal character and prestige, backed by his large army, had maintained a firm peace in the Punjab and upheld the treaty of friendship with the British. He died leaving a fateful legacy – a divided, ambitious family, a weak heir addicted to opium, intriguing politicians, and a disintegrating army command. 'The break-up of the Punjab will probably begin with murder. It is their way,' Lord Ellenborough, governor general of India, predicted.[1] In fact no member of the ruling family would be sure of his life in the ruthless struggle for power fought out over the next four years.

During those desperate days the young Duleep Singh could hardly be considered an early candidate for head of state. His ambitious mother removed him to the countryside until such time as her intrigues could influence the dynastic struggle in his interest. A native painting of the period shows the three-year-old boy, a royal aigrette in the turban of his faith, riding in a canopied wagon drawn by two white stallions. He sits beside his bosomy mother, whose ladies loll behind. From the absence of shadow it would seem to be the height of noon; characters from the nearby village decorate the scene – a water-carrier, a hunter with his hawk, a woman pulling her two children in a tiny cart; every moving thing, including a hurrying hare, stirs up its cloud of dust. Other than such pictorial glimpses, there is little on record of Duleep Singh's earliest days. By the time the boy had reached the age of six, most of his relations had died or been murdered. A powerful faction backed him as the last surviving recognized son of Runjit Singh and on 18 September 1843 he was proclaimed maharajah in Lahore.

Though little Duleep Singh attended all the council meetings seated on the royal throne, and was paraded through the streets of Amritsar and Lahore high up in the silver howdah of the royal elephant, his mother and her current lover were the actual rulers of the state. The only threat to their power came from the ever-increasing ambition of the Sikh legions, now ruled by regimental committees rather than the palace generals. A test of strength came when the Rani Jindan's brother, Jewahir Singh, brought about the death of another brother who had the support of a powerful military group. It led to an occasion that must have been profoundly unsettling to the psyche of one small boy.

The troops had sworn to avenge the murder of their champion and summoned the suspect sirdar to appear before them. He had no choice but to face the large force of clamorous soldiery outside the gates of Lahore. To enhance his prestige and for a measure of protection he sat the young Duleep Singh beside him on his elephant and was followed by the Rani Jindan and her attendant women. The rani, who had considerable influence over the troops, being regarded by them as 'the mother of the people', pleaded her brother's cause and offered extra pay for their support. Encouraged by their apparently accommodating mood he prepared to deliver his conciliatory address. Bugles suddenly sounded and drums began to beat, upon which signal his elephant was seized and made to kneel. Duleep Singh was snatched from the howdah at the same moment as his uncle was bayoneted through the side and a bullet blew out his brains. The terrified child was held that night by the soldiers, who feared that his mother, mad with grief and rage, might do harm both to herself and their maharajah. The following morning, when he was returned to her, she took him to see the mangled body and threw herself and him upon it, screaming and tearing her hair. It was some time before she could be restrained.

Real power now lay with the military committees even if they continued to recognize the rani as regent and Duleep Singh as maharajah. Their insistent demands for more pay and privileges undermined the fabric of the state; with an emptying treasury and a threat to replace her son on the throne with the little Shahzadah, son of the murdered Maharajah Sher Singh and thus grandson to Runjit Singh, the Rani Jindan and her ministers could by no means consider themselves secure. The only hope, they decided, was to weaken the immediate grip of the army by encouraging it to make war on the British, who were themselves preparing across the Sutlej for what they had long seen as an inevitable conflict with the Sikh nation. Inspired by evidence of the warlike intentions of the British and visions of the conquest of Delhi and even the entire subcontinent, the army insisted on going to war under the leadership of the very people who hoped to destroy its power by collision with a more powerful enemy.

Had it not been for the double-dealing of the rani's generals, it is likely that the ambitions of the Sikh army would have been realized. They crossed the Sutlej but obligingly held back from attacking Ferozepore, the forward British base. Mudki, Ferozshah, Aliwal, and finally, Sobraon: battles fought valiantly by both contestants, each one of which might have been a defeat for the British had not the traitorous commanders quit the field. With their further co-operation British troops crossed the Sutlej unopposed and on 20 February 1846 took possession of the Punjab capital.

On 9 March, the Treaty of Lahore was ratified by Governor General Hardinge, now a viscount, in his state tent outside the walls of the city. Duleep Singh sat on his right and a travelling notable, Prince Waldemar of Prussia, on the left. Around his neck the Duleep Singh wore an oval miniature of Queen Victoria, given to Runjit Singh when Lord Auckland was governor general. Hardinge described him to the queen as 'a very beautiful brave little boy, acting his part without any fear and with all the good breeding peculiar to the Eastern people.'[2]

Hardinge did not feel the time had come to annex the whole of the Punjab, but sizeable pieces of it were amputated in the British interest – Kashmir and Jammu were sold to the traitorous sirdar, Gholab Singh, who undertook to be a bulwark against Afghan or Russian encroachment from the north; a rich piece of the country between the rivers Beas and Sutlej was engorged by the British Raj. The rump of the Punjab was to be governed from Lahore by the durbar in the name of the Maharajah until he came of age.

So forceful was the character of Duleep Singh's mother, said by Herbert Edwardes, who knew her well, to have more 'wit and daring than any man of her nation',[3] that she easily established dominance over the durbar and, with her lover as prime minister, set out to rule the country in her own way. The ambitious rani was soon to find out, however, that under the terms of the treaty it was the British 'Resident', installed on her doorstep in Lahore and backed by the bayonets of the British army that she herself had invited into the city to maintain order, who was in effect dictator of the country. As Lord Hardinge expressed the situation: 'In all our measures taken during the minority [of Duleep Singh] we must bear in mind that by the Treaty ... the Punjab was never intended to become an independent state ... in fact the native prince is in fetters, and under our protection, and must do our bidding.'[4] The Resident, kindly Henry Lawrence, did his best to respect the sentiments of the durbar and the Sikh people, and for a time it seemed as if the rani was getting the better of him. But he tightened his grip when, fretting under the restrictions to her power, she began to intrigue against him. Her downfall was not long in coming.

At Lawrence's instigation, the title of rajah was to be conferred on the commander-in-chief of the Lahore army, a man whom she regarded as the arch-collaborator with the British and responsible for the recent banishment of her lover and former prime minister. In no way anxious to endorse her enemy's elevation she delayed her son's arrival at the ceremony for over an hour, much to the annoyance of the Sikh sirdars and the British officials who were kept waiting. When he finally appeared, the young maharajah firmly refused to obey the Resident's urgent order to mark the forehead of the commander-in-chief, Tej Singh, with the saffron sign of rajahship. According to Hardinge: 'When Tej Singh knelt at the little prince's feet, to have his forehead anointed by the Boy dipping his finger in the perfumed oil, he refused, and when he was pressed to do so he tucked his little hands and arms and resolutely resisted any entreaty ... It is known

6

that the Rani had drilled the Boy to play his part 2 days before.'[5] The rani was clearly in a defiant mood, for despite admonishment from Lawrence, she further asserted her will by forbidding her son to attend the celebratory display of fireworks that evening. Her ungovernable behaviour was to have untoward consequences: the governor general, who had earlier referred to 'the Billingsgate in which she has indulged, the anti-English side she has taken, and the scandalous profligacy of her conduct',[6] went further on hearing the report of her performance at the investiture and wrote to Lawrence that he could see no remedy but to 'remove' her from Lahore and that 'her general misconduct and habits of intrigue are sufficient to justify her separation from her son ... The British Government being the guardian of the Maharajah have the right to separate him from the contagion of her evil practice.'[7]

Less than two weeks after the investiture incident, the Rani Jindan was 'removed' to an uncomfortable provincial fortress. She was said to have been involved in a murder plot but no charges were laid against her in the knowledge that there was little concrete evidence, other than a few intercepted letters and reports from spies. On the morning of her removal Duleep Singh was packed off to the Shalimar Gardens with a new toy to occupy him. According to Lawrence, when he asked to be returned to the palace and his attendant informed him he could not do so until evening, he replied loftily: 'Perhaps I am detained in confinement, as I am not able to leave without permission.'[8] Later when he was told that his mother had been taken away he is said to have remarked that at least he had been allowed to keep his toy.

'I had entrusted my head to your care,' the rani wrote to Lawrence from her place of confinement. 'You have thrust it under the feet of traitors. You have not done justice to me. You ought to have instituted an enquiry, and then charged me with what you found against me ... Why do you take possession of my kingdom by underhand means? Why do you not do it openly? ... Do justice to me or I shall appeal to London headquarters.'[9] Without her son, the rani was without power and wrote passionate letters to Lawrence begging to be re-united with him: 'You have been very cruel to me!' she wailed. 'You have snatched my son from me. For ten months I kept him in my womb ... In the name of the God you worship and in the name of the King whose salt you eat, restore my son to me. I cannot bear the pain of this separation. Instead you should put me to death.'[10]

Lawrence wrote a conciliatory reply, assuring her that her son was perfectly happy and in good hands. 'I am very glad to hear from your letter that the Maharajah is happy,' she answered. 'Whatever you write may be true. But my mind does not believe that the Maharajah is happy. How can he, whose mother has been separated from him, be happy? ... Weeping, he was torn away from his mother and taken to Shalimar Gardens, while the mother was dragged out by her hair. Well has the friendship been paid. You never thought in your mind how the Maharajah who was very young, could live happily without his mother.'[11]

The gentlemanly Lawrence was moved to pity, and possibly to shame, by such maternal pleas, but Hardinge, who had motivated and taken full responsibility for her removal, was little more than cynical. 'We must expect these letters in various shapes, which a woman of her strong mind and passions will assume as best suited either to gratify her vengeance or obtain her ends ...'[12]

Whether as a result of losing his mother or not, Lawrence noticed that the boy looked 'downcast' and did his best to cheer him up. He hoped to persuade him that the English were not as bad as he had been led to believe, and to gain influence over him by tact and charm. The Resident arranged visits to the racecourse where he could 'mix with the European ladies and officers';[13] he took him to a display of fireworks, and a lecture illustrated by 'dissolving views' projected from a magic lantern. Lawrence thought that the boy needed to be removed from the indulgent and necessarily un-manly atmosphere of the zenana and given sterner training under English auspices: he proposed that some of his young civil servants might take on the task, but the Sikh sirdars, who may have wished to keep their maharajah's education in their own hands, protested on the grounds that he was 'still very young and timid'. Lawrence persisted and soon was claiming that those same sirdars were passing 'encomiums on the precocity of His Highness's intellect, which they ascribe to the visits of my Assistants'.[14]

His report indicated that his charge showed promise: 'The Maharajah's writing lessons were as usual shown to me, when I said that I hoped he read a little every day .... He then sent for the pictures drawn last Friday by Lieutenant Edwardes and seemed much pleased with them. With a reed pen he then scratched off several pictures of peacocks and men. He has a turn for mechanics and for drawing and writing, and is altogether a very intelligent and apparently well-disposed boy. His manners are particularly good and his temper seems excellent. I hope that as he becomes accustomed to us, we will be able to teach him some-thing; at present my main endeavour is to keep him from evil.'[15]

At the beginning of 1848 the strain of running the domestic affairs of the Punjab forced Henry Lawrence to return to England on sick leave. The old soldier, Henry Hardinge, retired at the same time to be replaced as governor general by James Andrew, tenth Earl of Dalhousie, a lowland Scot and lately president of the Board of Trade. Dalhousie was only thirty-five, but was capable of acting with an authority and determination that belied his poor health and unimpress-ive appearance. In public he expected his authority to be un-questioned: 'There can only be one master in all India,' he wrote, 'and while I am in India, I have no mind than it should be anybody else than the Governor General in Council.'[16]

Hardinge had assured his successor that 'it would not be

necessary to fire a gun in India for seven years to come'.[17] This wishful forecast was disproved within three months when, towards the end of April 1848, Lieutenants Anderson and Vans Agnew were murdered by the excited retainers of Moolraj, governor of the outlying province of Mooltan. The young officers had been sent to relieve him of a position he no longer wished to retain under the exasperating conditions of British fiscal supervision. Moolraj, who may not have instigated the murder, was further compromised by his men attacking the British escort and had no choice but to set up the standard of revolt in his fortress headquarters.

In his proclamation calling on the Sikh army to support him, Moolraj called for the release of the Rani Jindan – who had been moved to an even less comfortable accommodation following the discovery of a plot to murder the Resident – and for power to lie in the hands of their Maharajah rather than the usurping *feringhees*. Such was the aggravation caused by the monitorial concern of the British for the welfare of the common people that several of the important sirdars, including two members of the Lahore durbar, joined the rebellion along with substantial and revengeful remnants of the Sikh army. Thus, what had started out as a local incident, which might have been rapidly suppressed if British troops had been allowed to help the loyal forces immediately, developed into a situation which only powerful reinforcements could hope to contain. 'Unwarned by precedents, uninfluenced by example, the Sikh nation has called for war,' Dalhousie announced at a Government House banquet, adding, to the cheers of the assembled diners, 'And on my word, Sirs, they shall have it with a vengeance!'[18]

On 18 November 1848, having held back until the hot weather was over, Lord Gough proudly, if belatedly, entered the Punjab with his grand army of fifteen thousand men. A proclamation was addressed to 'all loyal subjects of the Maharajah' to assure them that the British had come 'not as an enemy to the constituted government, but to restore order and obedience'.[19]

On 13 January 1849 Gough's army met twice their number of Sikhs in a ferocious battle:

> Chillianwallah, Chillianwallah!
> 'Tis a wild and dreary plain
> Strewn with plots of thickest jungle,
> Matted with the gory stain.
> There the murder-mouthed artillery,
> In the deadly ambuscade,
> Wrought the thunder of its treachery
> On the skeleton brigade.[20]

Thus sang George Meredith to commemorate the three thousand British who were left dead or wounded in the ravines and underbrush. The old Duke of Wellington, still an oracle on Indian affairs, called for Napier to take command and threatened to lead the troops himself unless he did so. The army's reputation was happily restored by the reduction of Moolraj's fortress from a lucky hit on the powder magazine and a notable victory at Gujrat over the main Sikh army of thirty-four thousand men which led to a total surrender.

While all these great events were being enacted, Duleep Singh remained in Lahore and in almost complete ignorance of what was being effected in his name. He only knew that a young companion, the son of a rebel sirdar, was placed in confinement, and he cannot have failed to observe that a British regiment was put to guard the palace. Treaty or no treaty, Lord Dalhousie was committed to the annexation of the Punjab. Despite Henry Lawrence's threats to resign, it was decided to depose the young maharajah whom, under the Treaty of Lahore, the government was committed to protect and maintain.

From his camp at Ferozepore, on 30 March 1849, the governor general issued the manifesto that sonorously spelt out the wrong-doings of the Sikh nation and proclaimed that the kingdom of the Punjab was at an end. Generous promises and moral justification were interspersed with questionable charges and grim admonishment. It was left to Mr Henry Eliot, secretary to the government of India, to convey to the

Maharajah and his 'council of regency' the precise terms to which they were expected to submit:

1. His Highness the Maharajah Duleep Singh shall resign for himself, his heirs, and successors all right, title and claim to the sovereignty of the Punjab, or to any sovereign power whatever.

2. All the property of the State, of whatever description and wheresoever found, shall be confiscated to the Honourable East India Company, in part payment of the debt due by the State of Lahore to the British Government and of the expenses of the war.

3. The gem called the Koh-i-noor, which was taken from Shah Sooja-ool-moolk by Maharajah Runjeet Singh, shall be surrendered by the Maharajah of Lahore to the Queen of England.

4. His Highness Duleep Singh shall receive from the Honourable East India Company, for the support of himself and his relatives, and the servants of the State, a pension of not less than four, and not exceeding five, lakhs* of the Company's rupees per annum.

5. His Highness shall be treated with respect and honour. He shall retain the title of Maharajah Duleep Singh Bahadoor, and he shall continue to receive during his life such portion of the above-named pension as may be allotted to himself personally, provided he shall remain obedient to the British Government, and shall reside at such place as the Governor General of India may select.[21]

Dalhousie had little sympathy for the boy who was supposedly his protégé and who had now been relieved of his throne and his fortune. He did not see why a person he had earlier referred to as 'a child notoriously surreptitious, a brat begotten of a bhishti, and no more the son of old Runjit Singh than Queen Victoria is',[22] should be treated with more than cursory justice. He thought it necessary, however, to justify his action to his critics in London and wrote to Sir John Hobhouse, chairman of the East India Company, explaining the reasons for the confiscation of property that might be considered by some the rightful heritage of their juvenile charge: 'that the means of mischief hereafter might

---

* Lakh = 100,000 rupees. Then worth about £10,000.

not be left to the Maharajah'; and 'that the great debt which
is due to this government today for the expenses of war might
be diminished by the amount of the property'. The letter
continued:

Whatever my 'affectionate friends' at Leadenhall Street should,
or may, think, you at least will find no fault with my having
regarded the Koh-i-noor a thing by itself, and with my having
caused the Maharajah of Lahore, in token of submission, to surrender it to the Queen of England. The Koh-i-noor had become
in the lapse of ages a sort of historical emblem of conquest in India.
It has now found its proper resting place.

The pension of the Maharajah is fixed at not less than 4 lakhs.
His own stipend, I mean, and always meant, to be 1,200,000 Rs.
like the Raja of Sattarah. He has a large territory but he is a
boy . . .

The Maharajah is allowed to remain for this year, as the hot
weather is on. Next year he must go.

I am sorry for him, poor little fellow, although it is a superfluous compassion. He does not care two pence about it himself
– he will have a good and regular stipend, ('without income tax')
all his life, and will die in his bed like a gentleman; which under
other circumstances, he certainly would not have done.[23]

The members of the regency council were by no means
anxious to incur the odium of signing away their country
to the British, but Eliot cunningly played on their fears of
losing estates or salaries and persuaded them to accept on
the grounds that if they refused he had no authority to say
that they would receive any consideration whatever. When
the document, known as the Treaty of Bhyrowal, was presented to the Maharajah, Eliot reported that 'the alacrity with
which he took the papers when offered to him, was a matter
of remark to all, and suggested the idea that, possibly, he had
been instructed by his advisers that any show of hesitation
might lead to the substitution of terms less favourable than
those which had been offered'. Eliot described the final scene
in a manner which the Maharajah's future guardian, John
Login, described as 'undignified exultation'. 'The whole

ceremony was conducted with grave decorum. No Sirdar was armed. The costly jewels and gaudy robes, so conspicuous in the Sikh Court on other public occasions, now were thrown aside. I did not observe the slightest sign of wonder, sorrow, anger, or even dissatisfaction, upon the countenance of any one present ... As I left the Palace, I had the proud satisfaction of seeing the British colours hoisted on the citadel under a royal salute from our own artillery, at once proclaiming the ascendancy of British rule, and sounding the knell of the Khalsa Raj!'[24]

Thus the most important piece of real estate on the subcontinent became an integral part of the British Raj and the warlike Sikhs submitted gracefully to the well-intentioned operations of the British civil servants. Their former maharajah, son of the founder of the nation, was taken in hand by a Scottish doctor.

On 6 April 1849, Duleep Singh was formally introduced to his new 'Superintendent', Dr John Login, a native of Orkney, who had started his career as a medical officer in the Bengal army. He had served the company both in a medical and lately in an administrative capacity with a dedication that earned him the respect of the civil establishment. Henry Lawrence had entrusted him with command of the Lahore citadel and its prisoners of state – Moolraj and the recalcitrant sirdars – as well as giving him charge over the treasury of the kings of Lahore. It may have been the doctor's moral rectitude that persuaded the Resident to offer him the permanent post of guardian to the Maharajah – a job which could hardly advance his career in the service – so that he would not have him looking over his shoulder in the new administration of the Punjab. His salary of £1,000 a year was to be paid from the Maharajah's stipend.

Login described his first meeting with the boy in a letter to his wife Lena, who had for health reasons returned to England some time earlier with their children: 'The little fellow seemed very well pleased with me, and we got on swimmingly. I told him that now you had gone to take my little ones to England, I was left alone, and wanted someone to care for and be kind to ... He seems a very fine-tempered boy, intelligent, and handsome.'[25]

Login's other charge, the royal treasury, contained much of the riches accumulated by Runjit Singh – a profusion of gold and silver, religious relics, jewels of immense size, golden thrones, cashmere shawls, magnificent armour and weapons, embroidered tents, bejewelled saddles, and a portrait of Queen Victoria. Among this magpie's hoard, which Login had to sort out and catalogue, was the object described in his inventory as THE DIAMOND, the legendary Koh-i-noor referred to in the treaty, which Runjit Singh had 'persuaded' his old ally Shah Shuja of Afganistan to part with. The Koh-i-noor, 'mountain of light', had passed from conqueror to conqueror as a symbol of power and glory and was regarded as the greatest treasure in India. The great uncut stone, the size of a pigeon egg, was at that time mounted with two other diamonds in an enamelled armlet. Dalhousie decided that it should be presented to Queen Victoria with the compliments of the East India Company and it was accordingly dispatched to England in a metal box guarded by two soldiers. It was agreed that the Maharajah could retain a small part of the treasure to be selected by his guardian, a concession that may have indicated a guilty awareness that the hoard could be considered 'family' rather than 'state' chattels claimable under the treaty.

'Now that I know what I can keep for him out of the accumulated property I must take care that his possessions are not diminished by pilfering,' the ever-conscientious doctor wrote to his wife. 'Poor dear little fellow,' he continued, 'so far he seems mightily pleased with me, and I do hope we shall continue to like each other; he is very lovable, I think ... His studies at present are Persian and English. For amusement he is passionately fond of hawking, and thinks of nothing else. He is busy getting up a book on the subject ... this takes up his whole attention, and renders him indifferent to all else for the time being . . . He has painters continuously near him at this work and himself tries to draw and paint a little. I want you to send me out for him a nice paint-box and materials for his use, and a good book of instructions in the art of drawing and painting, till I can get him good lessons. Send also some mechanical toys to amuse him, also geographical puzzles or dissected maps, plates of animals etc. fit for a boy of his age to amuse and interest him.' Login added a positive idea for his charge's future: 'I think the Maharajah shows a great desire to hear about England. Sir H. Lawrence wished he could be educated there, and not left to grow idle and debauched in India, with nothing to do. He will surely have as much to live on as any of our nobles, considering what he has *lost* and we have *gained*! Why, then, should he not be brought up to the life of one (in the highest sense of the word) – he is young enough to mould.'[26]

Login decided that the Maharajah should have a party for his eleventh birthday. 'Don't you think it would be proper to make up a party from the Residency to offer him their good wishes?' he asked Henry Lawrence, who was now back in the saddle. 'A little civility and attention shown on this, his first birthday since he lost his throne, would be kindly taken. It need not be in the least *official*, merely friendly; but as the natives will all do their best to do him honour, I think our party should *not* sport *solah* hats and shooting jackets on this occasion.'[27]

'Solah' hats would have in any case been superfluous on that occasion as it poured with rain. The Maharajah himself was dressed 'most splendidly', wearing the diamond aigrette and star and various other jewels that Login had rescued from the treasury and handed over to him on that day as a 'birthday present'. 'When I congratulated him on his appearance,' he wrote to his wife, 'he innocently remarked that on his last birthday he had worn the Koh-i-noor on his arm.' The boy's observation on receiving his own possessions as a present might have been less 'innocent' than the doctor supposed. But the party was voted a success and Login had certainly tried his best: 'Everything was done that was in my power,' he wrote to his wife, 'to give the anniversary due honour, so that he should feel the difference in his position as little as possible, and not contrast unpleasantly with the last, when he was a reigning King. No doubt, in spite of all, he did see and feel a great difference, poor little man! But nevertheless he thoroughly enjoyed himself, and was as delighted with the fireworks as any boy of his age could be. Luckily the evening was fine though the deluge of rain in the morning was dreadful and upset all my fine arrangements.'[28]

A colourful impression of Duleep Singh at this period was provided by Helen Mackenzie, wife of a company officer who was taken by Dr Login to visit the Maharajah in the Shish Mahal, or Glass Palace, with its walls and ceilings covered in a mosaic of little bits of coloured mirror: 'Dalip Singh is about eleven years old, with beautiful eyes and nose, but the lower part of the face is too full. He met us at the door and took Dr Login's hand: a gold chair was set for the little prince, and a silver one on his left for Dr Login. A box of toys had just arrived from Sir F. Currie, and both the little Maharajah and his servants were anxiously waiting to see its contents....'[29]

Helen Mackenzie made a number of charming sketches at Lahore. Duleep Singh asked her to make one of him and she depicted him 'richly dressed in yellow velvet and silver, with a sort of crimson tunic underneath, and magnificent pearls round his throat'. She noted: 'His hawk is always in the hall, and when he drives out he carries it on his wrist; it is a mark of royalty.'

The next big party to be attended by the Maharajah was on the splendid occasion of the state visit of the governor general attended by all his staff and accompanied by the contentious commander-in-chief of the army, Sir Charles Napier, conqueror of neighbouring Scindh. Dalhousie described his arrival at Lahore on the morning of 28 November 1849:

The chiefs came out to meet me, and the troops were in consider-able strength – there was an abundance of God Save the Queens, and lowered colours, and roaring salutes: and as the camp was pitched just under the walls of the citadel of Lahore, a fine mass of building, and as I knew that Chutter Singh, and Shere Singh, and Moolraj, our *prisoners*, as well as the little Maharajah, were looking down on us, the sight was rather a fine one in sentiment as well as gay externals . . . The little Maharajah is an engaging little fellow, and has quite won my heart. He appears to be happy, enjoying his hawks and his fun, and already very fond of Dr. Login who has had charge of him.[30]

The governor general on his elephant was met by the Maharajah on his and taken for a conducted tour of the city. Afterwards there was a garden fête at the residency for the soldiers, where the Maharajah expressed great interest in the Highlanders in full dress – 'Login, tell him they are my countrymen,' said Dalhousie.

On a visit to the treasury, which Login had to admit had just been broken into by British soldiers, the governor general selected various additional jewels for the queen's collection and two sets of historic arms and armour. Added to the selection was an item that it must have been sad for its owner to part with, described by Dalhousie to the queen as 'a suit of his own little caparison, which he was accustomed to wear at the head of the boy-regiment which was formerly kept up for him at Lahore. The Maharajah begged that the Arms might be presented on his part, and with his respects, to His Royal Highness the Prince of Wales . . . It is a curious specimen of modern native workmanship.'[31] Queen Victoria failed to acknowledge the Maharajah's charming gift.

The queen might have been expected to disapprove of the fact that her statesmen in India had separated a sovereign prince not only from his country and possessions but also from his mother, and Dalhousie was anxious to assure her that all was for the best. In one of his regular reports to her he wrote: 'At Lahore, the Governor General had much communication with the little Maharajah. He is an intelligent and engaging child, most sensible of kindness, and apparently as happy as the day is long. He is old enough to be sensible of what he has lost, but old enough too, to appreciate what he has gained. He recollects what he saw four years ago, intimates that he knew the risks of his own fate – has no desire to return to his mother, who "put discredit on him", he says, "by beating him every day," and he wishes to remain as he is. . . .'[32]

The Maharajah's mother had in fact escaped from her latest place of detention. The resourceful lady had disguised herself as one of her maidservants and, being always veiled, had easily deceived the guards. In the role of a beggar she had reached Nepal and taken sanctuary with the ruler, Jung Bahadur. 'The Ranee Jindan is, even by her own relatives, looked upon as *exceptionally* bad, even among these licentious people.' Login wrote. 'I trust she won't come this way. He [Duleep Singh] told me gravely that he won't trust himself among the Sikhs again and declines to go out for a ride or drive unless I accompany him.'[33]

There was indeed some danger that her partisans might try to abduct her son from British protection. Even such a hard-headed man as Colonel Hodson, Lawrence's agent at Peshawar, could write: 'Punjabees recently arrived here from below assert that a plan has been concocted and matured for carrying the little ex-Maharajah from Lahore to the Hills, and that should a favourable opportunity occur, it will certainly be attempted. This may be moonshine, but as long as the Ranee is alive and free, we may expect plots ad infinitum.'[34] It was clear that the Punjab was no place for its ex-king.

I shall be truly glad when it is settled what is to be the future destination of Duleep Singh [Login wrote to his wife]. Sir Henry and Lawrence both advise his being sent to England at once; but Lord D. is not fond of suggestions, so we all wait for his decision. Sir Henry says that the Dhoon, with a large estate, might not be a bad thing. Either of these plans would suit me; but if it was decided to send him to some place in Central India, and to bring him up with no other expectation than to be a mere pensioner, debauched and worthless like so many others, then I feel it is no

work for me, and I'll wash my hands of the charge, take my fur-
lough and join you in England; but all this is in wiser hands than
mine, and I leave it there contentedly.[35]

The wise men at Government House decided that the
Maharajah should be removed to Futteghur, a small station
on the Ganges, the other side of the country.

is ancestral
n escort of
valry. The
ng that the
by parti-
der house
position to
ingh's six-
mother: as
be allowed
e given that
uleep Singh
panion had
English boy,
e, Dr Login
act as tutor.
nd attentive,
ot altogether

850 and in-
for the next
an East India
cted, having
best to get it
doctor wrote
have to live
til I can get
all not feel is

unsuited to the M

home through no f

though indeed no

park andlay on the

were put in order

others – and each h

Login took great

establishment on be

only thing missing f

sence of his wife, Le

eighteen months an

return to his side. 'I

plaintively, though h

warmed her heart: 'I

jah (and Shahzadah)

tians, in our domesti

for the character of an

afterwards have weig

them to think better

what their idea of la

healths must be, if the

better and acquiring r

bell of Kinloch, obe

return. In advance of l

erly correspondence

pictures of herself and

tained a paint-box, as

Boys' Own Book which

of his hand' and 'the

study.'[6]

The 'companion',

and the Maharajah s

not seem to be Duleep

give the little fellow a t

plained, 'in fact for stu

not been trained to do

difficult to get him to a

CHAPTER 2

Tea With Tommy Scott

THE removal of the ex-king of the Punjab from his ancestral lands was a minor military operation involving an escort of infantry, horse artillery and several squadrons of cavalry. The governor general's marching orders added a warning that the boy might be rescued or 'inveigled away at night'[1] by partisans instigated by his mother, who was then under house arrest in Katmandu and not in fact in a strong position to intervene. Included in the convoy was Duleep Singh's six-year-old nephew, the Shahzadah, and his Rajput mother: as another rallying point, the little boy could not be allowed to remain at large in the Punjab. Instructions were given that the child should be treated as a companion to Duleep Singh but 'as in all respects his inferior'.[2] Another companion had been promised when they reached Futteghur, an English boy, Tommy Scott, son of a company officer. En route, Dr Login recruited a young man called Walter Guise to act as tutor. Login described him as: '... amiable, patient, and attentive, of mild manners ... rather slow, perhaps, and not altogether the man who would suit later on'.[3]

They reached Futteghur on 19 February 1850 and inspected the property that was to be their home for the next four years. The house, formerly occupied by an East India Company 'nabob', looked forlorn and neglected, having been empty for several years. 'I must do my best to get it soon to look bright and cheerful,' the worthy doctor wrote to his wife. 'I'm afraid, however, that we shall have to live among bricks and mortar for a long time, until I can get it to look what I wish it to be, and what I shall not feel is unsuited to the Maharajah, who has lost his own splendid home through no fault of his own.'[4] In its favour the house, though indeed no palace, was surrounded by an attractive park and lay on the banks of the Ganges. Scattered bungalows were put in order – British installed in some, Indians in others – and each household established their own routine.

Login took great pride and pleasure in organizing the little establishment on behalf of his landlord and paymaster. The only thing missing for his complete contentment was the presence of his wife, Lena, who had been away in England for eighteen months and was showing no great inclination to return to his side. 'I do so need you to assist me,' he wrote plaintively, though his reasons for requiring her cannot have warmed her heart: 'I am anxious to give this young Maharajah (and Shahzadah) a favourable impression of us as Christians, in our domestic state, and to make him acquire respect for the character of an English lady. His opinion of them may afterwards have weight among his countrymen, and dispose them to think better of our ladies than they do ... Just think what their idea of ladies dancing the polka and drinking healths must be, if they had no opportunity of knowing them better and acquiring respect for them!'[5] Mrs Login, a Campbell of Kinloch, obeyed the call of duty and arranged to return. In advance of her departure she entered into a motherly correspondence with the Maharajah and sent him pictures of herself and her children. Her first gift parcel contained a paint-box, as earlier requested, and a copy of *The Boys' Own Book* which, according to Login, was 'seldom out of his hand' and 'the book above all others he prefers to study.'[6]

The 'companion', Tommy Scott, duly arrived and he and the Maharajah soon became fast friends. Study did not seem to be Duleep Singh's strong point: 'I wish I could give the little fellow a taste for learning,' his governor complained, 'in fact for study of *any* sort; but you see he has not been trained to do anything of that kind, and it is so difficult to get him to apply his mind for even five minutes at a time. Poor Guise has a lively time of it, and needs great patience.'[7]

The good doctor had to act as mother and father to Duleep Singh and, though he disapproved of the custom of child marriages, set about finding a suitable bride for his charge, a matter which had been in abeyance since negotiations initiated at Lahore for marriage to an infant cousin had broken down. 'I have been making enquiries about a wife for my little boy,' he wrote home. 'He says I am his "Ma-Bap" and he trusts me to do what may be necessary for his happiness. He will have nothing to do, he says, with Shere Singh's sister to whom he was betrothed, so I am left quite at liberty to choose for him. I have heard of a little daughter of the Rajah of Coorg, at Benares. She is being educated like an English child, and her father has asked, and has obtained permission, for her to visit England to have her education completed. She is only eight years old, described as fair and good-looking, and also intelligent, with decided marks of good blood and lineage about her.'[8] The Rajah of Coorg, who had been deprived of his small and hilly territory in South India, was living in Benares in exile. As he had lost most of his treasure, stolen during the evacuation of his territory, his daughter Gouramma could by no means be considered an heiress. Lord Dalhousie, who was anxious only that the Maharajah should not marry a Sikh, expressed his approval. There had, in fact, been talk in the Indian household that the Maharajah would marry his brother's widow, mother of the Shahzadah, which would have been permitted by Sikh custom. She was a Rajput, who had broken caste by marrying a Sikh; Mrs Login was to describe her as 'the most absolutely beautiful woman she had ever met',[9] but the Maharajah had given no sign of interest in her. He expressed more enthusiasm at the mention of the little princess from Coorg, but when Login consulted the appropriate Sikh elder on the subject he was told that she would be quite unsuitable on the grounds that she had been in the habit of drinking tea and eating plum-cake with the English ladies at Benares and had therefore broken caste.[10]

Life at 'Futteghur Park', as Login called the place, continued on its leisurely way. There were lessons and games for the boys, hawking and hunting in the country and riding out in the hours of cool. In his passion for hawking, a favourite sport among the Sikhs, the Maharajah now took an absorbing interest not only in flying his birds after game but also in their training and feeding. All along Login had tried to discourage his dedication on the grounds that the cruelty inherent in the pursuit 'might develop the tendency to barbarity which is so inherent in the oriental character'.[11]

Despite orders from Government House that he should not be given ideas of his own importance, Login encouraged the Maharajah to keep up considerable state. One of the more picturesque sights at Futteghur was the elegant cavalcade attending his daily rides – the prince on his high-stepping horse, hawk on outstretched wrist, accompanied by the Shahzadah and his English friends – Tommy Scott and Robbie Carshore, the padre's son – a retinue of fierce-looking Sikhs jostling behind, followed by a detachment of the Body Guard in scarlet uniforms and troopers of the famous regiment Skinners Horse, otherwise known as 'Canaries', in saffron. Sometimes he would go out on his elephant with its silver howdah, or ride in his smart carriage with its four grey arabs, driven by his English coachman, Thornton.

It was still thought necessary that he should be protected against his mother, several of whose emissaries from Nepal had been caught at the frontier. 'Honour thy father and mother' was one Christian precept that Login had made no effort to instil: 'As far as I can judge, not the least desire exists on the part of the Maharajah to communicate with his mother,' he reported to Government House. 'Having lately, in the course of reading history with him, met with an allusion to his being the acknowledged, though not the reputed son of Runjeet Singh, I told him that the conduct of the Maharanee, and the character she had acquired, exposed him to this imputation; he said, "Ah, yes; it was all too true!" And he had frequently made up his mind, while at Lahore, that he would have his mother killed, that she might not disgrace him.'[12] Such summary execution was not altogether unorthodox in the Punjab – Runjit Singh had killed *his* mother when, as a boy, he had found her in bed with a lover.

In November 1850 Dr Login took a month's leave so as to be in Calcutta to meet his wife and children on their arrival from England. While he was away an event took place that must have gratified him but at the same time given him some feeling of shame, that though he was the young Maharajah's mentor he had not fully appreciated what was going on in his mind. The twelve-year-old Sikh suddenly announced that he was going to become a Christian! Login might have taken some hint from a casually-dropped request in a letter from his distant charge: 'My dear good friend – We are all well here. Captain Campbell presided at our examination, and I got twenty marks; but Shazada got only ten. Will you kindly send me a nice bible, because Bhajun Lal was reading to me; and also to send me a chest of fine tools for carpenter's work.'[13] The Maharajah's next letter contained the un-expected affirmation: 'You will be surprised to learn of my determination to embrace the Christian religion. I have long doubted the truth of the one I was brought up in, and con-vinced of the truth of the religion of the Bible, which I have made Bhajun Lal read portion of it to me.'[14]

It was a delicate political matter, at a time when the ver-nacular press was free to present even the most controversial arguments, that the juvenile ex-head of a warlike and sternly religious nation, educated under British protection, should embrace an alien faith. Such an event would require the auth-orities to establish to the people of India, and to some people of England, that 'improper influence' had not been brought to bear. Religious tolerance was a cardinal principle of British rule and, though Christian missionaries were active through-out the country, the charge of proselytizing a prince would have convincingly to be rebutted. Login was called upon to provide an explanation:

The Governor-General desires to be informed whether you have had any reason to suppose, at any time since the Maharajah has been under your charge, that His Highness gave his attention to matters connected with the Christian faith. Whether you or Mr. Guise, or any European person who have had charge of him, or may have had access to him, have introduced the subject of our religion to his notice; have talked to him upon it, or engaged him in any question regarding it? Whether the young gentlemen who have been allowed to reside with him as his playfellows have talked to him, or have been talked to by him thereupon ... and where the bible was procured, which His Highness says has been read to him by an attendant, and who that attendant is?[15]

Dr Login would have been proud enough to consider himself the true progenitor of the Maharajah's conversion. Though he was quite aware that it was against the rules to evangelize, he had done his best to set a Christian example. 'I trust that God helping us, we shall be enabled as "written epistles" to manifest the spirituality and benevolence of a Christian life, if we cannot otherwise preach to him,' he had written to his wife soon after he was appointed guardian.[16] His frequent homilies on 'frankness', designed to correct what he regarded as an inborn deceitfulness in the Indian character, and the setting out for copying and translation of such precepts as 'Do unto others as you would they should do unto yourself' was intended as a discreet projection of the Christian ethic.

What may have influenced the Maharajah more than anything was the behaviour of the English boys on the station who were his friends; his exclusion from their intriguing religious observances, their hints that in their eyes he was no more than a heathen, and irritation that the rules of his caste forbade him taking food in their company, must have undermined his confidence in his own faith. In fact he had confided his intention to Tommy Scott some time earlier and sworn his best friend to secrecy. That Tommy Scott might have had something to do with it did not go unconsidered by Dr Login. In his report to the governor general he observed: 'Considering the relative character and disposition of His Highness, as compared with Master Scott, to whom he first made known his intention of becoming a Christian, I cannot consider the latter altogether passive in the matter; or if he did exert any influence over the Maharajah's mind, in leading him to adopt the same faith, it could only have arisen from His Highness's friendly regard for the boy, and the admiration of the honesty and truthfulness of his character, which he has frequently expressed.'[17]

Knowing Login's Christian zeal, the governor general might have held him totally responsible. Lengthy statements of innocence were taken from all concerned, and there was some relief when the Indian 'attendant' referred to offered himself as a convenient scapegoat. The gentleman in question, Bhajun Lal, was a young Brahmin; he had been educated at the American Presbyterian Mission where, though still observing the rules of Hinduism, he had acquired more than a toleration of Christianity. Bhajun Lal was ordered by Login to write a full report of the matter. He described such steps towards apostasy as might be held to put no one at fault:

As you want to know the circumstances of His Highness Maharajah's breaking his caste since you left, I have the honour to explain before your honour, what all I have known from the time when I was employed in His Highness's service.

When the Maharaj began to learn out of a English book, by name of *English Instructor*, there were some lines at the back end of the book with a few words about Christian religion. You once said to Maharaj, 'These are records of our religion; if you want to read them, then read, and if you don't want, you can leave them,' but His Highness say to me, 'Never mind, I will read them, because I want to know everything'; then they were read. As I was with him at all the times, he used to ask me questions about our religion (Sudras): What is the benefit of bathing in Gunga Dee? Would it take us into heaven if we still do other wicked works and bathe in Gunga? I replied, and said, 'Maharaj, it's written in our Shastras,

27

but I do not know whether we would go to heaven or hell.' Then he said, 'Yes, but it depends on our works.' And so on he would speak.

In the month of Barsakh, Maharaj began to have some of our religious books read, and in one book there was written a paragraph about a Rajah who used to make charity of ten thousand cows every morning before taking his breakfast! This way the said Maharajah used alms of ten thousand cows during the time of his life. But it came to pass, that if any *one* of these cows came again or was bought by his servants without knowing it, and the Rajah made his alms of that cow again, by this he was cast into hell. Now when the Katha was over the Pundit gone, His Highness's servant Jewindah said to the Maharaj, 'See, is it not impossible that now the Rajah could get so much new cow every day?' Maharaj answered and said, 'Yes! it is quite nonsense; and that's why I doubt many things what the Pundit do say.'

Such conversations had been many times, but I always found him very conscious, and of high opinion, and not superstitious, and of a reasonable mind.

Now, Sahib, after some time you went to Calcutta, Maharaj saw one copy of Holy Bible into my hand, and asked of me, 'Will you sell this over to me?' I replied, and said, 'Maharaj, I don't want to sell it to you, but I can present you, if you can read a chapter out of it without any assistance.' So he did read, and I presented him my Bible. After some time, he asked me to read to him, and let him hear it, and according to his orders I did read. First day I read 6th chapter St. Matthew, and a few others during the whole week. Sometimes Bible, sometimes a few tricks, then sometimes out of *Boy's Own Book*; but I am sure I never heard any Englishman, talking or reading him any of their religious things.

After this week, then Maharaj disclosed his designs to Captain Campbell and to Mr. Guise, that he approves the Christian religion is true, and that of his own is *not* true. Then the gentlemen said, 'Well, Maharaj, if you understand it with your conscience, it is far better, and we would be only very happy if you would understand it.' But I well know and can certify that whatever Maharaj did say or do, he did it by his pleasure and opinion, but not by any man's beguiling.

When I did ask Maharaj, 'Do you really believe, or merely joking?' he then answered, and said, 'I really do believe, and I will embrace the Christian religion, because long before mine designation was to do this.'

After two or three days, on Sunday, I came back from my city house at twelve (because I often go to city on Saturday evening, and come back on Sunday at midday). Maharaj told to me, 'Bhajun Lal, I have become a Christian.' I then say, 'What did you eat?' He answered and said, 'I have not eaten anything, but my heart is changed. See now, I have not gone to play, nor like to play, on this day.' But when the cool of evening came, he went out hawking with his favourite hawk. When he came back into the house I asked him, 'Maharaj, how is it that you told me that you would no more play this day, but you went and played with your hawks?' He answered, and said, 'I forgot, and am very sorry for that.' After two days he began to say that he would like to take tea with Tommy Scott and Robbie Carshore. I said 'Very well, do whatever you like, but do only that thing which you well know will do good for you at the end.' On Wednesday I had some work in the city, and I took leave of him at twelve and went; and when I came back at evening, I found Maharaj, T. Scott, and R. Carshore, in Maharaj's room, sitting at a table, and *he* (the Maharaj) was boiling the water. As soon as he saw me, he came out of the room and told me, 'See now, I am going to make tea with mine own hands, and then we all three take together.' I answered, and said, 'Very good, Maharaj, do whatever you like; but I tell you one thing, that you must not take tea, or do anything, until Dr. Login Sahib comes back.' He replied, 'That you do not know if Dr. Login will allow me to do it, and then I will be very sorry!' After this he went and made the tea with his own hands, and took with T. Scott and R. Carshore; but all whatever he did, he did with his pleasure, and was very anxious if Dr. Login will like him to do his wilful work. He will be very much pleased and glad, to hear if you will allow him to break his caste, and he will be very happy in breaking his caste.

Sir, as far as I know, I have related with justice. Your most obedient, humble servant,

Bhajun Lal.[18]

The Brahmin's simple statement of events effectively reassured Dalhousie that no overt influence had been applied by the Maharajah's guardians and he was inspired to write

a jocular account of the conversion to his friend and confid-
ant in England, Sir George Couper:

My little friend Duleep has taken us all aback lately by declaring
his resolution to become a Christian. The pundits, he says, tell him
humbug – he has had the Bible read to him, and he believes the
Sahib's religion. The household, of course, are in a grand state.
Politically we could desire nothing better, for it destroys his possible influence forever. But I should have been glad if it had been
deferred, since at present it may be represented to have been
brought about by tampering with the mind of a child. This is not
the case – it is his own free act, and apparently his firm resolution.
He *will* be a Christian, he says, 'and he *will* take tea with Tommy
Scott', which his caste had hitherto prevented! This last cause is
a comical point in his profession of faith! I have thought it right
to report the thing to the Court for their orders. But, as you may
suppose, I have intimated that if the lapse of time shall show that
this is not a fantasy of the boy, that he knows the effect of what
he is doing and still persists in his desire to be instructed in Christian
truths, I can be no party to discouraging, still less to opposing it.
He is a remarkable boy in many ways.[19]

The governor general's assertion that the Maharajah's
political influence would be 'destroyed forever' now that he
had ceased to be a Sikh was to some extent counteracted by
the mother of the Shahzadah, who began to encourage her
son to feel that it would now one day be *he* who would be
restored to the throne of the Punjab. The little boy began to
put on airs and affected to avoid his uncle's company. Login
was sternly instructed by Dalhousie to bring the mother
to account: 'You will inform the Ranee that the Raj of the
Punjab is at an end for ever, and that any contemplation of
the restoration of her son, or anybody else, to sovereignty
there is a crime against the State. It is her duty to instruct
her son accordingly. If on any future occasion, either she or
her son is detected in expressing or entertaining expectations
of restoration to power, or to any other position than that
which he now occupies, the consequences will be immediate
and disastrous to his interests.[20]

Mrs Login, newly arrived from England, described a domestic confrontation with the lady which showed that even if power was no longer a matter for discussion, prejudice was. The rani wanted personal proof that the Maharajah had in fact broken caste and thrown in his lot with the *feringhees*. Mrs Login had taken the boy, who for some time had been 'keeping away', on a visit to his neighbouring relations.

There was the usual constraint observable during the visit; even the little Shahzadah seemed not at ease, and as if expectant of something about to happen. The Ranee offered refreshments, and called for fruit sherbet, for which she was famous. The tray appeared with only *one* glass upon it. This the Ranee filled, and offered with deep reverence to her Sovereign; but the Maharajah courteously handed the glass first to me. Drinking part of the contents, I replaced it on the tray. To my horror, it was immediately refilled, and once more presented by the Maharanee to the Maharajah. I exclaimed in a low voice, in English: 'Don't touch it, Maharajah!' But, rising and turning towards me with a courteous salute, he took the glass in his hand, drank off its contents, and abruptly turning on his heel, left the house, giving the slightest possible gesture of farewell to his sister-in-law, who gazed after him in consternation, now alarmed at the result of her experiment ... I took my leave, you may be sure, directly after this insult to my husband's ward, and was much touched to find the Maharajah was waiting outside, in order that I might not return without his escort. Asking him *why* he took the glass, and thus permitted himself to be thus affronted – 'What?' he replied, his eyes flashing, 'you would have me let them *insult you too*? They shall see that I honour you! And I am not ashamed to show thus that I have broken caste!'[21]

The Maharajah, who soon came to regard kindly Mrs Login as a mother, performed a further gallantry by presenting her with the tress of hair, long and abundant as a woman's, which, in accordance with the Sikh religious custom, he had worn twisted into a knob under his turban. He had wanted to shear his locks as soon as he announced he would be a Christian, in order to look more like the English boys, who had probably teased him as looking like a girl, but Login had dissuaded him from taking so drastic a step until he had been at least a year 'on probation'.

On Christmas Day 1851 Lord Dalhousie visited Futteghur with the primary purpose of meeting the Maharajah whom he had not seen since he had dethroned him at Lahore. The governor general and the boy were to be seen walking together round the little estate, inspecting improvements and chatting away like father and son. Dalhousie was said to have shown himself so thoroughly kind-hearted and genial that it was hard to realize it was the same man whom his detractors portrayed as uncompromisingly frigid and autocratic.

Lord Dalhousie asked the Maharajah for a portrait to remember him by, and George Beechey, who lived in Calcutta, was commissioned to paint it. Beechey, whose following in England had declined disastrously after the death of his more distinguished father, had married an Indian lady and become court painter and comptroller of the household to the King of Oudh. His picture shows a big-eyed, strong-nosed boy with a sensual mouth. He is decked out in jewels and wears Runjit Singh's miniature of Queen Victoria around his neck. He does not look as if he was in the habit of taking too much exercise and an over-indulgence in sweetmeats may have been one of his failings. 'If only you could keep down his fat!' Dalhousie wrote Login. 'But there you are not the best of examples!'[22] To the Maharajah he wrote: 'At last after a long delay upon the river, Your Highness's portrait has arrived. It is in excellent condition, not at all injured by the weather. It is really very like you and does great credit to Mr. Beechey as an artist. Your Highness has really done me a great favour in offering me the likeness of yourself. If it pleases God that I shall live till I am old, I shall look upon it with strong feelings long after my connection with this country shall have been dissolved and always with a renewal of the interest which I feel in yourself and in everything belonging to your fate and fortunes.'[23]

The Maharajah's future had been the main subject of discussion between Login and Dalhousie during his visit. What was to be done with him? Certainly he and his entourage could not rot away forever at Futteghur. Perhaps he might be given a really large estate in another part of India, which he could consider a substitute principality. Login put forward the old plan that the boy should go to England, but there had been an excess of Indian visitors to London around that time and Dalhousie did not approve of the attention they had been receiving, especially when they had some grudge against his government. The governor general, however, became almost enthusiastic about that idea when it came to the question of the Maharajah's marriage. How would they ever find a suitable Indian girl for a Christian prince? There was even then in London little Princess Gouramma, youngest daughter of the deposed Rajah of Coorg who had gone to plead his case for compensation – that same child who had been rejected earlier on the grounds of her breaking caste. While marrying off one daughter to Jung Bahadur, ruler of Nepal, the rajah had turned the other into a Christian. The Maharajah had read an account of her conversion in an English newspaper and after thinking the matter over for several days had himself suggested that a marriage with her might be negotiated. What to do with the princess, now called Victoria Gouramma after the queen had stood as god-mother, was a question already exercising the minds of the East India Company panjandrums in Leadenhall Street.

'I am an advocate for his going to England,' wrote Dalhousie to Login, having thought the matter over, 'and if it should help a marriage between him and the little Coorg, I shall be very glad for it will reconcile much which would otherwise be a considerable perplexity both in her case and his.' The governor general, who did not have much time for the 'rascally' Rajah of Coorg, went on to express his views about the daughter's christening with a certain degree of cynicism:

I have been greatly disgusted with the notoriety they have given this man [the Rajah of Coorg] in England, though I had carefully provided against it here and had warned them on the subject. It had been calculated to turn the girl's head, and his too, for he will now be more convinced than ever of his accomplishing his object of marrying her to an English nobleman. Whether he would prefer a Maharajah pucka to a nobleman in prospect, I don't know! nor do I feel that the Maharajah would do well to arrange any marriage until he has seen the young lady; for as a Christian, he can't get Ranees in duplicate, he may as well see how he likes her first ... The little heathen sister whom Jung Bahadoor took away with him to Nepal was really very pretty. The orthodox one is not nearly so good looking.

Consider these points, and let me know what you think. You are aware that I have been most anxious that there should be no fuss or display connected with Duleep's profession of Christianity, in order that I might feel satisfied in my conscience that the boy had not been, unintentionally by us, or unconsciously to himself, led into the act by any other motives than that of conviction of the truth. To that end your management of the matter has been most judicious and highly satisfactory to me, I should wish that course steadily pursued. I consider that the Coorg christening in St. James's Chapel, with royal godfathers and godmothers, and the name Victoria given her, has been a great mistake, calculated to make the child regard a sacrament as a Court pageant, and to lead all the world to believe (as I verily believe myself) that the father's motive was not so much that his child should be an 'heir of salvation', as that she should be a goddaughter of Queen Victoria: I do not think I am uncharitable in concluding that the man could have no higher motive who, while he was leading with one hand his elder child to Christianity, gave over the younger with the other to Hinduism and Jung Bahadoor! Let us avoid all such reproach. If Duleep is to go to England, let him be quietly baptized before he goes, and by his own name of Duleep Singh. Indeed I am prepared to advise his being baptized now, as soon as his minister can declare that he is sufficiently instructed, and is willing to be baptized at all, he is quite old enough to take the obligations directly upon himself, and to be baptized without the intervention of godfathers and godmothers.[24]

Though the governor general was prepared to encourage the immediate baptism of the Maharajah, Mr Carshore, the padre in charge of his religious education, would under no circumstances admit that his pupil was yet 'sufficiently instructed'.

Early in the spring of 1852 the Logins set out with the Maharajah on a short tour, as much for their own pleasure as their employer's education, before moving up to the cool of the hill station at Mussoorie where they were to spend the hot season. It must have been a stimulation to all concerned to leave the limited confines of Futteghur and proceed on a princely march complete with elephants, a herd of goats and a pack of greyhounds, and set up the red and white striped tents with their silver tent poles in delectable spots only ten miles' march apart. Their progress took them to Delhi, where the Maharajah was unable to resist adding to his already considerable collection of jewellery by purchases in the bazaar. At Agra, a breakfast was given in his honour by the English community who took over the Taj Mahal for the occasion. Login laid on other more educational experiences for his pupil – a visit to a printing foundry, an inspection of the electric telegraph station, and the headquarters of the Ganges Canal Works. The Maharajah wanted to take a look at the Hindu religious ceremony then in progress on the Ganges, which was attended by a large number of pilgrims from the Punjab. The authorities feared a demonstration and arranged for the main party to be sent in one direction as a decoy, while the boy made a hurried visit to the ghats on his elephant. He was recognized when leaving by a crowd of his former subjects, who hailed him with an enthusiasm that may have given him food for future thought.

As the main object of the Maharajah's move to the cooling hills was to enable him to pursue his studies more effectively, Login forbade attendance at the more amusing entertainments of a hill station such as balls, theatricals and race meetings, though the more sober pleasures of archery, cricket and picnics were permitted. The Maharajah, who had a talent for music, developed by his music master, Mr Hunter, formed a band and would play the flute or the cornopean in concerts on the Mall. Login also encouraged his charge to 'finance', the fees going to local good causes, a series of 'improving' lectures by local experts on such varied subjects as astronomy, the habits of bees, zoology of the Himalayas, and the peculiarities of the English language.

He made a number of new friends among the 'sons of gentlemen' on the station who would come every Saturday from Mr Maddock's school to join him at play. As well as Tommy Scott and Robbie Carshore his particular companions were the sons of Major Boileau of the Artillery, Frank and Charles; together they would go riding, hawking or coursing attended by Thornton, his English servant, and with an escort of troopers within easy hail. 'The [Boileau] boys have just arrived from England,' Login informed Dalhousie, 'and as they are very intelligent lads of fifteen and sixteen, who appear to have been carefully educated, and are very diligent and attentive to their Urdu studies, I have little doubt that their example will be in every way beneficial to His Highness.' That some sort of an 'example' was desirable was indicated in Login's following paragraph:

From all I have seen of the Maharajah's disposition, I am the more satisfied as to the great advantage and stimulus of example in his case. His disposition is naturally indolent, and nothing but his strong good sense, and his desire to be on an equality in knowledge and accomplishments with lads of his own age, enables him to overcome the natural slothfulness of his character. It is on this account that I am so anxious that he should be permitted to visit England, as he so earnestly desires it, while he is young, and while he can have an opportunity of mixing with lads of his own age, and incur less risk of being spoiled by too great attention.[25]

The season at Mussoorie was voted a great success. So much so that it was decided the Boileau boys should come back to Futteghur and continue to share their studies. Mr Hunter, the music master, who had made himself popular with the boys, also accompanied them back 'by request'.

After two years of probation and instruction in the mysteries of the Christian religion, the Maharajah, at the instigation of Login, wrote to the governor general saying that he had a 'strong desire' to be baptized and hoped that he might now be considered fit. Lord Dalhousie replied:

My dear Maharajah, I have received with the most lively satisfaction the letter in which you express your desire to be at once baptized, and to be admitted as a member of the Church of Christ. When you at first showed an inclination to believe in the truths which you found declared in the word of God, I advised you not to act hastily, to continue in your study of the Bible, and to test by time the strength and sincerity of your belief.

You have followed my advice, and I have learnt with real pleasure from the statement of the Archdeacon and Mr. Jay that they have found you quite fit to receive the baptism you desire to obtain. I, on my part, most readily assent to your wish, and I thank the God and Saviour of us all, who had put into your heart a knowledge of, and a belief in, the truth of our holy religion, and that you may show to your countrymen in India an example of a pure and blameless life, such as befits a Christian prince.

I beg your highness to believe in the strength and sincerity of the regard in which I shall ever feel towards you, and to remain, now and always, Your Highness's sincere and affectionate friend.[26]

On 8 March 1853 what the governor general described as 'a very remarkable event in history, and in every way gratifying' was enacted at Futteghur – the baptism of Maharajah Duleep Singh. 'This is the first Indian prince,' Dalhousie wrote to George Couper, 'of the many who have succumbed to our power or have acknowledged it, that has adopted the faith of the stranger. Who shall say to what it may lead? God prosper and multiply it! I have never from the hour in which I signed the decree had one moment's hesitation or doubt to the justice or necessity of my act in dethroning the boy. If I had such a doubt, the sight of the blessed result for him to which that act has led would now have thoroughly consoled me for what I did then. As it is, my mind is doubly content as to what he lost; immeasurably content as to the gain he has found in his loss.'[27]

The christening took place at the Maharajah's house rather than in the church, which at that moment was under repair. Login insisted on the minimum of display but all the chief people of the station were there and several of the native staff who were eager to watch the strange ceremony. Mrs Login described 'the earnest expression on the young boy's face, and the look, half-sad, half-curious, on those of his people present by their own wish'. In the absence of Jordan water, Mrs Login suggested the use of water from the nearby Ganges, not so much as a concession to Hindu custom as on the grounds that the river would 'henceforth be sanctified to Duleep Singh with a new and holier association'.[28]

The great occasion was described by the Maharajah's religious instructor, the Reverend William Jay, to his friend Robert Montgomery, then judicial commissioner to the Punjab at Lahore:

The service was inexpressibly solemn and affecting, and everyone seemed deeply moved. The boy answered the questions put to him in a firm, reverent, and decided tone, and nothing as far as man's eye can see could have been better. For the last ten weeks I have been reading very carefully with him the Gospels, and it is astonishing to remark his great improvement. Three months ago I said I would rather resign my Chaplaincy than baptize a person so unprepared as I thought the lad then was. Many and many a time have I felt shame to the very heart's core that I could have uttered so rash, hasty and sinful a speech. For I believe that few people have ever received the sacrament of baptism in greater sincerity or inner faith than the boy who has this day been admitted into the Christian Church. Much of his future life will humanly speaking depend on Dr. Login, who has managed his interests with much wisdom, although with him too I must very foolishly now and then be vexed, because he does not see everything in the same way that I do, about parties and entertainments etc. May God grant that the young Maharajah indeed be a child of Grace.[29]

Now that the Maharajah had become a complete Christian, Login began to press the point of the visit to England and made the boy put his request in writing for onward transmission to Government House: 'I wish to say that I am very anxious to go, and quite ready to start whenever his Lordship gives me permission. I do not want to go to make a show of myself, but to study and complete my education, and I wish to live in England as quietly as possible,' Such a contrived text was probably formulated by Dr Login to satisfy the Court of Directors in London, whose permission it would be necessary to obtain.

To Login's covering letter Dalhousie replied:

We are at one in thinking he should go to England. It is my opinion, as it is yours, that he should go while he is yet what we should consider a boy. I shall therefore ask permission from the Court to let him go next Spring, if you consider him ready and desirous, as before, to go. I will not disguise from you that the Court may not give a very gracious assent; the visit of Jung Baha-door, whom they spoiled, and still more, the present visit of the ex-Rajah of Coorg, whom, in spite of all my precautions and warnings, they have lifted wholly out of his place, making a fool both of him and of themselves thereby, has disgusted the Court and the Board of Control with native, and especially with princely, visitors. Still I hope they will agree, and still more, I hope that the Maharajah will not expect pompous receptions, and will rather seek quiet and privacy while he shall remain in England.[30]

To Couper he wrote: 'He is dying to see Europe and all its wonders. He told me he used to dream every night he was visiting the Duke of Wellington.'[31]

At the beginning of 1854 the Court of Directors of the East India Company in London duly agreed that on the governor general's recommendation they approved a visit to England by the deposed Maharajah of Lahore. Dalhousie personally informed him: 'I am very happy to tell you that I have this moment received the permission of the Court of Directors that you should visit England. In the belief that this intelligence will give you pleasure, I hasten to convey it to you with my own hand. I have not time to write another word beyond the assurance of the pleasure it will give me to see your Highness again.'[32] In his covering letter to Login, he added: 'I hope he will do me credit, for they have had a sickener of native grandees at home lately.'[33]

Duleep Singh was anxious not to be separated from his younger nephew, the Shahzadah, with whom he was again good friends. The government, who were glad enough to see a possible claimant out of the way, gave permission for him to accompany the Maharajah to England. His mother did not wish him to go, and he tried to enthuse her with pictures of England from the *Illustrated London News*. He was to get only as far as Calcutta before the outraged rani petitioned the government to prevent his sailing. A mother's plea could hardly be gainsaid and he was hauled back, protesting, by her emissary. 'I have sent you a huge memorial from the mother of the brat,' Dalhousie wrote to Login, 'accusing you of many enormities, of which child-stealing is the least!'[34]

The Maharajah was filled with excitement at the idea of crossing oceans, seeing new lands, and visiting the country of his guardian and favourite playmates. Inspired by stories in *The Boys' Own Book*, he talked of entering a public school and taking his place among boys of his own age. This suggestion did not commend itself to the governor general: 'The proposal to go to a public school won't do at all' he wrote to Login. 'He is much too old, and would be thrashed without a doubt periodically. Even a university would not do.'[35]

In April 1854 the Maharajah's party set off for Calcutta, the port of departure for Europe. He was provided with a mounted escort, and orders had been given that he should be greeted with the full honours of a twenty-one-gun salute. 'Pray impress upon His Highness,' Dalhousie instructed Login, 'that while in India he receives all the honours of his rank – in England he will be entitled only to courtesy.'[36]

At Lucknow they stayed with the famous Colonel Sleeman, scourge of the murderous *thugs*. An ardent ethnologist, he had studied the settling of northern India by distant peoples. He did his best to explain how the Maharajah was descended from the Jutes, and as many old families in Kent were also of Jute descent, he would find they were all his cousins! The Maharajah presented Mrs Sleeman with a ring, which, unlike Queen Victoria, she was unable to accept because of company rules forbidding their employees to accept gifts from natives. The old colonel suggested to Login that the Maharajah offer it 'to the first pretty Kentish girl he sees, and claim brotherhood with her, on the authority of an old Indian officer, his friend, Colonel Sleeman. If she is of pure Kentish descent, he may feel assured that they are members of the same great family.'[37]

At Benares a new member was attached to the Maharajah's suite, the twenty-year-old Pundit Nilakanth (Christianized as Nehemiah) Goreh, one of the first Brahmins to be converted to Christianity. He had been working as a missionary among his own people and was a candidate for holy orders. He expressed an earnest wish to go to England and the head of the mission to which he was attached was persuaded to allow him. A term of three years was agreed upon with 'food and raiment' as his only remuneration, and he was to act as tutor in oriental languages to the Maharajah. Bhajun Lal was persuaded by his family to stay behind in India, where he became a prosperous tentmaker. Mrs Login maintained that though he had 'very strong' Christian convictions and had certainly helped the Maharajah in his conversion, he had not, in his own case, 'the courage to throw off the bondage of Hindooism'.[38] Tommy Scott was returned to his now-widowed mother, and Mr Guise was paid off with a bonus of 5,000 rupees.

Dalhousie was then in Calcutta, and Government House was full, so the party was installed in the weekend residence at Barrackpore, a short boat trip up the Hooghly. The Maharajah was invited to dinner and Dalhousie was able to report favourably to his friend George Couper, recommending the boy to his care, and asking him to see that he was not exploited by the missionary societies:

He is at an awkward age, and has dark callow down all over his face, but his manners are apparently nice and gentlemanlike, and he now speaks English exceedingly well. He is attended by

Dr. Login, an excellent man for the office, whom I should ask leave to introduce to you ... I earnestly desire this boy should make a good impression in England, and equally so that he should not be spoiled and made a fool of ... I look upon him as in some sort, my son, and am really solicitous for his success and well-being ... I hope you will discourage any idea you may detect of taking the boy to public meetings, especially Exeter Hall ones – there to be paraded as a Christianised prince. I have warned him against it but I am a little afraid of the temptation when it comes close; and wish to guard against it, for it would be very bad for the boy.[39]

On 19 April 1854, the Maharajah and his party sailed for England. Lord Dalhousie's letter of farewell to his ward was delivered before departure along with a beautifully bound bible:

My dear Maharajah, Before you quit India, I have been desirous of offering you a parting gift which in future years might sometimes remind you of me.

Since that day when the course of public events placed you a little boy in my hands, I have regarded you in some sort as my son. I therefore ask you, before we part, to accept from me the volume which I should offer to my own child, as the best of all gifts, since in it alone is to be found the secret of real happiness either in this world or that which is to come.

I bid you farewell, my dear Maharajah, and beg you to believe me always, with sincere regard, your Highness's faithful friend,

Dalhousie.[40]

CHAPTER 3

Visits to Queen Victoria

THE Maharajah Duleep Singh arrived in England in midsummer 1854. He had been gratified on the journey with the use of the khedive's carriages in Egypt and by twenty-one-gun salutes from Malta and Gibraltar. As Dalhousie had made clear, such official tokens of respect would stop as soon as he reached England; certainly Mrs Claridge, proprietress of Mivart's Hotel in Brook Street, organized no special reception when the Login party moved in. But there was soon to be recognition in the form of a summons to meet the queen at Buckingham Palace and on the afternoon of 1 July the first encounter took place between the fifteen-year-old boy and the thirty-five-year-old woman who was to be the greatest influence in his life. In her journal, Queen Victoria made the first of many entries concerning her exotic subject whose background she had studied in a memorandum from his sponsor, Sir Charles Wood, secretary to the India Board: 'After luncheon, to which Mama came, we received the young Maharajah Duleep Singh, the son of Runjeet Singh, who was deposed by us after the annexation of the Punjaub. He has been carefully brought up, chiefly in the hills, and was baptised last year, so that he is a Christian. He is extremely handsome and speaks English perfectly, and has a pretty, graceful and dignified manner. He was beautifully dressed and covered with diamonds. The "Koh-i-noor" belonged to, and was once worn by him. I always feel so much for these poor deposed Indian Princes.'[1]

The queen was so impressed by the handsome young man in his dashing Sikh costume that she at once decided that he

43

must be painted by her favourite artist, Winterhalter, who was then in London working on portraits of members of her family. Meanwhile, within a week of the first presentation, there was an invitation to a big dinner party at the palace, and it was perhaps to show off her latest find that she asked some of her closest friends and sat the Maharajah at her right hand. The entry for 6 July in the journal describes the occasion:

. . . Mama, &c, the Maharajah Duleep Singh, the Abercorns, & Etta, the Van de Weyers, the D^{ss} of Sutherland, L^d & L^y Churchill, Sir C. & L^y M. Wood, Sir G. Bonham &c dined. The Maharajah sat next to me & is extremely pleasing, sensible & refined in his manners. His young face is indeed beautiful & one regrets that his peculiar headdress hides so much of it. He speaks English remarkably well & seems to prefer doing so, more than his own language, which he thinks he will forget. So far he does not feel the cold, likes the climate & is pleased with everything. He regrets India not being nearer, to enable more Indians to come here, 'as it would open their eyes'. The Maharajah seems to be very fond of music. Sir C. Wood told me that the young man had been horrified by the iniquities and cruelties he had witnessed that it gave him quite a horror of returning to the Sikh country. Ld Hardinge said that the Maharajah had been in the arms of Jewahir Singh, on an elephant, when the latter had been shot; his mother, the Ranee, was a very violent woman, who now lived in Nepaul.

Of course she must write and tell Lord Dalhousie about her meeting with the young man who was still to some extent his responsibility: 'The Queen wishes to tell Lord Dalhousie how much interested and pleased we have been in making the acquaintance of the young Maharajah Duleep Singh. It is not without feelings of pain and sympathy that the Queen sees this young Prince once destined to so high and powerful a position and now reduced to so dependent a one by our arms; his youth, amiable character, and striking good looks; as well as his being a Christian, the first of his high Rank who has embraced our faith, must incline every one favourably towards him, and it will be a pleasure to us to do all we can to help him and to befriend and protect him.'[2]

Lord Dalhousie, in his reply, was to take some credit for the creation of such a paragon: 'The Governor General has read with grateful pleasure the sentiments Your Majesty has expressed regarding Maharajah Duleep Singh. Naturally from the peculiar relations in which they have stood towards each other, and from the frankness & confidence which the boy has always shown, the Governor General feels a strong and genuine interest in his welfare. He feels some pride in the acquirements, such as they are, in the manner, feelings, & above all, in the character of the Maharajah, contrasting so honourably as they do, with those of other youths in India of his age.'[3]

Sittings to 'our dear Winterhalter', as the queen referred to him, were to start almost at once in the White Drawing Room at Buckingham Palace. The queen, who was a fair artist herself, would often drop in to see the work in progress. 'Went to see Winterhalter painting,' she wrote in her journal for 10 July, 'where we found the Maharajah in his full dress with Dr. Login and Col. Phipps [Keeper of the Privy Purse]. The former is a Scotch gentleman, a Dr., who has had charge of the Maharajah for 4 years, indeed ever since the annexation of the Punjab. He seems a sensible clever man, much attached to the Maharajah & anxious to keep him out of all mischief. He has come here to learn & see, but not *at present* to enter society, excepting here and there, to a quiet dinner . . . Winterhalter was in ecstasies at the beauty and nobility of the young Maharajah. He was very aimiable & patient standing so still and giving a sitting of up to 2 hours.'[4]

Winterhalter, who had painted most of the royalty of Europe and was used to problems of presentation, made the Maharajah stand on a dais so that he could more easily elongate his rather stocky figure. The painter explained that he wanted his sitter to 'grow into' the picture. As he was never to grow taller the effect is more flattering than factual.

At the next sitting the queen met Mrs Login, whom she

45

described as 'a pretty, pleasing person, quite like a mother to the Maharajah'. 'We were present for a while at the Maharajah's sitting, which went very well,' the queen entered in her journal for 11 July. 'He was again in full dress. The portrait of me, set in diamonds, which he generally wears, was the gift of Ld Auckland to his father, as well as the ring with my miniature, which he had on today ... We showed him a drawing of himself & a view of Lahore done by young Hardinge, which seemed to interest and please him; Dr. and Mrs. Login told me many curious & interesting things about the Maharajah, his family, & India generally.'[5]

Two days later Pundit Nehemiah Goreh, the Maharajah's convert attendant, was brought along for her to meet. 'Albert talked with him for an hour about the Brahmin and Christian religions,' noted the queen. There was further informative talk about India – 'Dr. Login says that the Sikhs are a far superior race to the other Indians ... that the women kept up superstition, as we both observed they did in many countries. They were very ill educated and schools for girls were much needed. If they could be started it would be an immense change.'[6] The queen drew a lively miniature sketch of the pundit and another of the Maharajah which she pasted in her journal for the appropriate day. She tinted the Maharajah's turban (his 'peculiar headdress') gold and the Pundit's monkish robes a sombre brown.

During one sitting the queen drew Mrs Login aside and asked her in a low voice if the Maharajah ever referred to the Koh-i-noor and if so did he seem to regret it. Mrs Login replied that he had often spoken of it in India but not since he had been in England. The queen then said that she felt a certain delicacy about mentioning it to him and, now that it had been re-cut, even of letting him see it. She asked Mrs Login to find out his feelings on the subject. While riding in Richmond Park, Mrs Login casually asked if he would like to see the Koh-i-noor again? The Maharajah's response was encouraging enough for her to make a favourable report to the queen. In her *Recollections*, Mrs Login described the embarrassing occasion of the meeting of the Maharajah with the 'mountain of light', now reduced to half its size by a diamond-cutter from Amsterdam:

She came across to me at once on entering the room, the Maharajah being on the platform, posing for the artist, asking eagerly if I had executed her commands ... The Queen seemed as pleased as I had been at Duleep Singh's response to my question, and, signalling to the Prince Consort, who was engaged in conversation with the painter at the other end of the room, they held a hurried consultation in whispers, despatching one of the gentlemen-in-waiting with a message. For about half-an-hour they both remained, watching the progress of the portrait and conversing with those present, when a slight bustle near the door made me look in that direction, and beheld, to my amazement, the gorgeous uniforms of a group of beef-eaters from the Tower, escorting an official bearing a small casket, which he presented to Her Majesty. This she opened hastily, and took therefrom a small object which, still holding, she showed to the Prince, and, both advancing together to the dais, the Queen cried out, 'Maharajah, I have something to show you!' Turning hastily ... Duleep Singh stepped hurriedly down to the floor, and, before he knew what was happening, found himself once more with the Koh-i-noor in his grasp, while the Queen was asking him 'if he thought it improved, and if he would have recognized it again?' Truth to tell, at first sight, no one who had known it before would have done so, diminished to half its size, and thereby, in Oriental eyes, reft of much of its association and symbolism. That this was what he felt I am inwardly convinced; yet, as he walked towards the window, to examine it more closely, turning it hither and thither, to let the light upon its facets, and descanting upon its peculiarities and differences, and the skill of the diamond-cutter, for all his air of polite interest and curiosity, there was a passion of repressed emotion in his face, patent to one who knew him well, and evident, I think, to Her Majesty, who watched him with sympathy not unmixed with anxiety – that I may truly say, it was to me one of the most excruciatingly uncomfortable quarters-of-an-hour that I ever passed! For an awful terror seized me, lest I had unwittingly deceived her Majesty as to his intentions, seeing him stand there turning and turning that stone about in his hands, as if unable to part with it again, now he had it once more in his possession! At last, as if summoning up his resolution after a profound struggle, and with a deep sigh, he raised his eyes from the jewel, and – just as the tension on my side was near breaking point, so that I was prepared for almost anything – even to seeing him, in a sudden fit of madness, fling the precious talisman out of the open window by which he stood! and the other spectators' nerves were equally on edge – he moved deliberately to where Her Majesty was standing, and, with a deferential reverence, placed in her hand the famous diamond, with the words: 'It is to me, Ma'am, the greatest pleasure thus to have the opportunity, as a loyal subject, of *myself* tendering to *my* Sovereign the Koh-i-noor!'[7]

Dalhousie was not amused when he heard the story. 'Login's talk to you about the Koh-i-noor being a present from Duleep to the Queen is arrant humbug,' he grumbled to Sir George Couper. 'He knew as well as I did it was nothing of the sort; and if I had been within a thousand miles of him he would not have dared to utter such a piece of trickery. Those "beautiful eyes", with which Duleep has taken captive of the court, are his mother's eyes, – those with which she captivated and controlled the old Lion of the Punjab. The officer who had charge of her from Lahore to Benares told me this. He said that hers were splendid orbs.'[8]

There was no reference by the Maharajah then, or at any other time, to the other magnificent jewels from Runjit Singh's treasury deviously retained by the East India Company and presented to the queen after the Great Exhibition of 1851 as a reward for her interest in their exhibit: 'The jewels are truly magnificent,' she had then noted. '... The very large pearls, 224 in number, strung in 4 rows, are quite splendid and a very beautiful ornament. The girdle of 19 emeralds is wonderful and also of immense value. The emeralds, square in shape and very large, are alternatively engraved, and unfortunately all are cut flat. They are set round with diamonds and fringed with pearls. The rubies are even more wonderful, they are cabochons, unset but pierced. The one is the largest in the world, therefore even more remarkable than the Koh-i-noor. I am very happy the British

Crown will possess these jewels, for I shall certainly make them Crown Jewels.'[9] In her graphic account of the Maharajah's confrontation with his family diamond, Mrs Login gave no hint that behind the Maharajah's gallantry there might lie a touch of irony. He was later to refer to the queen as 'Mrs Fagin',[10] a receiver of stolen goods.

'Winterhalter has got the whole figure beautifully & the likeness is so grand,' the queen wrote in her journal.[11] It was indeed a magnificent picture – the proud young oriental prince in his blue and gold striped blouse with matching turban decked with jewels, her portrait in miniature on the fifth row of pearls around his neck, and in the background, instead of the conventional column and curtain, the amber plains of the Punjab stretching to the pearly cupolas of Lahore. So handsome was her prince that the queen decided Marochetti must do a bust of him, which she had tinted by Millais just as Mr Gibson in Rome had done his 'Venus'. She ordered an engraving of the painting to be published, and suggested to Winterhalter that he do a companion piece of the little princess of Coorg, for whose future she was already developing ideas.

When the queen moved down to Osborne, her Italianate palazzo on the Isle of Wight, the Maharajah must of course be asked to visit, inspect and be inspected by the family. His day of arrival – 21 August – coincided with a difficult moment in the Crimean War and that morning the queen had been discussing Lord Raglan's latest grave dispatches from Sebastopol with the secretary for war, the Duke of Newcastle. But she seemed in high spirits that afternoon as she went out driving with the Maharajah at her side. In her journal she noted:

We took a drive out towards Carisbrooke, & came back by Cowes & over the Ferry. We took the Maharajah with us, who had arrived early in the afternoon, also the Duke (Newcastle) & the two ladies ... The Maharajah sat next to me, very handsomely dressed & with his jewels on. Speaking of Heera Singh (the older brother of Gholab, who was murdered), whom the Maharajah remembered well saying 'My uncle murdered him', I observed that he must have seen many terrible things. He answered sorrowfully, with a very expressive look 'Oh, Yr. Majesty. I've seen dreadful things; when I think of it it makes me shiver. I am certain they would have murdered *me* too, had I remained.' This thought reconciles me to having had to despoil him of his Kingdom, & he is convinced of the wisdom of this himself. We were struck by his anxiety to improve himself, his intelligence & at the same time gaiety.'

The following day she wrote:

We breakfasted in the Alcove, with the truly amiable Maharajah, who is so kind to the children, playing so nicely with them. We then walked him to the Barton & showed him all over the Farm, the cattle, the machinery &c, the latter interesting him particularly. The Duke of Newcastle, & Dr. Login joined us – At ¼ to 3 started with the 4 eldest children, the Maharajah & all the Ladies and Gentlemen joined us to go on board the 'Victoria & Albert' where Sir J. Graham joined us ... We steamed out to the Needles, inside of which we lay & watched the gun practice on the 'Arrow', a new gun boat, just built for the purpose. Coming home I had a most interesting conversation with the Maharajah, about his motives for becoming a Christian, entirely at his own wish, & with what determination, & in the face of the great opposition, he carried it through. I was much touched and impressed by his fervent & strongly religious turn of mind. His sister-in-law would hardly speak to him since his conversion. They used to kiss each other but now she only kissed his hand '& then bathed afterwards'. He still thinks & hopes his nephew *will* become a Christian.

The queen was so 'touched and impressed' by the conversation she had with the Maharajah about religion that she committed her thoughts to paper in the form of a long memorandum:

I asked the Maharajah yesterday ... *what* had made him think of becoming a Christian. *'Nothing at all,'* was his answer, no one whatever had urged him, quite the contrary – but when the Brahmin (who has since not had the courage to *own* his faith and has become a shopkeeper at Benares) began reading to him the different stories in their religion about Cows – & eating in the fingers

& the perdition it wd. be if he bathed in one place & not another, he began to doubt it very much & settled in his *own* mind that he wd. become a Christian but was so afraid that he wd. be prevented doing so by his own people & by Christians that he was determined to wait till he went to England & then at sea he thought he *might* break his caste. He asked permission to go to England & this was not granted; though Dr. Login was away at this time he continued having portions of the scripture read to him & when the act of the stoning of St. Stephen was read to him 'The tears came into my eyes, & I said this religion must be true.' Shortly after he was determined to take this step wh. considering the indignation of his own people was a very bold one. However he was so fearful that he wd. not be allowed to do it, that, 'I was determined to break my caste without asking for permission so that they cd. not prevent me. Accordingly I proceeded to take tea with them in my room & sent my playfellow, a young Englishman, to tell the other; & one of my servants came & stood in the door & called & said "Mind what you are trying to do & wait till Dr. Login comes." And I said Go. I am yr. master & you have nothing to say & I shall do just what I like. So I took the tea, & from the moment I had done that I grew bolder & bolder.' Then at first they wd. not allow him to embrace Christianity – as they wd. not believe him but allowed him to have instruction for 2 yrs from Mr Jay & Dr Carshore both clergymen & at the end of that he was baptised; he is an Episcopalian but prefers the Presbyterian Religion but don't mind to wh. he belongs as long as it is a good Christian religion. The Presbyterian Religion the Indians call 'The Englishman's religion'. I told him that the *real* truths & the *really essential* points were very simple and that to be a Christian & to do *one's duty* was what was necessary, wh. he entirely believed in & seems extremely fervent, sincere, & religious in his feelings. He is aware of the difference & defects of the Catholic Religion, wh. resembles he says the Brahmins. Already at Lahore – when no Christians approached him – he had the idea & laughed at their absurd practices with the cows – tying a string around their tails, he used to pull them by their tails. He expressed himself thoroughly for the strict observance of the Sunday – thinks that is right & 'wd. not like to run about & play' but to sing hymns & play on the organ. He has not yet taken the sacrament, & said 'I should not wish to take it until I am well prepared.' Altogether I was much struck by the very fervent &

strongly religious turn of mind of the *poor* young Prince –
When I told him how many people wd. wish to make a show of
him as a Convert – & that I warned him against it & said I had
spoken strongly to Dr. Login & Sir Charles Wood on the subject,
he replied that was the very last thing he wished for – or had ever
thought of & that I might be sure he wd. never allow himself to
be used in that way; that his wish had been to come here quietly
– that he did *not* know where he shd. ultimately settle & here his
voice faltered, & his countenance became sad, & he seemed quite
overcome as he proceeded & said 'Wherever I am I shall always
pray for yr. Majesty' & that his feelings wd. ever be those of gratitude
& attachment'. Poor Boy he touched me deeply. I said I always
would take the gtsts. interest in him – as I always have done.

He is most anxious that missionaries shd. go out to India particularly to the Punjab – for that now was the time; – that the idea
of those Indians who were *not* converted from conviction was that
by becoming Christians they obtained every earthly advantage,
and eternal happiness hereafter, that there were hardly any Indians
(of rank I infer) of responsibility in India (he alluded to the Rajah
of Coorg) who might behave very well here – but became the *g'test.*
blackguards in India.[13]

It is clear from entries in the queen's journal that on that
visit she thoroughly enjoyed the Maharajah's company and
did her best to make him feel at home in her family circle:

August 23. Our aimiable young visitor again at breakfast with
us, then the Boys took him to the Swiss Cottage, whilst I read in
the Alcove ... We rowed out to the 'Arrow' & examined the great
gun & the immense shells which are fired from it. But somehow
we were not struck by the practicality of the whole thing. The
gun boat draws so much water that the whole advantage to be
gained by it, would seem to be lost ... At a little before 3 we all
went to see the people marching to their dinner before the Fête,
& we walked through the tents to the dinner, Arthur taking the
Maharajah's hand ... The gentlemen, Capt. du Plat, Mr. Gibbs,
Mr. Saumaraz & Mr. Talbot (both of the yacht) took part in running races, playing leap frog &c. There was Blindman's Buff, foot-
races, football with the legs tied, wheelbarrow races &c & dancing.
At the last it was dipping for oranges, bobbing for gingerbread
&c no one enjoyed it more than our young guest, who laughed

heartily & was greatly amused. Our children were constantly near him & chatting with him & he carried little Leopold, who is so fond of him, in his arms.

August 24. After breakfast, we walked with the Maharajah, taking him round the pleasure grounds, showing him the plants & flowers in the garden all of which he was pleased & interested in. He planted a fine deodara & was amused at having to shovel in the earth with a spade. When we came in we took leave of the Maharajah, shaking him warmly by the hand & wishing him many happy returns of his approaching birthday, when he will be 16, & would have come of age and taken the reigns of govt. into his own hands, had we not been obliged to take the Punjab!

The young Maharajah was especially popular with the royal children. Little Prince Leopold, suffering from haemophilia, was his favourite and he would carry him around on his back so that he would not fall and could keep up with the others. The two older boys, the Prince of Wales, and Prince Alfred, became good friends. On this first visit to Osborne they did sketches of him and he photographed them with the help of Prince Albert, an early camera enthusiast, in clothes that had been sent from India.

Prince Albert's photographs of the Maharajah were more professional and clearly show his everyday costume of the period – the Sikh cashmere tunic worn under a single-breasted velvet coat richly embroidered in gold, and European-style trousers with a thick stripe of gold embroidery down the seams. As well as other assorted jewels, he invariably wore several rows of pearls around his neck, and a pair of long emerald and pearl earrings.

The Maharajah had almost been one of the family. 'I was quite sorry to see him go,' the queen added in her journal. 'I take quite a maternal interest in him & I pray he may be protected, guided & kept as good & innocent as he is at present.'[14]

Lord Dalhousie, who received an account of the visit to Osborne from Sir George Couper, then comptroller to the queen's mother, seemed to think that contact with the great might indeed affect the Maharajah's 'innocence' and give him ideas above his, or even the governor general's station:

It is very good for the Maharajah to have seen the Royal Family under such an aspect as you describe at Osborne [he wrote in reply]. But I am a little afraid that this exceeding distinction will not be for his future comfort. If he is to live and die in England, well and good, but if he is to return to India, he is not likely to be rendered more contented with his position there by being so highly treated in England; and, after breakfasting with queens and princesses, I doubt his much liking the necessity of leaving his shoes at the door of the Governor General's room, when he is admitted to visit him, which he will certainly be again required to do. The 'nightcappy' appearance of his turban is his strongest national feature. Do away with that and he has no longer any outward and visible sign of a Sikh about him.[15]

Dalhousie would almost certainly have been among those who disagreed with the queen on the matter of protocol regarding their protégé, a question which she had been considering since his first visit to Buckingham Palace. Where exactly should a deposed maharajah, allowed certain honours under treaty, stand in the complicated hierarchy of European society? Charles Phipps, who had become responsible at the palace for matters relating to the Maharajah, projected the Queen's view that it would hardly be right and proper in feeling, that he should be treated as any foreign nobleman as that would mean his *placement* after all foreign ministers and chargés d'affaires. Her prime minister, Lord Aberdeen, regarded his position as 'anomalous and exceptional' and recommended that it 'was expedient for the Queen to shew him such special marks of regard as would be due to a Foreign Prince in whose welfare Her Majesty felt an interest'.[16] Other weighty opinions were sought and given and in the end it was agreed what the queen had already decided – that the Maharajah should take the rank of Prince, equal to those European princes bearing the title of Serene Highness.

That an Indian prince should take precedence over an English primate caused some raising of eyebrows and the queen's indulgence brought disparaging comments from old hands at the East India Company, who may have persuaded Aberdeen to follow up his first letter with the oblique suggestion that she was spoiling him:

Lord Aberdeen is rejoiced to learn that Your Majesty has had reason to be pleased with the Maharajah and feels that Your Majesty's gracious condescension is a source of pleasure to Your Majesty, as well as of deep gratitude on the part of the young Prince. But while indulging these feelings, Lord Aberdeen humbly begs to remind Your Majesty that too great distinction may ultimately prove disadvantageous to the Maharajah himself. Any such honour as would forbid the possibility of an easy intercourse with your Majesty's subjects might produce such an effect. But Your Majesty will perfectly be able to judge how far this may properly be carried; and Lord Aberdeen ought perhaps to request Your Majesty's pardon for presuming to advert to the subject.[17]

In this instance the queen was not prepared to tolerate even this most delicate corrective and expressed her attitude in a tart memorandum:

With regard to the young Maharajah. The Queen wishes to observe to Lord Aberdeen we have *not* paid or intend to pay any extraordinary distinctions to him but have merely treated him in strict accordance with the opinion given us by Ld. Aberdeen's message in which he stated that 'he shd. be *treated* as a *Pce.* in whom the Queen took an *interest*' & we accordingly treated him *just* as we do *all Princes* (not speaking here of those who belong to *Royal Hs's* – like Pce. Ed. of S-Weimar, the Pce. of Hesse or Pce. of Nassau who mixed very freely with Society) – and the Queen does not apprehend this will in any way interfere with his free intercourse with Society. He has been on a visit to Hardinge – intends paying some more in the country generally; he dislikes *large parties* which is perhaps as well for his own sake – tho' he likes small ones.[18]

The visit to Lord Hardinge, referred to by the queen, was the start of a tour organized by Login to give the Maharajah some idea of country life and to inspire him with a desire to settle down in England on an estate of his own. Hardinge, who had been governor general when the Sikhs were first subdued and had succeeded the Duke of Wellington as commander-in-chief of the army, lived at South Park in Kent. The queen had given the Maharajah a hunter for his birthday, which had been sent down in advance, and he went for pleasant rides through the local byways. Some puzzlement was caused when he propounded Colonel Sleeman's eccentric views about the common ethnic origin of the Sikhs and the Kentish Jutes. Highlights of the Maharajah's progress were a visit to Scotland, where he stayed with Lord Dalhousie's daughters near Edinburgh, and with Lord and Lady Morton at Dalmahoy; there was a week with Sir Charles Wood at Hickleton Hall in Yorkshire; Earl Fitzwilliam demonstrated the latest in agricultural machinery at Wentworth and Lord Hatherton showed off his new system of irrigation in Staffordshire. He made a number of new friends and impressed everybody with his candour and simple good manners. Sir Charles Wood, who was keeping an eye on him, reported to the queen that the Maharajah was 'one of the most charming young men he knew'.[19]

Lord Dalhousie, when he had an account of the trip from Login, was less than sanguine about the idea of the Maharajah becoming an English landlord in his own right. 'I am altogether incredulous as to the probability of the Maharajah ever entertaining such a wish. The habits and idea of his whole life, from his cradle until now, have been little calculated to inspire him with a desire for incurring the trouble of managing a landed estate, and I do not believe that all his visits to Lord Hatherton's irrigation, or to the great cattle show, or to the tile drains and deep ploughing of East Lothian, are likely to create this taste in his mind.'[20]

On his return there was a visit to Windsor, duly recorded by the queen in the journal:

November 13 1854: Albert went to see the Maharajah Duleep Singh, who had arrived. Mama &c, the Maharajah (as well as Dr. Login) came for 2 nights. Sir H. & Ly. Seymour, Sir Hugh Ross,

Mr. Murray &c dined. The Maharajah sat next to me at dinner, dressed in his beautiful clothes & wonderful pearls & emeralds. He liked his trip to Edinburgh very much & also visited Sir C. Wood & Ld Hatherton. His studies are proceeding well ...

November 14: The Maharajah breakfasted with us & afterwards talked with Albert about his studies. He is very anxious to learn, which he had not been until he realised how much he was going to associate with Europeans. He had learnt nothing from books, till he left Lahore, it being unusual for the Sovereigns of the Punjab to *learn* ... We took the Maharajah over the State Rooms, Library & Armoury. He seemed particularly pleased with some very valuable Indian illuminated works in the Library, one of which Dr. Login had brought over with great difficulty in '39, & even at great personal risk from the Khan of Herat. We took care to avoid showing the Sikh cannon sent by Ld Gough.

Dr Login's tutorial role was, however, not to go unappreciated or unrewarded. He was soon to be knighted, though he modestly disclaimed that he deserved it. 'It has been as much a spontaneous act of Her Majesty's favour,' he wrote Dalhousie, 'as it is possible to be, and can only be considered in the light of a compliment to the Maharajah and a token of Her Majesty's high approval and encouragement.'[21]

The next visit to Windsor was early in the New Year.

Jan 26 1855: Mama &c, the Maharajah D-S (staying over Sunday) dined, & the latter sat next to me. He does not seem to mind the cold, & has been trying to skate. He is getting on well with his studies & has got a new tutor, bright, & young enough to be a companion for him.

Jan 27: Our young guest was at breakfast, looking extremely well, talking away with our Boys, anxious to hear about *their* lessons. He is very fond of carpentering & turning, also of fencing, which is not known in India ... Albert went out shooting & took the Maharajah with him, & in the afternoon he walked with me, Bessie W. & Eleanor P. He was in his beautiful golden coat, lined with fur. We walked through the Slopes, by Adelaide Cottage, to the gardens, where we went into some of the Greenhouses. The

Maharajah was very talkative. He said he was learning to dance, & meant to do so while he was in England – though *not* in India. He will not be going out into Society this year, but next year before he returns to India, which he will do, visiting France, Germany, and Italy on the way ... Dinner as yesterday, the Maharajah leading me in, & I sitting between him & the Duke of Argyll. The former was gay and talkative, talking about his own country, its peculiarities & customs. His anxiety to learn & improve himself is very great.

Jan 28: A sharp frost. After our breakfast we walked out with all the children & our aimiable young Indian friend, who is most popular with them. A few flakes of snow fell when we went out – service at 11, Maharajah being in our pew with us, which *seemed* like a dream ... The poor Boy is evidently nervous, and the early experiences of cruelty, murder & violence have made a deep impression upon that young, gentle and timid mind.

Jan 29: It had again frozen hard in the night & was rather dull. The Maharajah took leave of us at 10. He certainly has a very beautiful face, & such a charming expression.

The queen was concerned about the Maharajah's reaction to the cold weather and tried to insist that he wear woollen underclothes. 'Indeed, Ma'am I cannot bear the feel of flannel next to my skin!' Lady Login quotes him as replying. 'It makes me long to scratch and you would not like to see me scratching myself in your presence!'[22]

The Maharajah was next to see the queen at a levée at St James's Palace, one of many royal occasions he was to attend in the future. The queen observed, in her journal for 29 March 1855, how he was 'sparkling with jewels'. At a dinner that week, when as usual he was seated next to her, she noted he looked 'very well', adding 'but he is timid in society & retiring though always *à la place*'. Count Bernstorff, the Prussian ambassador, complained about the Maharajah's *placement*, invariably next to the queen, and was sharply rebuked for his impertinence. '*She is astonished,*' the queen wrote to Clarendon, 'at any Ambassador pretending to dictate *who* is to be at the Queen's table ... She trusts to Lord Clarendon kindly & *civilly* but firmly pointing this out to Count Bern-

storff and showing him the inutility of making himself disagreeable, always finding fault with everything, which the
Queen *knows* he does, for he constantly writes home every
sort of things which produce ill blood at Berlin.'[23]

The Logins, after moving from Wimbledon to Roehamp-
ton, established themselves in Kew at Church House – a
'grace and favour' house acquired through the influence of
Lord Dalhousie's friend Sir George Couper. This information caused the ailing governor general to write to Login:
'You have done a tidy bit of business in getting a house out
of the Court, and I advise you to rest content with that, and
not seek for more "marks of consideration", or they may
be anxious for his return to Futteghur.'[24]

Meanwhile, it having been agreed that a public school or
university 'would not do at all', the Maharajah's educational
programme proceeded under Login's direction and a report
of progress was sent to Colonel Phipps at the palace, for
onward transmission to the queen: 'I am happy to say that
the Maharajah continues to go on very well. He has fairly
settled to his studies and takes greater interest in them than
he did. Besides giving a couple of hours daily to classical and
mathematical masters on four days a week I have arranged
to give him object lessons very frequently ... I propose to
make the Crystal Palace his special school of instruction.'[25]
Practical demonstrations in botany, lessons on the har-
monium, and visits to places of educational interest rounded
off the curriculum.

We strongly dissuaded Dr. Login from engaging any English
Tutor for the Maharajah [the queen, who had experience of such
matters in her own family, entered in the journal], but only
Masters, which Dr. Login being himself the Tutor, he said he could
do. His task had been a very pleasant one, owing to the very aimiable disposition of the Boy & his extreme truthfulness – an exception to Orientals in general – that his own good sense & the principles of Christianity had helped to make him overcome the natural
indolence of disposition, inherent in all Easterners. I observed how
important it would be that he should not fall into bad hands, which

Dr. Login hopes to be able to prevent; but it would depend a great deal on who was with him. He was very resolute & determined & had shown a great deal of determination in coming here, many of his people having tried to persuade him not to do so.[26]

Login's further report to Lord Dalhousie indicated that Prince Albert, also, was concerning himself in the problem of educating an 'indolent Easterner':

The Maharajah continues to apply himself to his studies, and has made much more progress than formerly, because he now puts some heart in his work. At present he devotes his attention to the German language, which, from its affinity to the Sanskrit and Hindu, is, he thinks, more likely to be useful to him than French. Perhaps his intercourse with the Prince Consort has been a spur to his application in this particular branch. He has great facility in acquiring languages, however, and this is likely to be very useful to him if he travels. Among his other accomplishments, he is learning photography, with much success. This has been greatly encouraged by the Prince Consort, who has taken great interest in his progress.[27]

Duleep Singh, in fact, became an ardent photographer and was apt to present his friends with their often unrecognizable 'likenesses'.

Since boyhood the Maharajah had shown a keen interest in field sports and he was enthusiastic when Login suggested renting a sporting estate in Scotland, as was becoming fashionable in those days for gentlemen of means from the South. Castle Menzies, in Perthshire, the property of Sir John Menzies, was decided on. As the dusky laird of this fortress-like retreat, the kilted Maharajah was to become something of a local legend, as were his retainers, who included six wounded veterans of the Crimean War. His valet, Thornton, formerly coachman at Futteghur, and Russell, the butler, also donned the kilt, the latter sporting the royal dress tartan complete with silver embellishments. Another servant, a handsome young dragoon who had been in the charge of the Light Brigade at Balaclava, was one of the sights of Perth-shire as he strode through the village with all his medals jang-ling on the Maharajah's blue and green livery.

Guests at the house were mostly friends of the Logins and included senior officials from the India Board who might one day come in useful. Though the Maharajah was to meet in neighbouring houses older men such as Lord Breadalbane, who asked him to stay at Taymouth, and such notable figures as Archbishop Tait, William Wilberforce, Delane of *The Times*, and the great Quaker John Bright, the only person of his own generation he made a friend of was Ronald Leslie-Melville, heir to Lord Leven and Melville.

In Scotland, Login was distressed to find that his ward's interest in falconry showed no signs of lessening and he would exercise his birds by flying them at grouse. Login con-sidered the sport involved unnecessary cruelty and tried to keep him concentrating on his shooting. It was sometimes said of the Maharajah that he showed indifference to suffer-ing, so the Logins, as well as other peripheral advisers, were on the look-out for what they called 'signs of an Eastern nature'; the story of 'the poor woman's cat' became a cele-brated contribution to the myth. Lady Login's version told how at dinner at the castle there was a 'good deal of chaff' about a cat which 'someone', presumably the Maharajah, had shot while returning from the day's sport. Login said that he hoped it was not some poor woman's cat, to which the Maharajah had replied that he did not care if it was as it had no business there. Afterwards, in the drawing room, some of the ladies were saying how cruel the Maharajah was, but Lady Hatherton's intense admiration for him prompted her to try to prove everyone wrong. She disguised herself as the village woman whose cat had been killed and was 'dis-covered' in the billiard room bewailing her loss and demand-ing compensation. Alec Lawrence, Sir Henry's son, was moved to tears, but the Maharajah stood unmoved, his eyes blazing with anger. Finally, shaking a billiard cue at the importunate woman, he burst out: 'Yes, cry! Cry until you are tired. Don't let your brutes cross my path. Not a penny shall you get from me!' Then he roughly showed her the door, at which point Lady Hatherton dropped her disguise. The Maharajah's look of consternation and embarrassment was quickly brushed on one side. Waiving his profuse apologies for discourtesy, Lady Hatherton declared that she had 'only admired his princely air of command', and felt him to be 'every inch a king'.[28]

CHAPTER 4

The Rejection of Princess Gouramma

NOT long after the Maharajah arrived in England, the queen tried to forward one of her special little projects – the making of a match between the Maharajah Duleep Singh and her thirteen-year-old goddaughter, Victoria Gouramma of Coorg. Charles Phipps, who was perforce beginning to take a personal interest in the fortunes of the queen's young protégés, wrote to Login from Osborne concerning the possibility of an alliance:

> The more I think upon the subject, the more it appears to me that these two young people are pointed out for each other. The only two Christians of high rank of their own countries, both having the advantage of early European influences, there seem to be many points of sympathy between them. They are both religious, both fond of music, both gentle in their natures. I know that the Queen thinks that this would be the best arrangement for their happiness *provided that they were to like each other* – of course, without this no happiness could exist. Of course the Queen takes a great interest in the little Princess, as Her Majesty considers Herself as *more* than a Godmother to her.[1]

Gouramma was at the time living in the care of Mrs Drummond, the wife of an Indian army major who had ingratiated himself with the Coorgs at Benares. The rajah was regarded by India House as an 'old reprobate' and his influence over his daughter as 'dangerously Hindoo'.[2] He was really quite a well-meaning man and liked to see his daughter as often as he could. Mrs Drummond, however, kept her away from him as much as possible, even taking a house in

Edinburgh. The two young Indians had already met on several occasions, at Kew and at Castle Menzies, and anxious accounts had been exchanged between their elders on the development of the relationship. The queen wrote to Lord Dalhousie: 'The young people have met and were pleased with each other, so that the Queen hopes that their union will in the course of time come to pass. Her little God-daughter has been here lately and though still childish for her age (she is nearly fourteen) is pretty, lively, intelligent, and going on satisfactorily in her education. Of the young Maharajah ... we can only speak in terms of praise. He promises to be a bright example to all Indian Princes – for he is thoroughly good and aimiable and most anxious to improve himself.'[3]

Probably because he felt he was being pressed into what he regarded as an arranged marriage, such as he had been led to believe was not the European way, the Maharajah swore to Login that he was determined to remain a bachelor. When the queen learned of the reluctant suitor, she consulted Lord Dalhousie, whose reply from Ceylon, where he was resting on his way back to England dying of cancer, carried undertones of disapproval of an interest he regarded as undue:

Lord Dalhousie will be most willing to give you his best advice and aid to the young Maharajah Duleep Singh, in whom your Majesty is pleased to take so much interest. The boy has the qualities and dispositions of Eastern blood and if he can be formed and can be kept a well-bred and well-conducted gentleman, it is the utmost that the most sanguine could expect to make of such material.

The Maharajah's vow of celibacy will not prove irrevocable, and Lord Dalhousie is to express respectfully his entire concurrence in the view which Your Majesty has always taken of the alliance which would be best for him. Very early in life he showed that he could be obstinate beyond all belief when he pleased; and if he does not himself acknowledge the advantage of an alliance with the Princess, no power on earth will make him form it ...[4]

It was not until the end of 1856 that the queen came to realize that her little plan was unlikely to succeed. She had the matter out at Osborne:

The Maharajah breakfasted and lunched with us. [After Church] Albert had a long conversation with the Maharajah, who poured out all his feelings & wishes to him, which Albert seemed pleased with & thought very sensible. I have not the time to enter into all the details, but will just allude to the principal ones, some of which are embodied in a Mmdum. which has been sent in to the East India Company. His principal wish is to become of age, & to have more money allowed to insure his life for his eventual children, should he marry, & to purchase land in England as well as in India, to be able to move about, without having to get the permission of the E.I. Company. This, civilised as he now is, he feels much the need of. He wants to spend his time in India & England, or rather more Scotland, as he feels he could no longer live exclusively in India – his health even not being able to stand it. He also spoke of requiring company, Sir J.Login being too old for him, mentioning a very nice young man, nephew to Ld Leven, who is now going to travel with him. Albert pointed out to the Maharajah the dangers of falling into bad hands, which he is quite alive to, & dreads more than anyone. Albert said that a good wife would be the best companion for him, to which he replied that he did not wish to be hurried or pressed about that, as he did not wish to marry till he was 23 or 24. It was such a difficulty. He could not marry a Heathen, & an Indian who would become a Christian only to please him, would be very objectionable. Were he to marry a European, his children would be half-caste, which would not do. Albert then spoke of our idea regarding Gouramma, to which he replied that he could not marry her, – that he liked her very much, thought her a very nice little girl, whom he would like as a friend but *not* as his wife. She did not at all come up to his idea of a person he could marry. He *must* have time, & he wished to see the world. Albert told him he must beware of designing mothers, who might try to catch him, & if he lost heart, it might be too late. He replied that he was also quite aware of this. Poor boy, I feel so much for him, for he is so good & so well principled. But I am sorry about Gouramma, who I know would wish to marry him.... The Maharajah is so civilised & like other people that one forgets what he was.[5]

It had been agreed that the Maharajah should 'come of age' at eighteen, instead of sixteen as was the practice among the

Sikhs. He therefore attained his majority on 4 September 1856. From the beginning the East India Company had shown no great zeal in granting the allowance to which their ward was entitled under the terms of the treaty. They had not yet submitted an account and had been withholding sums of money, made available after the death of family pensioners, to which he thought himself entitled. Now that he had reached his majority, he became more assertive and began to press the men of Leadenhall Street for an immediate and more generous settlement. At the same time, chafing perhaps under the earnest supervision of Sir John Login, he wanted freedom to travel without permission and to live where he liked instead of having his residence directed or approved.

Sir Charles Wood, to whom he sent his application for a review and an accounting of his affairs, was slow to reply, and there was a suggestion that he wait until he was twenty-one, like everyone else in Britain. On the other hand there was the question of whether he was a British citizen at all. The Maharajah became restive. The queen, who had a copy of his petition, was keeping an eye on the situation, and could see that her young friend was becoming nervous and depressed by the uncertainty over his future. She took matters into her own hands by putting her heartfelt views in a memorandum to the president of the Board of Control:

Osborne, Oct 15th, 1856.
Upon the Maharajah Duleep Singh.
The Queen has seen the Memorandum which the Maharajah Duleep Singh has sent to the East India Company. She thinks all he asks very fair and reasonable, and she trusts that the E.I. Company will be able to comply with them. As we are in complete possession since '49 of the Maharajah's enormous and splendid kingdom, the Queen thinks we ought to do *everything* (which does not interfere with the safety of her Indian dominions) to render the position of this interesting and peculiarly good and aimiable Prince as agreeable as possible, and not to let him have the feeling that he is a *prisoner*.

His being a Christian and completely European, (or rather more

English) in his habits and feelings render this much more necessary and at the same time more easy.

The Queen has a very strong feeling that everything should be done to shew respect and kindness towards these poor fallen Indian Princes, whose kingdoms we have taken from them, and who are naturally very sensitive to attention and kindness.

Amongst all these however the Maharajah stands to a certain degree alone, from his civilisation and likewise from his having lost his kingdom when he was a child, entirely by the faults and deceits of others.[6]

Lord Stanley replied that any claim by the Maharajah on the British government would be considered 'with a disposition to deal with it in a spirit of liberality and fairness'. He ended: 'The question now at issue must be reported on by the local authorities previous to decision here.'[7] Which was his way of saying that he was getting a difficult matter off his hands by passing it on to the government of India.

To further the Maharajah's education, and perhaps to take his mind off problems about his future, the Logins decided that a long holiday on the Continent would be to everyone's advantage. His friend Ronald Leslie-Melville, now an Oxford undergraduate, was persuaded to come along, and John Bright and his daughter Helen would join them at Genoa. The travellers set out with a few servants in attendance, including Thornton and Mr Cawood, the Maharajah's secretary. They went by train to Marseilles, which was then the end of the line, and on by carriage to Cannes.

The Maharajah was in top form. At Nice he was entertained by Lady Ely, and met the young Lord Dufferin, who as viceroy of India, was to feature in his life thirty years later. In Rome he caught a glimpse of Pope Pius IX, who made a special benediction as he passed in his carriage, but was thought by the Maharajah to have 'made snooks'[8] at him. Joining the penitents ascending the Santa Scala at St John Lateran on their knees, he bet he could race them all to the top. At Tivoli he sat in a fountain and told everyone he was Neptune. He followed hounds along the Appian Way and at a ball at Princess Doria's met the King of Bavaria and Queen Christina of Spain. He flirted with the ladies and twice declared himself in love. The fashionable Mr Gibson, who had already sculpted the queen, was prevailed upon to start a bust of him.

Venice proved to be a failure. Both the Maharajah and Ronald Leslie-Melville went down with malaria. Ronald became so ill that his parents were summoned from London. It was mid-May before the Maharajah arrived back from Switzerland, where the doctor had sent the two of them to recuperate.

Whilst the two young men were resting at Geneva, news came of a mutiny by native troops at Meerut, forty miles north-east of Delhi. On Sunday, 10 May 1857, sepoys of the Third Cavalry ran amok through the town. Delhi fell within twenty-four hours. The rebellion spread along the valley of the Ganges to Bareilly, Benares, Allahabad and Cawnpore. It was not until the end of September that an assault force of Sikhs, Gurkhas and Afghans subdued Delhi, by which time three thousand British and Indian soldiers had been killed. The Sikhs had proved to be a vital element in the suppression of the mutiny, though their inspiration was said to be more a desire to get at the throats of the Muslims in Delhi than a sense of loyalty to the British Raj. A number of people known to the Maharajah were involved in the affair – Frank Boileau, his boyhood friend, was wounded at the siege of Delhi; Sir Henry Lawrence, whom he remembered from Lahore days, died of wounds in the Lucknow Residency; Tommy Scott, come to Lucknow to take up a commission in the Indian army, found that his mother, brother and sister had been killed there. At Futteghur, also in the Lucknow district, the Maharajah's old house, which had been left in the charge of Sergeant Elliott, formerly Login's assistant at the Lahore treasury, was ransacked and badly damaged. Elliott, his wife and children, and Walter Guise, the Maharajah's former tutor, had tried to escape, along with two hundred others to the imagined safety of Cawnpore. They had piled into boats, but by the time they arrived, the Ruler, Nana Sahib, had changed his allegiance and ordered his men to massacre everyone on the river. Bhajun Lal, the Maharajah's first religious instructor, remained loyal and did his best to save what was left of the property at Futteghur.

With many of his friends among the victims, people thought it odd that Duleep Singh was never heard to express any outright condemnation of the rising, and the queen's friend, the Earl of Clarendon, went so far as to complain to her that the Maharajah had shown 'little or no regret for the atrocities of the Mutiny ... or sympathy for the sufferers'.[9] Lord Clarendon may not have appreciated that by this time the sufferers were Indians, against whom the British were taking savage reprisals, despite the instructions of the governor general, Lord Canning, who was given by his compatriots what was meant to be the pejorative cognomen of 'Clemency'.

The queen was quick to defend the Maharajah from the charge:

Though we might have perhaps wished the Maharajah to express his feelings on the subject of the late atrocities in India – it was hardly to be expected that he, naturally of a negative, though gentle and very aimiable disposition, should pronounce an opinion on so painful a subject – attached as he is to his country with all his aimiability and goodness – an *Eastern Nature*, he can also hardly, a deposed Indian Sovereign, *not very* fond of the British rule as represented by the East India Company, and above all, impatient of Sir John Login's tutorship, be expected to *like* to hear his Country people called *fiends* and *monsters*, and to see them brought in hundreds, if not thousands, to be executed. His best course is to say nothing – and he must think [so]. It is a great mercy he, poor boy, is not there.[10]

Clarendon, who had probably heard the famous cat story, wrote again saying the Maharajah was rumoured to have a cruel nature. It looked as if he was trying to influence the queen against him. She once more rose to his defence:

The Queen is much surprised at Lord Clarendon's observing that 'from what he hears the Maharajah was either from nature or early education cruel'. He must have changed very suddenly if this be true, for if there was a thing for which he was remarkable, it was his extreme gentleness and kindness of disposition. We have known him for three years (our two boys intimately), and he always shuddered at hurting anything ... His valet, who is a very respectable Englishman, and has been with him ever since his twelfth year, says that he never knew a kinder or more aimiable disposition. The Queen fears that people who do not know him well have been led away by their present very natural feelings and distrust of all Indians to slander him.[11]

However, even Login was not above criticizing the Maharajah's seeming lack of concern about the fate of his friends in India, and Clarendon had quoted him in support of his contention. Login, when challenged, explained his position to Phipps:

I *have* been a little disappointed that he has shewn so much indifference on the subject of the treacheries and cruelties perpetrated in India by the mutineers – and that he has scarcely admitted the propriety of abstaining from some of the usual gaieties at this season, in consequence of the sad intelligence we received from India of many whom he knew there, and to whom – like his late tutor, Mr Guise, and others – he had often expressed goodwill; and I have endeavoured to find excuses for this want of sympathy in the natural tendency of young men of his age, in his position, to allow nothing to interfere with their sports and amusements. When Lord Clarendon therefore asked me what the Maharajah thought of these occurrences in India, I could only say candidly that he did not show very great interest in them, and that at this season his whole attention was taken up with shooting and other field sports: but nothing I said to his Lordship could I think lead him to consider the Maharajah to be of a cruel disposition.

He may sometimes, when he sees that any of the sentiments which he expresses cause surprise or wonder, exaggerate them a little for amusement, but always with a tendency rather to deprecate than exalt himself in the estimation of those he converses with'.

It is very likely that this impression may have arisen from the Maharajah's own conversation or remarks he may have made to the Ladies whom he met at Taymouth who are at this time more than usually observant of any traits in character which they consider to be peculiarly oriental.... His habit of talking (about training falcons), and a certain expression about his mouth, which a lady at Taymouth pointed out to me as very indicative of Oriental character, have no doubt led them to attach an idea of cruelty to his disposition, which may, I fear, be injurious to him ... The Maharajah certainly had no sympathy for the Hindoo and Mahomedan sepoys in India, nor any other wish than that we should effectively put them down. He does not consider them to be his countrymen, nor refrain from expressing abhorrence of their conduct whenever it is mentioned, but although he even goes so far as to suggest modes of punishment for them – perhaps as effectual as ridiculous ('High caste Brahmins to be employed as turnspits to roast beef for English soldiers!') his feelings are not so strong as to overcome his natural indolence ...[12]

It was not until 29 December 1857 that the Court of Directors of the East India Company officially agreed that the Maharajah might manage his own affairs. Login's representations in favour of his ward had not endeared him to that establishment; in addition, he had expressed disapproval of many of their actions in India, and given the palace information and advice that contributed to the decision taken to end the company's rule the following year.

Now that he was free from restraint, the Maharajah immediately decided he would go off on a trip on his own account. He selected Sardinia, which he had heard offered good sport for his hawks and the chance of bagging a wild boar. The queen, like an anxious mother, watched over this trying of his wings: 'The Queen and Prince would hope to see the Maharajah before he goes abroad,' Phipps wrote to Login. 'Would Sunday next be too late a day to name for that purpose? The Queen desires me to say, that she hopes the Maharajah will not think of going abroad without somebody as a sort of A.D.C. as companion. Her Majesty thinks that to go quite alone would hardly be compatible with his rank and station ...'[13]

Their meeting took place on 14 February 1858 at Buckingham Palace. 'After luncheon saw the good M. about his journey to Sardinia and Corsica, & taking a gentleman with him. He suffers from our trying winter & will have to remain abroad until the beginning of the summer,' she entered in her journal. There was another meeting the following week. As usual, the Maharajah sat next to her at dinner: 'The M ... talked very sensibly and nicely about India, & thought the effect of its being *really* governed by me, would be very great; as things were before, it was not understood. He is looking for someone to travel with him.'[14]

The Maharajah agreed to take a Dr Parsons, and on 2 March, with a small entourage and a load of equipment, he set off. His first letter was to Lady Login: '... Dr Parsons, I think, is a very nice man; he seems to know something about everything, and enters into all my amusements. I fear I shall not enjoy this trip as I had hoped, as they try to please me too much, and I fear very much that if I do not take care I shall be spoilt for ever afterwards. They act towards me as I daresay Sir John remembers, as Dr Drummond used to do to the Duke of Atholl. He used to call him "His Grace" at every word, and if the Duke happened to drop anything, he used to rush forward to pick it up ...'[15]

The shooting in Sardinia, which the Maharajah thought looked 'very like India', was not much good. He came to the conclusion that 'there is no place in the world for sport like England'.[16] On his return he was happy to find that Login had finally negotiated the lease of Mulgrave, a fine estate in Yorkshire, with a considerable acreage of grouse moor.

Mulgrave Castle, a handsome battlemented building in grounds laid out by Capability Brown, belonged to the Normanbys. As Lord Normanby was ambassador to Florence, and his son in Nova Scotia, he was happy to rent his place to the Maharajah while he was serving abroad. He was related to Charles Phipps, and it is likely that the introduction came through him. An earlier Phipps, Constantine, had received another dusky visitor at Mulgrave in the previous century,

Omai, the 'noble savage' brought back from Tahiti in a ship of Captain Cook's fleet. The estate lay above the cliffs, near Whitby, and apart from the grouse moor, had some excellent mixed shooting.

Early in September, the Maharajah wrote to Lady Login from Mulgrave. She had lately been persuaded by the queen to take charge of Victoria Gouramma from her previous guardians, the Drummonds, under whose jurisdiction she had been caught out in a romantic 'scrape' with a stableboy, which had caused a local scandal and come to the ears of the queen. 'I wish you would arrange to pay me a visit soon, *before* you get tied down with the Princess; for I do not think it would do any good to bring her here. Any time will suit me, and please invite any of your friends you would like to meet you. What do you say to the Cunninghames, Alexanders, Pollocks and any others you like?'[17]

Colonel [now Sir Charles] Phipps was one of the first visitors, and must have enjoyed himself, for his report enabled the queen to write in her journal: 'Nov. 12 1858: Sir C.Phipps has been staying with the M. for a week at Mulgrave which he has taken for some years, & said nothing could have been better managed nor anyone do the honours with greater tact or less presumption, than did the M. He was extremely high principled & truthful with most gentlemanlike & chivalrous feelings, but rather indolent, & not caring to learn or read, this due probably to his Indian nature.'

Not content with his Yorkshire moor, the Maharajah, now that the lease of Castle Menzies had expired, was renting a lodge from Lord Breadalbane, Auchlyne, on Loch Tay. It was probably while he was up at Auchlyne that summer that he met a visitor to nearby Loch Garry House, Loch Tummel: the flamboyant sportsman and traveller, Samuel Baker. Baker, later to be dubbed 'Baker of the Nile', was twenty years older than Duleep Singh; the two of them, however, got on so well that they planned a shooting expedition that would take them through Hungary and down the Danube. They would go that very winter.

Before leaving Vienna to join his new friend, Duleep Singh had a serious talk with the queen at Windsor. He had heard nothing from the India Board concerning his financial affairs, about which, the queen agreed, 'there has been very culpable neglect and dilatoriness'. At the same interview, he fed her curiosity about India, being able to give her first-hand opinions about 'the means of educating, civilising and conciliating the people'.[18]

The very next day she wrote off to Lord Stanley at East India House:

The Queen feels still more anxious for the settlement of the Maharajah Duleep Singh's affairs, which have been now for two years before the East India Company. He deserves every attention from his strong claims and from his very aimiable and excellent character, which render him almost a single exception amongst the Indian Princes. The Queen thinks it would do Her Government little credit, if, while she had possession of his vast Empire, the finest portion of Her Indian dominions, we grudged him the small compensation which he receives in return. He only asks for a settlement of what he was promised by Treaty ...[19]

Stanley replied that the delay was due to lack of attention to the matter in India, where it had been referred, and that he had written personally to Dalhousie's successor, Lord Canning, that unless he got on with the business it would be dealt with in London.[20] Not content to leave the matter there, the queen herself wrote a letter to Canning. It was just after the Proclamation of Crown Rule, and she referred to her 'great satisfaction and pride ... to feel herself in direct communication with that enormous empire which is so bright a jewel of her Crown, which she would wish to see happy, contented and peaceful'. She hoped that 'the publication of Her Proclamation might be the beginning of a new era drawing a veil over the bad and bloody past'. In conclusion, she urged on Lord Canning 'a speedy settlement of the Maharajah Duleep Singh's pecuniary affairs, which this truly aimiable and excellent young Prince is very anxious about – Lord Canning knows his interesting history, his very

strong claims on the British Government, and his very peculiar situation from being a Christian, and as civilised (if not
much more so) as any European, and we need not repeat,
as Lord Canning knows this, the sincere interest we take in
him'.[21]

Sam Baker was thought by the royal circle to be 'bad company' and unfit to be guide and counsellor to a young man
travelling abroad. Once again the queen pressed the Maharajah to take an equerry but, in spite of hints from Phipps, he
preferred to remain free. The great Danube expedition began
with a rendezvous with Baker at Vienna. Word had got
around that the celebrated Maharajah had arrived and gossip
flourished wherever he went. The English papers went so far
as to print a report that he had fallen in love and was about
to become engaged. Baker seems to have been annoyed by
the rumour, describing the story as 'utterly without foundation'. It is not unlikely that both he and the Maharajah had
been attracted to the seductive Hungarian girl, Florence Finnian, who was to become Baker's second wife, and there was
some confusion as to whom she was bestowing her favours
on. 'The most ridiculous stories were current wherever he
went,' Baker wrote to his friend Lord Wharncliffe, 'we both
being suspected as political agents and our movements telegraphed on in advance.'[22]

As the Danube steamer had stopped for the winter, they
hired 'a sort of passenger rowing boat', which managed to
get the two hunters down river in foul weather, as far as
Widdin, a journey which took nearly six weeks. 'We were
delayed constantly by ice and headwinds,' Baker wrote to
Wharncliffe, 'and at last we got such a squeeze from a large
flow that we sprang a bad leak and accordingly quitted the
boat at Kalifat and footed across Wallachia to Bucharest.'[23]

Wallachia was fine sporting country with first-rate coursing and partridge shooting as well as large numbers of
bustard, swans, geese and duck, but the Maharajah had been
too miserable in the harsh winter to enjoy himself. As Baker
put it, 'he was of too soft a texture for the successful pursuit

of large game in mid-winter in a wild country'.[24] By the time they reached Bucharest, where they encountered Florence Finnian, the Maharajah had had enough both of the climate and of Baker. Leaving Baker to his own devices, the Maharajah pushed on as quickly as possible to Constantinople, where he felt too ill even to accept an invitation to dinner from the British ambassador. He moved on by the next boat to Italy and so to Rome, where he knew the Logins were just then due to arrive.

The Logins were surprised to find the Maharajah already waiting for them. They had come with two of their children, but above all their trip was envisaged as an educational experience for Princess Victoria Gouramma, who had settled down well in their care. The Maharajah told them, according to Lady Login, that 'his expedition had been rather a fiasco, his guide – an old *habitué* of oriental cities – had not proved a wise counsellor to a young and inexperienced charge'.[25] From that unqualified statement it might be construed that in that corrupt oriental city of Bucharest, Samuel Baker had led the innocent Maharajah astray.

The Logins hoped that he had come in such a hurry to Rome in order to see Victoria Gouramma. But perhaps his experiences with Baker had made him more wary of gossip, for he told Lady Login that he was afraid of visiting them too often 'in case of false reports being circulated'. He went so far as to say that it was very unfortunate that the princess was there at all.

I have avoided throwing the Princess in his way [Lady Login reported to the queen], and quite agreed with the determination he at first expressed, of not getting their names mixed up together. But by degrees he has come back to us on the same footing, and constantly spends his evenings with us in familiar intercourse, without any invitation, and the circumstance of our boy and girl being with us brings him more into contact with the Princess. He has been talking to me more than once about his future prospects, marriage etc. and seems fully alive to the difficulties in his way of marrying an Englishwoman of the birth and rank to suit his position. The great interest Your Majesty takes in the Princess is not without its effect upon him, and even the kind attention shown her and us by the Prince of Wales is remarked upon by him, as proof of Your Majesty's favour.[26]

If not exactly a beauty, Victoria Gouramma was a lively young girl, and something of a flirt, making eyes at all the young men, even the eighteen-year-old Prince of Wales, who was then in Rome with his governor, General Bruce. The Maharajah seemed to disapprove of her lack of serious-ness, but, for whatever reason, it was soon apparent that a domestic situation had developed in another direction that Lady Login regarded as 'a bewildering and uncomfortable *dénoument*', in fact a 'bombshell'. She explained it all in a long letter to the queen:

Madam, When I had the honour to address Your Majesty so lately, I did not anticipate the necessity of so soon again doing so, but as I am very greatly concerned at the purport of a conversation I have just had with the Maharajah, I am desirous of losing no time in making it known to Your Majesty.

The Maharajah had met the Princess Gouramma, a few evenings ago, at a small party, and I observed that he sat by her talking for some time. The next day he asked for a private interview with me, and, after saying that he thought the Princess much improved in manner and appearance, and that he felt a sincere interest in her as his countrywoman, he said that he considered it only right and honourable on his part to tell me at once that he could not ask her to be his wife; that, from what he had observed of her lately, he had made up his mind that she was not calculated to make him happy, as he did not feel the confidence in her he would in an English girl.

I was much distressed at this, for I had hoped that she was con-ducting herself so as to make a favourable impression, but he said repeatedly: 'I could never marry her! I could never feel more than pity for her! She would not be a safe wife for me! I don't seem to trust her! and I dread so any trouble after marriage!'

He then went on to say that he felt very unhappy about himself, that he saw the necessity of altering many things in his own con-duct, and of endeavouring to live more as became his profession of Christianity, and his position in society; but that his temptations were so great, and he felt himself so weak to withstand them, that unless he could have some definite object in view, and some reward to strive after, he feared for the future; that up to this time his life had been aimless, that he felt he had no ties to bind him, no home or kindred that he could claim as his own, but that if this could be altered – if a hope could be held out to him that he might, at some future period, be permitted to try to win the love of one he had loved and known since childhood, he would undergo any probation it was thought fit to impose on him, and strive, with God's help, to make himself worthy of her ... (Here he named a young relative of my husband, who had her in his care and charge.)

On observing the effect this utterly unexpected announcement had upon me, he became so confused and nervously excited that he could not express his meaning clearly, and therefore begged I would give him no reply at present, but allow him to come next day and talk it over calmly, and, in the meantime, if we should feel inclined to reject his idea (as he feared might be) that we would reflect deeply on the effect such a decision would have on him.

I hope I need not assure Your Majesty that neither my husband, nor myself, had the slightest suspicion of the Maharajah's sentiments, and that we were quite unprepared for his request, which caused us the greatest anxiety and pain on her account, even more than on the Maharajah's; and though we felt ourselves in a very peculiar position towards him, as his only Christian parents, and in a great degree bound to give him every aid we could, still, at the same time, this young girl's happiness and welfare must be paramount with us.

When he came the next morning, he said much of the great difficulty he should always find in becoming acquainted with the real disposition and character of any young lady he might meet in society; that in no other family could he be domesticated as he was with us; that he had known her temper and disposition thoroughly, and watched her closely, and had long felt that she was in every respect what he wished for in his wife; her truthfulness and purity he could rely on, and her religious feelings he reverenced. But if we, whom he trusted and regarded as parents, could not accept him into the family; if we, who had taken him from his own country and people, and cut him off (though at his own request) from all prospect of mixing with his own race, should refuse to regard him as one of ourselves, to whom could he look?

I earnestly hope that in the reply we have given we have been rightly directed, and that, with God's blessing, the event may result in good. We have told the Maharajah that in our peculiar situation, and as Christians, we cannot altogether refuse his request, though we must adopt such measures as shall, as far as possible, render our present concession as harmless as possible to the other person involved, as she must be our first consideration; that in the earnest hope that this may lead him to a higher view of the duties of his position, and of his Christian profession, if it was found that for the next three years his conduct gave us confidence in his sincerity, and in the depth of his present feelings, and in the event of his obtaining Your Majesty's gracious approval, we would allow him to plead his own cause with the young girl, who would then be of age sufficient to make the decision for herself. In the meantime, he bound himself, on his honour, not in any way to make her aware of his sentiments – we, on our part, being careful that they shall see as little as possible of each other in the interim.

We have told him that we hold out this inducement to him, solely in the hope that, before this period expires, he will see his true position more clearly, and meet with someone more suitable in every respect as we in no wise covet such a destiny for our charge. We felt that to deprive him of all hope, considering the position we have held towards him, would have been both unchristian and injudicious, and might have led to him becoming utterly careless.

There were many circumstances which I cannot detail by letter, which have strengthened us in resolving on this reply. My first impulse was to return straight to England, instead of going on to Naples, in the hope of being permitted to lay everything personally before Your Majesty. On second thoughts, knowing that Your Majesty desired that the Princess should be as long abroad as possible, and that her health would be benefited by a stay at the seaside, I have decided to adhere to our first intention. Need I express to Your Majesty with what deep anxiety I shall await at Naples the expression of Your Majesty's opinion on the course we have thought it our duty to pursue with respect to the Maharajah?

I have the honour to be, Madam, with most dutiful and grateful respect, Your Majesty's most humble and most devoted servant,

Lena Login.[27]

Lady Login then proceeded to take it out on poor Gouramma, giving her a lecture on the 'unfortunate impression' that her freedom of manner[28] had conveyed to the Maharajah. According to Lady Login, 'she was so abashed to find what a gentleman's impression of her really was, that I had every hope the lesson might prove an effectual cure ... I was extraordinarily pleased and touched, by the humility with which she received my lecture.'[29] As the queen had once hinted that a foreign nobleman might make a suitable match for Gouramma, Lady Login suggested that she 'could arrange to make the acquaintance'[30] of members of the Prussian court, in attendance on the mad King Frederick William IV, then staying in Rome. Efforts in this direction came to nothing.

The awaited reply from the queen, voiced through Sir Charles Phipps, reached Lady Login at Sorrento and must have reassured her that she had taken the proper course of action:

Her Majesty fully comprehends, and sympathises with the conflicting feelings with which you must have received the unexpected declaration of the Maharajah, and Her Majesty thinks that, considering all the circumstances, the decision at which you arrived was not only the soundest and the most prudent, but also the kindest and the most likely to be beneficial towards the Maharajah. If his attachment to this young lady is deeply rooted and really sincere, it may afford him a sufficient object to strengthen and render permanent his good resolutions, and thus establish a strong motive for good, so much wanting in an indolent and self-indulgent, though generous, honourable, and upright nature, such as his. The Queen has therefore no doubt that you answered him both wisely, and in accordance with that affectionate regard which you and Sir John have ever shown him. Her Majesty hopes that the conversation you have had with the Princess may have a good effect, and that a marriage with some other eligible person may be effected. It would be desirable that any such prospect, with a person whom you would approve should in every way be encouraged. It is most probable that union with a sensible and kind husband, whom she could respect and look up to, might have the most desirable effect upon her character.[31]

The queen had asked her eldest son, while in Rome, to keep a friendly eye on the Maharajah. The Prince of Wales sent her word that he was showing an unhealthy interest in the Roman Catholic religion. She replied: 'I do not *myself* think there is any danger of the Maharajah's being *converted* to Catholicism as he thinks it so like the *Hindoo religion*, wh. he himself abjured.' She added a request: 'Would you tell Gibson that when he has finished the Maharajah's bust that I would like him to send me a cast of it?'[32]

When the Login party departed for the south, the Maharajah remained in Rome. He wrote a pathetic letter to Lady Login in Sorrento referring to his 'lonely life' and having 'no one who cares for me'. 'As there is no Miss P. this year to buy a bracelet for,' he continued, 'perhaps you will buy a pair of earrings and bracelet ... for someone else, whose name, I fear, I dare not mention.' He then suggested that 'to make up for his disappointment' she should bring the forbidden girl to stay with him at Mulgrave, promising Lady Login would see 'nothing in his conduct that would give the slightest suspicion'. He ended by asking for a lock of the loved one's hair, adding: 'I ask this though I don't expect to get it'. He did not, and Lady Login was to see that a letter he sent her was returned unopened.[33]

He wrote her another letter, she told Phipps, 'lamenting his proneness to yield to temptation and in despair at his own weakness and folly'. 'He intends to go to England immediately,' she ended, 'in the hope that something may be settled for his future guidance by the Indian Council, and I believe he means to apply for permission to travel through India for a short time.'[34]

The Maharajah returned to England in the middle of May 1859. On the twentieth he had the long-awaited response from Lord Stanley concerning his financial affairs:

I have the satisfaction to inform your Highness that I have received a dispatch from His Excellency the Governor General under date Jan. 3 1859 respecting the permanent adjustment of your allowances, and that in accordance with the recommendations therein contained, I propose on behalf of H.M.'s Govt. to fix these allowances, at an annual rate of Company's Rupees – (C.R. 250,000) to commence from the attainment of your majority according to the Laws of England. Adverting however to the letter addressed to your highness by the Court of Directors on 29th. Dec. 1857 acceding to your request to be allowed to take upon yourself the management of your own affairs, Her Majesty's Govt. are willing, from that date to fix your allowance at Company's Rupees (C.R. 150,000) instead of the 120,000 heretofore drawn by your Highness. It will be understood that the permanent allowance of Company's Rupees (C.R. 250,000) (which will be paid in India) is to include the sum formerly paid on account of the Futteghur Establishment and is to be in satisfaction of all claims.[35]

'In satisfaction of all claims' was a phrase the Maharajah was to subscribe to a number of times in future negotiations with his masters. He was by no means happy to have his annual allowance fixed at a mere £25,000 a year and asked that it should be raised to £35,000. His request was regarded as 'unreasonable'. As Sir Charles Wood remarked: 'With £25,000 he is far above the average of peers and *noblemen* in this country and indeed I believe that the overall income of the House of Lords is under £10,000.'[36] So, £25,000 it had to be, with £200,000 to be settled on the Maharajah's heirs, if any.

Now that the Maharajah was a man of property, with Auchlyne and Mulgrave to keep him busy with shooting and fishing and entertaining his friends, the queen again suggested he should appoint an equerry to look after his affairs. The sort of man he wanted, Phipps advised, should be 'a gentleman by birth, education and position, agreeable in his manners and knowing something of English Society'.[37] The Maharajah who had had enough of supervision from Login, continued to resist the idea, but when his former governor proposed that Colonel Oliphant, described by the queen as an 'agreeable, sensible, straightforward man',[38] should come and visit him at Auchlyne and they could see how they got on together, he did not disagree. Oliphant, formerly chairman of the Court of Directors of the East India Company, had lately met 'heavy losses' and was willing to handle the Maharajah's affairs for a salary of £800 a year. 'I am very glad I have followed Sir John's advice and asked Colonel Oliphant here,' the Maharajah wrote to Lady Login. 'He seems quite happy fishing, though he meets with indifferent sport, the water being so low. I have been away, at Susie, in order to get a shot at the deer, and I have been sitting up at night watching for them, when they come to eat the corn. Colonel Oliphant does not give any trouble, and I really am thinking of doing as Sir John advised, and asking him to come to me when I require an equerry, but it must only be now and then, not to live with me always. I think this would meet the Queen's wishes too.'[39]

By November, the Maharajah had still not had satisfaction from the India Board. 'My patience is exhausted!' he wrote to Login. 'Do, for *goodness sake*, get the Government to settle with me and pay my arrears as soon as possible! I *do believe* they will take *another year* to settle my affairs! I trust to you to stir them up for I dread getting into debt!'

The same letter, written from Eaton Hall, where he was staying with the Grosvenors, indicated that his heart was again fancy-free. 'I am going to a ball this evening, and expect (tell Lady Login) to meet the lovely Lady F-!'[40]

The Maharajah spent most of the winter of 1859 at Mulgrave, where Lady Normanby was allowed to return whenever she liked. She wrote to her son in Canada:

22nd. Sept. 1859
We stayed a fortnight at dear old Mulgrave and enjoyed it extremely. Nothing could be more courteous and considerate than the Prince. He left us very much to ourselves and seemed very anxious that we should consider ourselves at home. He keeps the place beautifully. The only thing to complain of is what I was always complaining of to you, the quantity of rabbits, but I think he sees himself he has too many. The fact is that the quantity of Hares and Rabbits at Mulgrave prevent the growth of the underwood. I always wondered why the shoots of the trees did not shoot

up again as in other places, and I found out this year that they get eaten down as fast as they appear.

Consequently the Cover gets bad for Pheasants. He has had wonderful sport with Partridges, killing 730 brace in the first six days with two guns, and he says he could kill 150 any day he liked. He had a Pic Nic one day at the Grotto and another at the Hermitage. He is going to build a greenhouse at the South Slope, and already made a very good Hot House behind the House. In short I think he seems anxious to improve and leave a good reputation behind him. He was very anxious we should prolong our stay, but I thought it would not be right to fix ourselves on him any longer.... The Prince has put a very good Billiard Table into the Library. It stands very well there, tho' it is not exactly the thing for a Library, but I suppose it is the only use he could make of it; at any rate I do not suppose he is a reading man.[41]

In another letter Lady Normanby wrote:

The Maharajah is very well inclined, and a very good Christian if they will not ride him too hard. The only thing is he is very like you, and says he cannot find anything in the Bible that obliges him to have *only one wife*. He don't like that. 'Suppose,' he said 'when I have been married to her I find I don't like her, what must I do?' He is half Indian still. He used to make the most extraordinary mixture for his dinner every day, which was cooked by his Indian cook ... First he had a large plate of rice, which bye the bye I advise you to try as it is excellent. It was first slightly fried as for curry, and then thrown into a Pan with a little Nutmeg, Coriander Seed and Black Pepper, *well pounded* and only about a pinch of it, but well mixed with melted butter, very hot, into which the rice must be thrown and stirred until each grain is separate ... then put the curry upon it, but he used to add curds and a sort of mixture that looked like soft spinach, but was sage or some other herb. All this he used to eat with Chuppity – I think he called it – and a sort of Indian girdle-cake, very heavy and made with fat instead of butter ... So you may try your hand at it and see how you like it.[42]

Now that there was little likelihood of a marriage between the Maharajah and Gouramma, Lady Login had asked the queen to relieve her of her duties as a chaperon, since to bring them together had been her reason for taking the job. The young princess had accordingly been placed in the charge of Colonel and Lady Catherine Harcourt, who lived at Buxted Park in Sussex. Lonely and miserable with her strict and fussy guardians, poor Gouramma had turned for comfort to the staff and had fallen in love with the under-butler, a young man named George Christmas. Gouramma was caught by the Harcourts in the middle of the night downstairs, without her stays, but with a dressing gown over her petticoats. When challenged she had pretended she was planning to run away, and was about to leave for the station. An intercepted letter to her lover starting 'My own darling' and ending 'from your dear sweet angel' had given the game away.[43] She sent him a volume of Longfellow's poems and told her maid that if they sent her anywhere else, and would not let her marry George, she would destroy herself. Lady Catherine was outraged and 'declined to take any further responsibility'. The consensus of opinion was that Gouramma was deranged and a psychiatric doctor was called in to advise. The queen, more sensibly, thought she was over-excitable, and recommended a trip abroad to avoid the growing scandal.[44] The Prince Consort took the view that 'the feeling of inferiority to European civilized society may have depressed and made her desperate'.[45]

Gouramma's future seemed totally compromised until the Maharajah made a decisive contribution to it by a successful piece of matchmaking. He introduced her to Colonel John Campbell, Lady Login's brother, a dashing widower with several children. He was about thirty years older than Gouramma but they were sufficiently attracted to each other to get engaged. The Logins received the news without enthusiasm and complained that they had not been consulted.

The queen, however, was delighted to hear that her difficult goddaughter was at last settled and 'a quiet and comfortable, though not brilliant home was secured for her'.[46] The marriage took place in July 1860.

The Maharajah was up at Auchlyne for 12 August 1860.

On the thirteenth he killed ninety-three brace to his own gun. With two friends they bagged nearly three hundred brace in three days. Colonel Oliphant, who was now officially appointed to the household, went up to Caithness to look over another property the Maharajah had his eye on, belonging to Sir George Sinclair, with fishing on the Thurso river. Sir John and Lady Login came up for a visit, but they had left before the arrival of the newly-weds, Victoria Gouramma and John Campbell. The Logins brought with them the Maharajah's boyhood friend Frank Boileau who, as second-in-command of the 2nd Sikh Cavalry, had been severely wounded in the siege of Delhi, three years earlier.

The Maharajah, especially in moments of loneliness, had given much thought to what remained of his family in India. He had managed to get a small pension allocated to the Shahzadah, and he had sent the Pundit Nehemiah Goreh to Katmandu to find out what sort of life his mother was now living. The pundit, instead of going himself, sent a letter which was intercepted by government agents, and he was forbidden to communicate with her, except through the British Resident. Report had it that the Rani Jindan was half-blind but still belligerent, and surrounded by unsuitable friends. Spurred on by a new sense of filial duty and the growing realization that his mother's role in the rape of the Punjab had been inspired by patriotism, he decided that the time had come to concern himself with her well-being.

CHAPTER 5

Mother and Son

❦

TOWARDS the end of 1859, Duleep Singh decided definitely to go to India, partly to get some tiger shooting, a major sport in which he had not yet participated, and partly to see his mother again and arrange for her to be moved from Nepal to India. Colonel Ramsay, the Resident in Katmandu, had written to Login:

The Government will be in a dilemma respecting the ex-Maharanee of Lahore, unless they or Duleep Singh are prepared to allow her a permanent subsistence in our provinces. Jung Bahadoor longs to get rid of her, for various personal reasons, and declares that if she ever sets foot in the British provinces, she shall never be allowed to re-enter Nepal, or receive a stiver from his government. He declares she now gets 20,000 rupees per annum, which he grudges exceedingly. He also wants her mansion, which is on his own premises. They are always quarrelling, and she contrives to wound him on a tender point, his vanity.[1]

The Maharajah's plan was regarded with some suspicion. Neither the queen nor Colonel Oliphant was in favour, and some efforts were made to dissuade him. But the Maharajah was not to be influenced: just before leaving he wrote to the queen saying he must go. He thanked her for all her kindness and ended with this valediction: 'Whatever may be my future destiny I shall ever retain the most grateful and happy recollection of every circumstance connected with Your Majesty's great kindness to me, and it shall be my most earnest endeavour so to conduct myself through life, as to be more worthy of such distinguished favours.'[2]

The Maharajah arrived in Calcutta in early February 1861.

Apart from organizing his mother, he wanted to find out how he felt about India, its people and customs, from all of which he had been cut off for almost seven years. He was now thoroughly English, and he found on arrival that at first he could hardly understand a word of his native tongue. There was also sport to be looked forward to: he brought three gamekeepers with him and his baggage included a rubber boat with a swivel duck-gun as well as the latest in rifles for tiger shooting.

He was accorded the regulation salute of twenty-one guns, and an ADC to Canning, now designated viceroy, went on board ship to welcome him and take him to Spence's Hotel. The authorities evidently wanted to keep him happy and retain his goodwill: there were dinners at Government House and receptions organized by the Anglo-Saxon establishment of the great commercial city. 'He has an escort,' Lord Canning wrote to Sir Charles Wood, who had asked him to do his best for the Maharajah. 'In short, I believe he is altogether satisfied as far as the dignities are concerned.'[3]

Although the political implications of the Maharajah's return were played down as much as possible, there was some apprehension that he might, perhaps with the encouragement of his mother, attempt to return to the Punjab and make trouble with the Sikhs. To someone on the boat, who had asked him if he intended to visit his birthplace, he had replied: 'The English Government does not trust me.' At their first meeting, Canning, who had already met the Maharajah in England, asked what he meant by the remark. The Maharajah, embarrassed at finding that his words had been reported, replied hotly: 'If you do trust me, why do you not let me go where I like?' Canning explained with sweet reason that it was not that they distrusted him, but that the risk of his presence in the Punjab was too great as it would certainly stir up old memories in the volatile Sikh community possibly causing unwelcome demonstrations; and he did not wish to have forced on him 'the necessity of restraining and perhaps punishing persons for showing a feeling which, in itself, is natural and creditable to them'. Duleep Singh acquiesced, according to Canning, 'with tolerable grace'. That the viceroy's apprehension had limited foundation was indicated when a Sikh regiment landed at Calcutta on its way back from China where it had formed part of an allied force against Peking. 'The men heard of his presence,' Canning wrote, 'and on two or three occasions large numbers of them went to the hotel and sat down quickly to get a sight of him. Upon his showing himself they made their salaams and went away. On one occasion there were about 200 of them, very orderly and not in uniform, but very determined to see their ex-Chief.'[4]

The Maharajah's meeting with his mother was soon to take place. It was ten years since their unhappy parting and it is likely that she extracted the maximum amount of drama from the reunion. According to Canning, the Maharajah was paying great respect to her and spoke of her 'very touchingly' but, Canning maintained, 'She is a she-devil nevertheless, and will make her impression on his feeble character if they continue together in India.'[5] As for the rani, she was soon filling his head with ideas of his destiny and teaching him to chew betel nut and *paan*. The Shahzadah, also, was there to meet him and hear of life in England. The young man still wanted to visit the country: perhaps a talk with his uncle on his disillusion with the Sikh religion and his request for a Christian bible was no more than the imagined key to an invitation to leave India.

The Maharajah was restless and unhappy in Calcutta, and not feeling at all well. He had had no shooting except at snipe outside the city. He abandoned one plan after another in quick succession: he would take his mother on a shooting expedition and afterwards to England; or he would install her in Eastern Bengal and make it his own sporting headquarters, but the government restricted his mother's movements. Or again, he would leave her near Calcutta and go off to Mussoorie to shoot. On the one hand he planned to visit Delhi, too close to the Punjab to please the government, and make his way across India to Bombay. On the other hand he felt he disliked India so much that he was half-inclined to leave immediately, in time to reach England for Derby Day. He also spoke of becoming a member of White's Club.

He was encouraged by a letter from Sir John Login, who was handling his claims in his absence, which implied that the India Office might be won over.

Sir Charles Phipps told me that now was the time to push the Government [Login wrote], as I should come in for all their blame in having the matter agitated, and that you could suffer no damage by my proceedings; and as he knew that I did not much care for their annoyance, so long as I had a good cause, he thought it by far the best opportunity for you to get the question advanced. So you see how coolly I am recommended to fight your battles. Well, be it so: it will be a great happiness to me if I can get our people to do what is liberal and right, to enable me to hold up my head before you, and to say that I am not ashamed of them. My dear Maharajah, it requires some knowledge of our national character to understand us: Because the Council of India do not benefit a single pie themselves, and they stand up for the interests of 200 million of subjects, they'll fight until they have not a leg to stand on, while all the time they have the most perfect goodwill to you, and would like to see you happy. However, it will all come right yet; I have every confidence.[6]

As the most tempting lure he could think of to encourage a return to England, Login included in his letter a description of a sporting estate with a good record for stalking then up for sale – Applecross, in the north-west Highlands. The Maharajah replied:

Oh! It is too cruel of you to write to me, so soon after coming out here, about an estate in Scotland; for now I cannot make up my mind to stay a day longer than is necessary to see my mother: Your letter has almost driven me wild; so you may expect me back sooner than I thought when I left. I have got the Shahzadah here on a visit ... He is a very quick, intelligent lad, but a thorough native in his manners, I regret to say. He wishes to marry another wife already.... He tells me he has no belief in his own religion,

and would like to go to England, if he could, without his mother
knowing! Now, I must tell you that India is a beastly place: I
heartily repent having come out, for I cannot get a moment's peace
with people following me, and all my old servants bother the life
out of me with questions. The heat is something dreadful, and what
will it be in another month? I hate the natives, they are such liars,
flatterers, and extremely deceitful. I would give anything to be
back in dear England, among my friends: I cannot think or write
about anything else but this property. Oh! buy it for me, if possible
... They gave me a salute of twenty-one guns, and *you* will be
amused to hear, an *escort of two sowars*![7]

Even the attraction of Applecross, an almost inaccessible
deer forest in Ross-shire, had not entirely made up the
Maharajah's mind. A few days later he wrote to Login: 'I
am trying to get a house outside Calcutta for my mother.
I have not yet settled whether I remain over the hot weather
here, going up to the hill, and then returning to England. I
am to have elephants from the Government for tiger shooting.
It is already very hot. Shahzadah is very anxious to come with
me to England, but does not expect to manage it.' In a postscript he added: 'Since I wrote this, my mother has declared
she will not separate from me, and as she is refused permission
to go to the hills, I must give up that intention; and I suppose,
we shall return to England as soon as I can get a passage.'[8]

The Indian government readily gave permission to the rani
to accompany her son to England. So pleased were they to
be rid of her that, fearing she might change her mind, they
offered to return her jewels and awarded her a pension of
£3,000 a year conditional on her departure.

Mother and son arrived in England in early summer 1861.
Sir John Login, with indefatigable energy, had found a suitable house for her two doors down from his own in Lancaster
Gate. He used his influence to clear her jewels through customs without the payment of duty, and helped in every way
he could. She told him, to his amusement, that had she
known what he was really like, and how extremely kind and
useful he would prove to be, she would never have arranged

to have him poisoned, as she had at one time contemplated.

The rani's household proved a source of wonder to the local urchins, who would peer through the railings down into the basement area, watching the Indian cooks at work over their pots, and sniffing the pungent smells of curry. Lady Login was soon to pay a visit. She found herself ushered into a large, heavily curtained room, in semi-darkness, to be confronted by an ancient half-blind woman huddled up on a heap of cushions on the floor. It did not seem possible to her that this could be the famous 'Messalina of the Punjab' she had heard so much about from her husband. Yet sometimes in conversation, when interest was aroused, there would be signs of a once shrewd and lively mind.

Within a few days the rani returned the call and Lady Login, in her habitually lively style, described the occasion in her *Recollections*:

My drawing-room ... was on the first floor, and I shall never forget the sight, as I viewed it from the landing, of the Maharanee being hoisted by main force up the long flight of stairs by several servants! In her case this piece of Oriental etiquette was perhaps not unnecessary, not only on account of her infirmities, but because, in addition to being a heavy woman, she had wished to pay me a special compliment by appearing in European dress; and as she could not entirely abandon her native garments for English under-clothing, she had donned an enormous bonnet with feather, mantle and wide skirt over immense crinoline, on the top of all her Indian costume! No wonder she was utterly unable to move hand or foot, and found it impossible to take a seat, encumbered with the crinoline, till two of her servants lifted her bodily up on to the settee, where she could sit comfortably cross-legged, her crinoline spreading all round her like a Cheese![9]

The final touches to her *toilette* were added by the timely arrival of the rani's jewels from the Customs House, which delighted her so much that she had lavishly decorated herself and her attendants with an assortment of necklaces and earrings, strings of pearls and emeralds, which she had arranged as a sort of fringe inside the brim of her bonnet.

Naturally the queen wanted to know all about the Maharajah's trip to India and on 2 July invited him to dinner at Buckingham Palace.

The M. D.S. & Col. Oliphant, Bessie Wellington & Ld Clyde dined. [She wrote in the journal.] Sat between Fritz & the M. who was very ill at Calcutta, & is so thankful to be back in England again. The Sikhs came in numbers to see him & he feels sure would have compromised him, revolted, & he would have then been imprisoned. He had found his nephew much improved – asking for a bible – wishing to learn, & not believing any longer in his own religion. He has brought his mother back with him; she is free from prejudice, not minding going about & being seen, & frequently wears European dress. She will even go to Church! The Sikhs generally & many of the Hindoos, he thought were much less strict than they used to be, about their observances.[10]

That autumn the Maharajah, now inseparable from his mother, took her up to stay at Mulgrave, which he continued to rent. He wrote to Lady Login in September 1861: 'I have been having capital sport these last few days, averaging forty brace daily ... I want your advice about getting a good likeness of my mother (in oils). The Normanbys are here, and beg to send their kind regards.'[11] Lady Normanby saw very little of the rani – 'She keeps herself very much within the house with her attendants,' she wrote to her son, 'sometimes dressed in a dirty sheet and a pair of cotton stockings, sometimes decked out in Cloth of Gold and covered with jewels ... It rather seems to me when I see queer Indian figures flitting about that "The Heathen are come into mine inheritance." '[12]

Login did not think it appropriate that the Maharajah should spend so much time with his mother, and even when she was at Mulgrave advised him to move her into neighbouring Lythe Hall which she declined to do. 'I am afraid the Maharajah is getting thoroughly under his mother's influence,' Login wrote to Phipps, 'and that the only hope of saving him from discredit, is to get him to live apart from her, as had been arranged, and to find some suitable companions of his own age to reside with him.'[13]

It was clearly the rani's influence that caused her son to introduce an explosive new element into the dialogue with the India Office. '... I very much wish to have a conversation with you about my private property in the Punjab and the Koh-i-noor diamond,' he wrote to Login the day before leaving Mulgrave for Auchlyne.[14] This was the first mention of 'private property' and an indication that the rani, who would have been fully informed on the matter of Runjit Singh's ancestral acres in the Punjab, was suggesting he lay claim to them as of right. Nor was that her only suggestion – she put into his mind that one day, according to an old Sikh prophecy, he would return in glory to rule the Punjab.

The rani's 'undue influence' over her son also encompassed the vexed subject of marriage. Lady Login, who may have felt that *she* was the one who should have been consulted first, commented waspishly on a letter from the Maharajah to her husband, which read: 'You will be glad to hear that my mother has given me leave to marry an English lady, and I think I have found one who will make me a good wife!'[15] 'Mark how the man of twenty-two has resumed the native custom of asking his mother's *leave!*' was Lady Login's response. Unfortunately the Maharajah failed to propose to the lady promptly, and lost her to another, but he consoled himself with an invitation to shoot over her husband's moors.

Having invested him with her new order, the Star of India, the queen 'talked to the Maharajah about his not going back to India, and the advisability of his buying a property in England and getting a good wife, whom we thought we might be able to find for him ... After dinner,' she continued in the journal, 'a long talk with Col. Oliphant about the Maharajah, whom he praised highly, but was most anxious he should not return to India ... Col. Oliphant spoke of his affection for his mother, but its being important she should not live in the same house with him. He hoped he might marry.'[16]

Only the deepest feelings of grief after the death of Prince Albert prevented Queen Victoria from offering some

comment on the Maharajah's disturbing new tendencies. Sir
Charles Phipps answered Login's report on her behalf:

I am very sorry to hear what you say about the Maharajah –
nothing could be so destructive to him as that he should succumb
to his mother's, or any other native influence. He is too good to
be lost; and, if I were in your place, I should certainly not, at such
a moment, forsake any position which gave me any influence over
him, or could possibly tend to prevent him doing anything foolish.
I do not think, if it were pointed out to him, he would do anything
wrong. I should have answered you some days since, but you may
conceive what this house is at present! For the very air we breathe
is an atmosphere of sorrow, and that is a bad medium in which
to transact business.[17]

Everybody was relieved when in June 1862 Duleep Singh
wrote to Sir John Login: 'I have decided to arrange for my
mother's return to India, and will see Sir Charles Wood on
the subject at once, to have a place of residence fixed for her.
I must see you soon, and will go up before I have to attend
the marriage of Princess Alice at Osborne, to which I am invited on July 1st.'[18]

There was, however, some difficulty in getting the India
Office to approve her return: Sir John Lawrence, brother of
Henry, and now a member of the Indian Council, wrote to
Login: 'There can be no doubt whatever that the Maharanee
is better out of India than living in that country. There she
is sure to do mischief; here, I admit, she will be equally the
evil genius of the Maharajah. It is for the Secretary of State
for India to decide *which interest is of paramount importance*.'[19]
Login, on receiving this temporizing reply, wrote to Phipps
for support. Phipps replied from Windsor: 'I quite agree with
you that it is most important for the welfare of the Maharajah
that his mother should not be prevented from returning to
India. I feel very much that, as long as he remains under this
influence, he will be retrograde in his moral and social character, instead of advancing to become an English gentleman,
as I thought he was doing.'[20]

On 10 March 1863, the Maharajah went to the wedding

of the Prince of Wales to Princess Alexandra of Denmark at St George's Chapel, Windsor. On the stroke of noon, the great West door was flung open, and Duleep Singh entered at the head of a procession of foreign princes. His view of the ceremony was almost as good as the widowed queen's, watching in seclusion from her specially built 'box'. The Maharajah's turbaned figure can be clearly seen in William Frith's ten-foot painting of the event, but Frith, who liked to sketch each figure from life, had to pursue him for over a year before even the first sitting could take place. While he was attending Frith's studio, the Maharajah insisted that his jewels be deposited each night at Coutts Bank.

The Maharajah, Frith thought, 'had a face of a handsome type, but somewhat expressionless'. He found it strange, he wrote in his autobiography, to be painting 'one who was a born ruler of a bigger country than England, who had been dragged across the sea, jewels and all, to assist at the wedding of a barbarian on a little Western island, and – what he may have considered an additional punishment – he was made to sit for his likeness, and compelled to lend his treasured jewels to be copied by an infidel whose neck it might have been his delight to wring if it had been in his power.' There was no cause, it seemed, for Frith to worry: ' "He is a thoroughly good young man", the Maharajah's servant told him, "he reads no book but the Bible, which he knows from cover to cover." '21

Pending a decision from India House, the contentious rani was installed in her own establishment at Abingdon House, Kensington, with an English lady companion. The Maharajah, who it was agreed would be more easily kept happy as the proud owner of an English estate, was encouraged to buy Hatherop Castle, a Tudoresque manor in Gloucestershire, at a cost of £183,000 advanced by the India Office. It was not long, however, before he discovered that the fenced-in grassland of the Cotswolds, though excellent for chasing foxes, did not lend itself so well to the conservation of game. More appropriate, he thought, would be Elveden Hall, newly on the market, where the open stubble of East Anglia could be relied upon to harbour a multitude of partridges.

On 1 August 1863 the Rani Jindan died, the Indian government's decision still unforthcoming. The Maharajah hurried down from Loch Kennard Lodge, in Perthshire, and Sir John Login was urgently summoned from his place of retirement in Felixstowe to advise on what to do. It was he who arranged that her remains should be temporarily held in an unconsecrated vault at Kensal Green Cemetery until such time as her son might take them to India for the prescribed funeral rites. As well as the weeping servants of the rani, a number of Indian notabilities then in London attended the funeral; a Methodist minister read the funeral service before the cortège left Abingdon House, and the Maharajah overcame his natural nervousness to make a moving speech comparing the Christian religion to the Hindu, and giving reasons for his own beliefs.

Two months later, on Sunday, 18 October, Sir John Login went upstairs after family prayers quietly humming 'Jesu, lover of my soul'. Minutes later he was dead. According to Lady Login: 'Duleep Singh's grief at my husband's death was indeed most sincere and unaffected, and many at the graveside spoke afterwards of the touching eloquence of his sudden outburst there, when he gave vent to the words, "Oh, I have lost my father! for he was indeed that – and more – to me!" And I remember the sort of tense expression on his face when, on his arrival, having come immediately when he got the sad news, he asserted solemnly: "If *that* man is not in heaven, then there's not a word of truth in the Bible!"'[22]

The Maharajah, who had just bought Elveden, and had not even had a chance to show it to Login, suggested he should be buried in a fine family mausoleum he planned to build there. But Lady Login wanted her husband at Felixstowe, and the Maharajah offered to pay for the erection in the churchyard there of a granite and marble monument, the designs of which were sent to the queen, at her suggestion, for approval. The Maharajah visited Lady Login at Felixstowe before leaving for India, combining his trip with some duck shooting on the Deben, for which he brought his own punt and duck-gun. He arranged that Login's pension should be continued in her name.

It had been a sad year for the Maharajah. He had lost his mother and his 'father'; his faithful valet Thornton had died as well as his secretary Cawood. In addition, Gouramma, who had lately given birth to a daughter, his goddaughter, was dying of consumption. His love affairs with English ladies had all gone wrong, and in his present sanctimonious mood, he had come to the conclusion that even if he found a lady of society to marry he would only be led into a life of idleness. He told Lady Login that what he wanted was a very young Eastern girl, 'a good Christian wife', he could train up to be what he called 'an help-meet'.

In a sudden spirit of enthusiasm he made a bet with Lady Login, committing its bizarre terms to paper: 'I promise to pay Lady Login £50 (fifty pounds) if I am not married by 1st June 1864, provided my health keeps good. N.B. That is, if I am not confined three months to my house, or ordered by my doctor (of course showing a "Doc" certificate) to go abroad.'[23] It may have been to increase his chances of winning that he went so far as to write to the principal of the American Presbyterian Mission School in Cairo, where on a visit during his first journey from India he had observed some charming pupils, to ask if they had any suitable girls to recommend. According to the records of the mission the Maharajah put it to them,

that from his peculiar position he was liable to many temptations as a young unmarried man, and he had determined, therefore, to marry, and had been making it for some time past a matter of special prayer that the Lord would raise him up a suitable wife, for he had determined to marry in the Lord. Her Majesty Queen Victoria had advised him to marry an Indian princess, who had been educated in England, but he wished one who was less

acquainted with the gaieties and frivolities of fashionable aristocratic life. His preference was decidedly for an Oriental, and as he
knew of no lady of rank in India who had been converted to the
truth he had concluded to inquire in Egypt if haply there might
be one found here whom the Lord had been preparing for him
in special answer to his prayer. Rank and position in life were nothing to him; what he desired was a young girl who loved the Lord
in sincerity and truth.[24]

CHAPTER 6

The Mission School Bride

THE Maharajah left England on 16 February 1864 with his
mother's corpse, and several of her servants. While his ship
was delayed at Suez, he hurried to Cairo and went straight
to the mission school. He observed a small fifteen-year-old
student teacher giving a lesson to a large, but disciplined, class
and decided she was just the girl for him. Her name was
Bamba Müller, and she was the daughter of an Abyssinian
lady – a Copt and therefore Christian – and Ludwig Müller,
a well-known and respected figure in the cosmopolitan
society of Alexandria, and partner in the German firm of
merchant bankers, Todd Müller and Co. The missionaries,
having received his letter of application, had also seen Bamba
as the ideal choice, especially as she was the only fully practising Christian in their care at that time. The Maharajah
saw her again when he presented the school prizes; speaking
to her through an interpreter, for she spoke only Arabic, he
persuaded her to accept his proposal and to await his return
from India. Even if the missionaries felt, as they phrased it,
'very heavily the responsibility of being in any way in-
strumental in transplanting a young, tender flower from its
native soil, in which it was growing in vigour and beauty
every day, to a region and climate where it might pine away
and die from withering blasts,'[1] they were prepared to give
their blessing to the match.

Until he came back from India, it was agreed that the missionaries should train Bamba to be a suitable bride to
a wealthy and well-meaning maharajah. 'I think it is desirable
that she should learn English and music, and to give her own

THE MISSION SCHOOL BRIDE

orders,' the Maharajah wrote from Suez. 'Do you not think it would be rather a good thing that she could go out driving a little, so that she may be accustomed to going unveiled? But her own feelings should be consulted as to this. I am having a pair of earrings made for Bamba, which I hope she will be able to wear.'[2] In addition to the earrings, there was another token, finished just before the Maharajah sailed: he sent it to the head of the mission with a covering letter that appropriately balanced the sacred with the secular:

I send you with this note a ring for Bamba, which kindly make over to her for me, and tell her it will give me very much pleasure if she will always wear both the presents I have sent her, whether we should be married together or not. Kindly tell her that she must pray to God for guidance and entirely commit herself to Him, believing that 'all things work together for good to them that love God,' and He who loved her, and gave Himself a ransom for her, will guide her in the right path. She does not know how much more anxious I am to possess her now since I heard yesterday of her determination to be entirely led by Him, and to live for His glory only. I pray God that it be His will her father may give his consent. I think (should everything go on all right) that Bamba should have one or two maid servants, in order that she may learn to give her own orders about different things about herself, for should she become my wife, she will not very well know how to get on at first, as I keep a large number of servants, and she must behave herself like a proper mistress before them.[3]

The missionaries saw to it that Bamba underwent an intensive course of domestic training. 'She, of course, had a great deal to learn,' one of them observed; 'how to sit, how to eat, how to handle her knife and fork etc. and many an awkward thing happened before she got accustomed to Frank [European] ways.'[4]

Then, having secured a firm option on a wife who seemed to be in every way what he had been looking for, the Maharajah continued on his journey to India. At Bombay his mother was cremated and her ashes scattered on the sacred waters of the river Godavari. On almost the same day

Victoria Gouramma Campbell died in London at the age of twenty-three, leaving behind her a baby daughter. The text on her tomb, selected by Queen Victoria, read, 'Other sheep I have which are not of this fold.' Her husband too was soon to meet an unhappy end. He was seen leaving his lodgings in Jermyn Street carrying a small bag supposedly containing her jewels and was never seen again. Murder was suspected.[5]

The Maharajah kept his stay in Bombay as short as possible, finding time, however, to hand over his mother's favourite slave, Soortoo, to the care of the Bombay mission; she had been a childhood playmate and was about his own age. He returned to Egypt by the next available boat to claim his bride and hopefully to meet the deadline of his bet with Lady Login.

Bamba had developed jaundice and had gone to stay with her father in Alexandria. The Maharajah called on arrival. 'It is marvellous how everything connected with the affair has gone on,' he wrote to the head of the mission in Cairo, 'and how Bamba's father has been led to fulfil his duties towards his child. May the Lord give him grace to take the Lord Jesus as his daughter does.'[6]

On 28 April the Maharajah called on the British consul, Robert Colquhoun, to inform him of his intention to marry, and request him to publish the banns. It was from Colquhoun's notification to Lord Palmerston at the Foreign Office that the first news of the remarkable suit reached London:

The Maharajah Duleep Singh has this day returned from Bombay – he waited on me this evening and informs me he is about to marry a young girl the daughter of a merchant here, she has been educated by the American Protestant Mission here – she is an illegitimate child, now recognised by her father, her mother an Abyssinian. The Banns will shortly be published at the Alexandrian Consulate.

His Highness tells me it is his intention to inform Colonel Phipps of the circumstance requesting him to inform Her Majesty to whom he is bound by the strongest ties of gratitude and respect, he seems to have well reflected on what he is about to do and I feel myself hardly at liberty to use any remonstrance where evidently his feelings are so deeply interested – your Lordship will pardon my troubling you on the subject – but perhaps you may think it right to inform the Queen of what I have written.'[7]

It was not the queen who was the first friend to hear of the impending marriage, but Ronald Leslie-Melville, to whom the Maharajah had immediately written the great news. Melville told Colonel Oliphant, who had already had a report on the preliminary courtship in Cairo, and Oliphant passed the gossip on to the palace.

I know not if you have heard from the Maharajah, or if any report has reached you from any other quarter that he is engaged to be married. He has not written to me; but to Ronald Melville, authorising him to tell me of it, so although he may not have announced it in due form, there seems no doubt that it is a fact. I hope the M.R. may have written to you on the subject, for consideration to the Queen; if not I must leave it in your hands to do what you think best. A month ago Mrs Oliphant had a letter from an excellent clergyman of Hull, Mr Deck, who had heard from a dear friend of his at Cairo that the Maharajah had been accepted by a young lady whom he thus describes: 'The Beautiful Girl who is soon likely to be the wife of the Prince is a very sweet girl with a face full of intelligence, a Decided Christian, between 15 and 16 years of age.' He added that unless we heard it from others we were to consider it strictly confidential which we have accordingly done. Mr Deck does not give her name, and no doubt she is a Copt. The Maharajah tells Melville she is the daughter of a Banker at Cairo, and that he would leave Bombay on the 14 April for Cairo, where I understood he was to be married. Both Mrs Oliphant and I have implicit trust in the account we have received of the Bride Elect, and there is good hope that his union with her will be all that his best friends can desire.
On the 13th of this month we flit from this to Hatherop, but whether to remain long or not, will depend on His Highness's choice between the 2 places, Hatherop or Elveden. At present his heart is in the latter, owing to its being such a place for sporting.
I trust the quiet of Osborne is restoring peace and health to our Dear Queen.[8]

That was all the queen knew about the matter. Why had the Maharajah not written to her, she wondered. She was so worried that she sent Phipps from Windsor to London, preceded by a liveried rider out of deference to the widowed Lady Login, to see if she had any more information. But for once Lady Login had to admit that she knew no more than anyone else. A fortnight was to pass before the queen had news direct: it came in the form of a letter from the Maharajah to Phipps.

I have hitherto hesitated not knowing whether I ought to write but fearing lest I should be considered negligent by the Queen who has been so gracious and kind to me that I take this opportunity of writing privately to you and of explaining what has prevented me from acquainting Her Majesty of my approaching marriage. The young lady is an illegitimate daughter (though adopted by her father) ... and it is her birth that has prevented me from telling you of this sooner knowing that there is such an objection to it in England. Therefore should the Queen hear of my marriage and be offended with me for not having told her of it be so good as to explain why I did not do so ... Finding out that she was a good girl and a true Christian and who only wished to serve God alone I asked her Father for her being convinced that a woman native to the East like myself would make me a better wife than a European.[9]

Though the fact of the fiancée's illegitimacy in no way disturbed the queen, there was outright disapproval in many quarters when the news got around of the Maharajah's proposed marriage. Lady Login, who had the information at second hand from her son that the wedding was set for 7 June, wrote to Phipps that there was just time to write 'to stop him and make him consider before he makes it impossible to go back'.[10] Colonel Oliphant had to have his say and wrote a letter to Phipps that can only be described as priggish:

There is indeed much cause for anxiety respecting the Maharajah's future, yet I am not without hope that things may turn out better than might reasonably be expected from the undesirable connection he has made and the haste with which he has entered into it. He seems to have acted with his usual impulsiveness probably without giving a thought about her Parents, who or what they were, but attracted by the personal appearance of the young lady and by the good account he heard of her. I take this to be the history of the engagement for I suppose they know little of each other's language and therefore could have interchanged but few ideas. Her youth is perhaps a good thing. She will more readily acquire good English manners and habits and ideas, and perhaps some things in H.H. that an English wife might not have liked, will in all probability be unobjectionable to the young German-Abyssinian (if she be so) whose tastes and habits are still unformed. What we all desired for him was that he might find a nice English wife yet this was no easy matter. Often and often have he and I talked on the subject and it was, I may say, continually in his thoughts, but poor fellow, I have reason to think that he had come to the conclusion that (as he termed it) a 'foreigner like himself' was distasteful to our Country women, and it is not impossible that some such feeling urged him on so hastily to the step he has taken.[11]

The Maharajah was to lose his bet by a week: owing to the necessity of posting the banns, the ceremony did not take place until 9 June 1864. The first report appeared in *The Times of India*:

The Marriage of Duleep Singh – The marriage of the Maharajah Duleep Singh took place at the British Consulate, Alexandria, on the 7th June, in the presence of very few witnesses. The young lady who has now become the Maharanee is the daughter of an European merchant here. Her mother is an Abyssinian. She is between fifteen and sixteen years of age, of a slight but graceful figure, interesting rather than handsome, not tall, and in complexion lighter than her husband. She is a Christian, and was educated in the American Presbyterian Mission School at Cairo; and it was during a chance visit there, while on his way out to India, that the Prince first saw his future bride, who was engaged as instructress at the school. Duleep Singh wore at the wedding European costume, excepting a red tarboosh. The bride's dress was also European, of white moiré antique, à fichu point d'Alençon – short lace sleeves, orange blossoms in her dark hair, with, of course, the usual gauze

veil. She wore but few jewels; a necklace of fine pearls, and a bracelet set with diamonds, were her only ornaments. The formula of
the civil marriage at Her Britannic Majesty's consulates in the
Levant is very brief. Both parties delcare that they know no lawful
impediment to their union; then they declare that they mutually
accept each other as husband and wife, and the civil ceremony is
over. This formula was pronounced by the Prince in English; the
bride, in a low but musical voice, read it in Arabic (that being the
only language with which she is acquainted,) and thus 'Bamba
Muller' became the 'Maharanee'. She showed much self-possession
throughout it all. A religious ceremony was performed by one of
the American ministers at the house of the bride's father; and the
newly married pair retired to the Prince's house at Ramleh, a few
miles from Alexandria.[12]

Perhaps because his new wife had caught jaundice and he did
not want to show her off to his friends at a disadvantage, the
Maharajah spent a month in Egypt among the missionaries
having what cannot have been a stimulating honeymoon.

The queen was among the first to hear of the Maharajah's
arrival in England and have a positive description of his bride
from someone whose opinion she knew would not be exag-
gerated. It came from Colonel Oliphant, the elderly equerry,
and was written from Claridges where the couple had just
been installed:

On Friday night I received a telegram from Paris from the
Maharajah saying he would be in London the next day, so Mrs
Oliphant and I started the next morning and found that he and
his bride had travelled all night, and had reached here two hours
before us. I did not write to you sooner, because I thought you
would like to know what we thought of her after a few days' acquaintance rather than the mere first day's impression. I am truly
happy to say that I can send you a very favourable report. In person
she is small and delicately made, has a sweet smile, winning expression, a soft black eye, and her complexion is like the late Princess
Gouramma. She is unable to speak English as yet beyond a very
little which of course prevents her from appearing to such advantage as she would otherwise do, but she is quite self-possessed and
has a natural dignity of manner which has struck all who have been

introduced to her. Lady Leven has just come in, and I am happy to report that her son Ronald, who was here last night, went home and told her that the Maharanee was such a nice little thing, so beautiful an eye and so pretty a hand, and such good manners and in short that his heart was quite relieved. If this is a young man's opinion, I think you may trust that mine is not more favourable than it ought to be. The Maharanee is just come into the next room and if I can add what Lady Leven thinks, I will. She is, she says, a sweet gentle girl. Lady L. has just taken her out in her carriage.[13]

Lady Login had not been able to visit the couple before anyone else, as no doubt she would have wished, because she was unwell and in deep mourning following the death of her husband. But her son Edwy represented her and thought the new bride was a 'perfect beauty'. She had a more reliable description from Lady Leven:

She is not the wonderful beauty that Edwy supposed; but she is remarkably nice-looking, with very fine eyes, and a sweet expression. In that respect she is better-looking than Gouramma, and a size larger. She looked simple and quiet, and rather dignified.

I asked the M.R. if her head was turned by her marriage? and he said that she knew nothing of her position and did not care for her jewels when he showed them to her ... I fancy she is entirely occupied with him. She is most submissive, and if asked if she would like to do anything, answers: 'Maharajah wish – I wish!' They are going immediately to the Highlands, and he is very anxious that Lord L. [Leven] and Ronald and I should visit them there, and I have persuaded Lord L. to agree. The rest of our party would go either to N. Berwick for sea-bathing, or stay at the Inn at Aberfeldy.

I should like to see more of this girl. He says her name is 'Bamba', which means 'pink', and that she was pink till six weeks ago, when she had jaundice!

He says that, *as* she is not strong, *he is doctoring her*! and the day he brought her here begged she might have nothing but cold water, because of some dose he had given her! I must remonstrate about this, or he will certainly kill her!

She looks as if she had a perfect temper, and seems a simple-minded girl, above marrying for rank, and her ready submission, if it does not last too long, will make them happy together.

The M.H. *will* interfere with everything concerning his wife's attire, and has the most absurd notions about the matter. I tried to convince him that the crinoline was not at all suitable for her and it would be better for her to dress in a modification of the Egyptian costume, which is infinitely more becoming.

You can fancy how it is now, with two dressmakers in the house, and he finding fault if she does not look like other people, and yet insisting on her dresses being cut short, and no trimmings of any kind, and choosing colours irrespective of the becoming! It is all from intense anxiety that she should look well, but I mean to try and persuade him to give up dress and medicine to professionals, and devote himself to her mind instead!

Mme. Goldschmidt* saw her here, and thought her very nice-looking, and all our girls were charmed with her.... And I hope she will make as good an impression on others as she did on us. I scarcely know why, but I feel as if I cared almost as much about his wife as I should about R's.[14]

Lady Login came up from Felixstowe as soon as she could to hear all about it direct from the Maharajah. He came to call on her in her lodgings in Hanover Square, not, however, to present his wife. He was anxious to claim the bet, which on the evidence, he seemed to have lost by a week. In her *Recollections* she paints a vivid picture of the meeting:

It was in the dusk of the late afternoon of a foggy day, and the remembrance often comes back to me of him, sitting there by the fire with the daylight slowly fading, while he told the tale of his wooing and marriage of this shy young child – for she was little more – who had no desire for the position he could offer her, and in her heart wished to be left to devote herself to the life of a missionary, for which she was being educated. He thoroughly enjoyed telling his story, and was in the highest of spirits, and triumphant over having just managed to 'win his bet' with me by speeding up the legal formalities and his own movements, to and from India, within the specified date!

To all my remonstrances as to the indecent haste with which he cut short his mother's 'cremation', so as to permit of his return quickly to Egypt, and to his having allowed pressure to be put on

* The singer, Jenny Lind.

a young girl to consent to such a hurried marriage, he responded only with peals of laughter, treating the whole matter as a joke. I can see his eyes rolling now, the gleam of his flashing teeth in the dark shadows, and his hilarious shrieks of mirth when I questioned him as to how he could possibly have conducted a conversation with his *fiancée*, if she knew no language he spoke, and he nothing of hers? 'Oh, that was quite simple! I had a dragoman to interpret!' 'Interpret, Maharajah? What do you mean? You never had a dragoman there when you were talking to her?' What could he say? 'Oh, quite easy, quite easy, I assure you! All I had to say was "I love you! Will you be my wife?" to him and he turned it into Arabic, and then her answer he translated to me!'

All this farrago was narrated with a succession of shrugs and expressive gestures, contortions of merriment and droll faces, as to make it extremely doubtful how much was in jest, and how much in earnest; but the bare idea of the situation, in the way he told it, was so irresistibly comic that I could do nothing but laugh with him, and had to abandon the attempt to show him how he had outraged the sense of propriety of the powers that be!

In August, the Maharajah and his wife retreated to Scotland until such time as Elveden, his newly acquired property in Suffolk, should be ready for occupation. Meanwhile it was hoped that the maharani, under the guidance of the 'amiable ladylike'[15] Miss Hart, on loan from the mission school in Cairo, would learn some English and general knowledge. Elveden took longer than expected to be made habitable, and meanwhile the young couple decided to return to Egypt for some early sunshine. They took Miss Hart back too, and by the middle of January were sailing on the Nile in the mission launch *Ibis*, which the Maharajah bought and fitted up for comfort. After visiting the Fayum, they took the boat to the Delta where they did some missionary work on their own account, distributing bibles and propagating the gospel to anyone who cared to listen.

CHAPTER 7

The Squire of Elveden

❖

ELVEDEN Hall lies about four miles from Thetford on the borders of Suffolk and Norfolk. It was originally owned by Admiral Keppel, the first Earl of Albemarle, but for the last fifty years had been the home of a sporting squire, William Newton. The cost to the Maharajah was £105,000, raised by a loan from the India Office at 4 per cent. By the time the adjoining estate of Eriswell, split with the rich Mr Angerstein, had been added, the property comprised some seventeen thousand acres.

It could not be said that the house was prepossessing; soon after he took possession, the Maharajah decided that it would virtually have to be rebuilt. The architect, John Norton, was commissioned to design a mansion in the Italian Renaissance style, and Cubitt & Co. were employed as contractors. The finished house was of red brick with Ancaster stone dressings; with its pillared portico, projecting wings and double bay windows, it had a solid look, though the ornamental urns at roof level and the four great chimney stacks gave it a certain air of fantasy. But the interior was even more fanciful: Norton's brief was to make the main rooms reminiscent of an Indian palace, and to give him some idea of what he had in mind, the Maharajah showed him a set of watercolours brought from Lahore and photographs obtained from the India Museum. The Shish Mahal, the Glass Palace, was the inspiration for the drawing room, with convex slivers of mercurized glass that sparkled in the light embedded in the plasterwork. The main rooms were embellished with elaborate pilasters and arches in the Mughal style; the grand marble staircase, built at a cost of £23 15s per tread, was set with splendid cast-iron banisters painted in sealing-wax red.[1]

The neighbours must have gazed in wonder when they turned up at the first reception and observed the extraordinary interior; with the 'Black Prince', as he was known locally, in full Indian outfit, his tiny wife by his side, holding court in the twinkling drawing room, its walls hung with cashmere shawls, and strange pieces of oriental furniture disposed among the familiar silk-covered ottomans, chesterfields and whatnots.

The Maharajah's predecessor, Newton, had been a keen shooting man and had improved the estate for that purpose during his tenure. His tradition was 'walking up', but the Maharajah, who had plenty of beaters at his disposal, proposed to lay out the property for the specific purpose of big drives, a system that had been developed in East Anglia in the previous decade but which he was conscientiously to advance by carefully planned plantations. Farming could be left to the tenant farmers: if agriculturally underdeveloped Elveden was soon to become one of the finest sporting places in the country, rivalling nearby Sandringham, purchased at about the same time by the Prince of Wales.

The Maharajah had chosen to live in an area that had the greatest concentration of sporting estates in the world. As well as Sandringham, there was Lord Walsingham's Merton, Lord Henniker's Thornham, Lord Albermale's Quidenham, the Duke of Grafton's Euston, and grandest of all, Lord Leicester's Holkham; not to mention numerous other lesser, but well-stocked, establishments. All the great shots came to Elveden, including the Prince of Wales, and the Maharajah's shooting guests included half the grandees in the land, among them Leicester, Kimberley, Dacre, Rendlesham, Abinger, Skelmersdale, Ripon, Bristol, Henniker, Walsingham, Westbury, Lovat, Balfour of Burleigh, Manchester, Londesborough, Atholl and Grafton. If the Maharajah was not quite so good a shot as Walsingham, Ripon or Hartington, he was rated the fourth best in Britain, even if his style of shooting pheasants was hardly elegant – he would sometimes sit on the ground and swivel himself around 'like a whirling dervish'. He held two records – 440 grouse to his own gun in a day at Grandtully, the estate he rented in Perthshire;[2] and 780 partridge for a thousand cartridges at Elveden. For the Grandtully feat he had three pairs of dogs working and rode from point to point on a pony. In an average season at Elveden the bag might be ten thousand pheasants, ditto partridges, three thousand hares and seventy thousand rabbits. For bagging the latter he took a ninety-nine-year lease on a sandy area known as Warren Lodge, where they could be shot from platforms erected in the trees. From these platforms the Maharajah liked to shoot them driven at him down wind and many hundreds were killed on such occasions, the skins ending up at the local factory where they were turned into fur hats.

An impression of the Maharajah out shooting is provided by T. W. Turner, who was to become head keeper at Elveden: 'I well remember seeing the Maharajah out partridge shooting ... It was in 1875 and I was a small boy of seven. These were the days of muzzle-loaders, and the Maharajah had three double-barrelled guns, and two loaders, who with their blue and green coats and waistcoats, powder flasks and leather shotbags, made a great impression on my mind. They were walking in seed clover, which was ideal for partridges to settle in, and to ensure this the gamekeeper was walking along the road flying a kite over the field, the kite being shaped like a peregrine hawk ... to make them lie close. I was so much impressed by it all that I thought, "When I get to be a man I will be a gamekeeper if I can." '[3]

Following the lead of Lord Rendlesham, the Maharajah tried to introduce the red grouse to the heathland, but like other neighbours who attempted it he found it did not work. He was more successful with the golden pheasant, and the sight of these elegant exotics strutting on the lawns beneath the cedars must have added to the magic of the scene. The

Maharajah trained several Icelandic gerfalcons to take the big brown hares on the open heath, but the quarry proved difficult to capture, being quick to take cover in his plantations. Wallabies and jungle fowl proved less able to compete with the chill East Anglian winters.

At Elveden the Maharajah had come into his own.

They had been at Elveden for over a year when an invitation arrived from the queen to 'dine and sleep' at Windsor; she was keen to see Bamba for the first time. The Maharajah hoped his wife had by now learned enough to do him credit. Lady Leven, who introduced Bamba, described the dress she wore for the occasion, and in which she was photographed: 'It had a full skirt, and Turkish jacket with wide sleeves; on her head was a jaunty cap, like a fez, made of large pearls, worn on one side with a long tassel of pearls hanging down to her shoulder. Her hair was plaited into several long, tight plaits, hanging straight down all round. This odd *coiffure* was apparently only for state occasions, normally it was coiled on top of her head in one immense plait.' Lady Leven described how the Princess Royal and Princess Helena, who were staying at the time, '*would* stay in the Maharanee's room to see her hair plaited'.[4] The queen kissed her, as an acknowledgement of her rank, and flattered the Maharajah with compliments about her. The two princesses made her sit between them all evening, cross-questioning her about Egypt and her life there. In her journal for 30 November 1865, the queen wrote: 'The good Maharajah (in his Indian dress) & his lovely little wife, beautifully dressed in Indian stuffs, covered with splendid jewels & pearls, like a Princess in a fairy tale, dined. He is so amiable & agreeable, but gets too fat.'

Indeed it could no longer be said that the Maharajah was the same slim youth that the queen had admired and Winterhalter had delineated. An anonymous writer, who called himself 'one of the Old Brigade' as author of *London in the Sixties*, described him as follows: 'It was only when His Highness assumed evening dress that visions of Mooltan, Chillianwallah, and Goojerat faded from one's brain, and a podgy little Hindoo seemed to stand before one, divested of that physique and martial bearing one associates with other warriors or Sikhs, and only requiring, as it were, a chutnee-pot peeping out of his pocket to complete the illusion.'⁵

Bamba's first child, a son, was born in June 1866. A small christening ceremony was held at Elveden, but eight months later the queen commanded them to Windsor for a second christening, at which she would be the godmother. Her journal entry for the occasion reads:

Directly after breakfast the Maharajah's baby was brought in by the nurse for me to see. I never beheld a lovelier child, a plump little darling with the most splendid dark eyes, but not very dark skin.

At 1, the Christening of the dear little 'Shahzadah' took place in the chapel. He is already 8½ months old and sits up. As he had already been baptised, the service was a different one, and the nurse held him all the time. I named him Victor Albert, the names the Maharajah wished to have. He and a Mr Jay, a Clergyman, who had christened the Maharajah himself, many years ago, were the sponsors with me. Lord and Lady Leven and Lady Sophy Melville, great friends of the Maharajah's, all my Ladies and Gentlemen, and Louise, Leopold and Baby were present. The dear little Maharanee sat with the latter, and the Dean of Windsor performed the service. Took leave of the dear young couple and my little godchild, to whom I gave some gifts ...'⁶

Poor Bamba did not take too easily to social life, and the heavy, masculine shooting parties must have both awed and bored her. But she was kept busy enough with her children, and in the first twelve years of her marriage produced three boys and three girls – Victor Albert Jay (born 1866); Frederick Victor (born 1868); Bamba Sofia Jindan (born 1869); Catherine Hilda (born 1871); Sophia Alexandra (born 1876); and Edward Albert Alexander (born 1879).

As his family responsibilities grew, the Maharajah began to worry again about his financial affairs. Elveden was mortgaged to the India Office and he would be unable to leave it to his son. Besides, there was some adjoining land he wanted to buy. In March 1868 he sought an interview with the queen, who had told him to call on her if he had any problems. 'After luncheon saw the good Maharajah,' the queen noted in the journal, 'who came in plain morning clothes, not nearly so becoming as his native dress. He wanted to speak to me about his own affairs & his anxiety, on his children's account to get his income increased.'[7]

The queen acted without delay. 'Saw Sir S. Northcote about the Maharajah's affairs,' she entered on 18 March, 'and told him that I was very anxious, if possible, that some further allowance be made for the children, though *I* knew and *he* knew he had no claim whatever.' This was the only occasion, in a long campaign to help, that the queen admitted there was no claim. If she in fact thought he had no legal claim, she was never in doubt about his moral one.

Sir Stafford Northcote, then secretary of state for India, ascertained that there was £13,585 not taken up under the mortgage agreement, and this was made available at a reduced interest rate. The next secretary of state, the Duke of Argyll, at the behest of the queen, further reassured him that, even if he had accepted previous arrangements as 'final', £15,000 a year would be available to his family after his death in addition to his own accumulations.[8]

As well as a qualified 'thank you' for his consideration, Argyll was soon to receive a puzzling request, sent from the Maharajah's expensively rented estate, Grandtully Castle in Perthshire. It may have been a 'try-on' to establish to what extent his movements in India might be circumscribed; it is also likely that it was the first hint that should his financial affairs not be taken care of to his satisfaction, he might move his family out of the country. 'I have the honour to inform your Grace that should circumstances permit it is my intention to proceed to India shortly with the view of purchasing 100,000 acres of waste lands at the foot of the hills in the North-Western Provinces or in Oudh, in order to make a further provision for my family, and to keep up our connexion with that country. I would feel very grateful to the Government if the above-stated extent of land could be made over to me in a ring fence and I be permitted to pay off the purchase money only on that portion of it which is brought under tillage annually, instead of being required to pay down the whole amount at one time.'9

There must have been some questioning looks at the India Office when the Duke of Argyll brought up the unexpected request with his council. In this instance his reply conceded nothing at all: '... whilst Her Majesty's Government have every disposition, as your Highness is aware, to comply with such reasonable requests as you may make for the advancement of the true interests of yourself and family, they cannot, I regret to say, recommend his Excellency the Viceroy to assent to the proposal which you have now submitted to me.'10

If the India Office rejected the Maharajah's continuing requests for cash, it was to some extent because he was seen to be living beyond his means, and a section of the public, especially that which voted Liberal, did not approve of conspicuous consumption by deposed, and presumably unworthy, maharajahs at the expense of India's innumerable poor. He was becoming known as something of a 'punter' and was often to be found in the clubs playing whist for up to £10 a rubber. His moral stance, also, was open to criticism – he was a popular patron of the Alhambra, and would turn up in the green room to display some minor piece of jewellery and inquire of the assembled *houris* 'What nice little girl is going to have this?' He soon concentrated his attentions on a member of the chorus called Polly Ash, whom he set up in a flat in Covent Garden complete with an annuity.11 Like the Prince of Wales, he enjoyed his visits to Paris. He was often seen at the tables there, and is said to have introduced to London *chemin de fer*, which he preferred to *baccarat*. One of the attractions in Paris was the courtesan Léonide le Blanc, whom he shared for a time with an unlikely pair, the Duc d'Aumâle and the young Clemençeau. The lady, it was said, had two sorts of writing paper appropriately designed for an 'amant de cœur' or an 'amant de poche'. It is not known for which category the Maharajah qualified. Another London lady who took his fancy was known as 'Marini', fair and aristocratic in appearance, who in fact had been a maid in a Knightsbridge hotel. If her manners were patrician, her voice was unmistakably East End, and she liked a brandy and soda for breakfast. The Maharajah's attentions were ardent – he had her send him a telegram twice a day, 'just to let me know you are alright'.[12]

There may have been some conflict in the Maharajah's mind between the Christian code of conduct indoctrinated by Login and the more liberated of some of his friends. Though rejected by White's, he had joined the Garrick and the Marlborough clubs and the followers of the Prince of Wales who were members of the latter, set an example that may have been nearer to his basic nature. But his other side wanted to make a more serious contribution to society, and it was to indulge him in this direction that Ronald Leslie-Melville suggested he have a go at politics. As a start, Melville had the duke of Richmond put him up for the Carlton Club and, supported by Lord Walsingham and Lord Colville, he was elected on 17 March 1873. It may have occurred to the stalwart Conservatives who composed the club that by contesting Whitby, in an area in which he had been so popular during his long association with Mulgrave, the Maharajah might have a faint chance of winning a Liberal seat and, even if he did not, might embarrass the incumbent member, who happened to be Gladstone's son Herbert, and thereby aggravate the 'Grand Old Man' himself.

When the Maharajah received the rank and status of a European prince, it was tacitly understood that he should not involve himself in politics, though Indian politics was probably what was meant. But the idea was in fact a good one: in the changing political and social climate of India, when the educated natives of that country wanted more and more to have a say in their affairs, an Indian in Parliament might stand for a symbol of their emancipation. As *The Times of India* commented: 'It should be worth a good deal for the

Indian people to obtain a representative so eminently qualified to give a valuable and sound opinion on questions affecting their religion, laws, feelings and prejudices, more especially a fine gentleman like the Maharajah – and according to
all we hear,' the editorial continued, 'no English gentleman
or nobleman plays that role with greater success, whether he
be regarded as a landlord, a patron or a host.'[13]

The queen did not think it at all a good idea that the
Maharajah should dabble in English politics, and she had been
advised that it would raise certain constitutional problems
connected with his legal right to British nationality. But why
should he not have a seat in the House of Lords and perhaps
some social gratification in being made a peer of the realm?
She put the question to the prime minister, who was visiting
her at Balmoral: 'Saw Mr Gladstone ... after luncheon &
talked to him about the idea of making the Maharajah a Peer,
which he thought was a very good one, whereas his standing
for Hse. of C., which he had hinted at, was quite inadmissible.'[14]

Gladstone was in an embarrassing position. He pointed out
to the queen 'the difficulty which would arise if it could be
said that I had advised the grant of a Peerage to the Maharajah
in order to get rid of the opposition at Whitby'. Nevertheless,
the great nonconformist conscience finally accepted what
was in fact that very *quid pro quo*. At Gladstone's suggestion,
the proposition was put to Colonel Oliphant, acting as the
Maharajah's adviser, by Sir Thomas Biddulph, Keeper of the
Privy Purse. 'If ... the Maharajah has entirely abandoned all
thoughts of Whitby ... I think that Mr Gladstone could
probably recommend the Queen to confer one.'[15]

In any case, when the Maharajah learned that the queen
was not in favour of his parliamentary plan, he withdrew
gracefully. So strong was her influence on him that he was
prepared to ditch his Carlton friends by undertaking not to
make political capital out of the affair by discussing it 'in the
clubs or elsewhere'. In any event Herbert Gladstone retained
his seat, but with his majority only 120 out of an electorate

of 2,050. It was perhaps to keep in with men of influence, who might sometimes be able to intervene in his interest, that he continued to use the Carlton more frequently than any other club and many of his more important letters were written on its paper. That he was quite at home there is indicated by a paragraph in *Vanity Fair*, the social and satirical journal eagerly read by every man of fashion of the day: 'His Highness Dhuleep Singh was much aggrieved the other day at the absence of fish-knives at the Carlton Club, and wrote a letter to the Committee petitioning them to allow him to introduce half-a-dozen for his own private use. Fingers were made before knives! A fact with which High Highness was at once acquainted.'[16]

Mr Gladstone did not, in the end, have to keep his side of the bargain: his party was beaten at the general election of 1875 and the Conservatives came into power with Disraeli as prime minister and the Duke of Argyll back again as secretary of state for India. Disraeli was under no obligation to fulfil Gladstone's pledge, but, at the queen's suggestion, he sent Argyll to discuss the position, which was already developing into a typical Maharajah mix-up owing to his suddenly deciding that he did not really want a title after all. Nor, it appeared, would his pride allow him to accept an honour for his children.

The story of the rejected peerage was told by Osborne Jay, son of the minister at Futteghur who had christened him:

Before I was ordained in 1880, I was acting for a time as Private Secretary to Lord Granville at the Foreign Office, and was asked by the Maharajah to attend him at Elveden at an interview with the Duke of Argyll, the Secretary for India.

Queen Victoria had always intended to make Dalip Singh English in all save name. She sent the Duke, therefore, on a special mission.

It was this, to offer Peerages for both Princes; a Marquisate for Victor, and an Earldom (or at least a Viscountcy) for Freddie.

His Grace's letter outlining this proposal had been sent to me beforehand by the Prince.

When, however, the formal interview took place in the great library at Elveden, a noble apartment decorated with gold Indian shawls upon the walls, the Duke conveyed the Queen's offer and the Maharajah immediately declined it.

'I thank Her Majesty', he said, 'most heartily and humbly convey to her my esteem, affection and admiration. Beyond that I cannot go. I claim myself to be royal; I am not English, and neither I nor my children will ever become so. Such titles – though kindly offered – we do not need and cannot assume. We love the English and especially their Monarch, but we must remain Sikhs.'

He walked across to a table and opened a drawer. 'This', he said drawing out some paper, 'is the design for my coat-of arms, drawn up by the Prince Consort and initialled by the Queen. I use them out of courtesy to Her Majesty, but I will not register them at the College of Arms; I am not English.'

The Duke said to me afterwards he had never seen truer dignity or more real independence of spirit. I have reason for believing that the Queen, when told of all this, shared his opinion.[17]

The motto selected for the Maharajah's coat-of-arms by the prince consort – '*Prodesse quam conspicii*' ('to do good rather than to be conspicuous') – was unlikely to have influenced him in what might have been seen as a conspicuous honour both to himself and his family. He may to some extent have felt that the offer of a peerage was no more than a polite way of denying him his freedom of operation within the British system. But if he now wore European dress on all but the grandest occasions and scrupulously observed the social conventions of his English contemporaries, the Maharajah was beginning to assess his position objectively, and was showing signs of a fundamental split in his nature, the Sikh in him struggling with the Anglo-Saxon overlay. Inflamed by the unaccommodating attitude at the India Office, he had begun to study the historical perspectives of his position, and a reading of Prinsep's classic and impartial *History of the Sikhs* and the relative government Blue Books in the British Museum, had made him aware of his people's past and of British perfidy in their suppression. And so, thanks to the limitations in cash the conquerors now imposed, his position even among his friends and retainers was being undermined. Fifteen thousand a year, all that remained after deduction of interest payable to the government, did not seem to go very far, nor did an advance of forty thousand pounds from Coutts, secured on his life insurance, do more than pay off pressing obligations.

On days of disquietude, the Maharajah would find relief in music and its composition. He was working on an opera and was seen alternating between two grand pianos in deepest concentration. The subject of the opera is not known; perhaps, like Massenet who in 1877 wrote *The King of Lahore*, he hymned his precursors in the heyday of their power.

On 1 May 1877 Queen Victoria was declared Empress of India. It may have been with the Maharajah in mind that she asked for a troop of Sikh cavalry to be sent over. This idea was firmly rejected by the India Office.

CHAPTER 8

The Sackville-West Report

NEW YEAR 1878 brought the Maharajah pleasure in the form of a letter from the queen-empress bestowing on Bamba her newly instituted female order, 'the Crown of India',[1] and chagrin in the copperplate handwriting of Messrs Coutts, bankers, who, while remaining 'his obedient servants', 'begged to remind him that he had undertaken to have by now considerably reduced his £40,000 loan and, though desiring to consult his convenience in every way, hoped that he would make arrangements to deal with the matter at an early date.'[2]

The Maharajah was probably not too intimidated by this unctuous reminder, but it brought into immediate focus his ever-increasing financial weakness: with five growing children to educate and bad harvests that raised the cost of living at the same time reducing his rents, he saw the necessity of once again approaching the India Office for help. Early in January he sent off to the secretary of state, Lord Salisbury, the dunning letter from Coutts and a new and more contentious projection of his case; ostensibly asking for no more than good advice, even if it raised the question of the retention of money freed by the death of family pensioners.

My Lord, I submit the following statement to Your Lordship for your advice and assistance.

After the first Sikh War the Indian Government constituted themselves my Guardian and solemnly promised to maintain me on the Throne of the Punjab till I attained the age of 16 years but so managed my affairs in the meantime that when the Governor of Mooltan rebelled against the Sikh Durbar they allowed a portion of my subjects to rise against my Government. As the late Sir Frederick Currie once informed me, had Lord Gough when first asked to send down the European troops from Simla complied with his request, the rebellion would have been nipped in the bud, but this delay on the part of the Commander-in-Chief, not only cost me my Throne for which I care very little, but also my private property both in houses and landed property and this when I had not even lifted my little finger against the British Government and when I and my property were alike under their Guardianship. I was sent as a prisoner to Futteghar, excluded from any communication with my family – I was allowed to take with me about £25,000 worth of plate, jewels etc. the only remains of my great wealth. I and this remnant of my property were guarded by the late Sir John Login and the Native Troops but even this small property was lost to me in the Indian Mutiny – I was offered by the Indian Government £3,000 to compensate me for this loss, a sum which I declined to accept.

My debts are mostly incurred in building and furnishing my house and concentrating on my property.

Upwards of £30,000 have been spent in the almost entire rebuilding of Elveden House and in partly refurnishing it, a sum Your Lordship knows is not large considering that many Country Mansions in England cost ten times as much and more. Had I been allowed to retain only one of the houses belonging to either my Brothers or Uncles the proceeds of the sale of it would have been more than ample to build me a better dwelling than I now possess and have left me a little more to amuse myself with. Out of the Four Lakhs and not exceeding Five Lakhs set apart for the maintenance of myself and relatives and the servants of my state, I have reason to believe that the whole of the sum allotted for that purpose has never been entirely spent annually and the amount now paid for those purposes is, I believe, greatly under the lower of these two sums. Though repeatedly promised by the Government, I have never yet received a fair statement of accounts as head of the family.

Your Lordship is aware that it takes the expenditure of the income of several generations to make a place and I have had to do this in a few years besides maintaining the position granted to me by my generous and gracious Queen in this Country and to add to my difficulties owing to the late dry summers and bad harvests we have had in Suffolk, a great many of the farms on my estate have been thrown on my hands and I have had to provide money to stock them in order to carry on the cultivation and Your Lordship as a landed proprietor need not be told what an expense and loss that is. Moreover all my property is settled on my descendants and I have no security to offer if I wished to raise money as at the present time I require some to go on with the Agriculture and Messrs. Coutts & Co. very naturally ask as you will see by their letter that my debt to them chiefly secured by Life Policies should be materially reduced – therefore my Lord I ask what am I to do?[3]

As was his custom in times of stress the Maharajah saw to it that the queen was made aware of his predicament and petition. On receipt of a copy, she wrote to Lord Salisbury suggesting that in view of her protégé's excellent behaviour and special circumstances he might be treated with generosity. Her secretary of state replied in a somewhat ambivalent style, accommodating enough, but leaving a line of retreat from possible royal displeasure via the veto rights of his council, at the same time sounding a warning of things to come:

Lord Salisbury with his humble duty to Your Majesty respectfully submits that the application of H.H. the Maharajah Dhuleep Singh is now under consideration at this office & that in dealing with it he will bear in mind the wishes expressed in Your Majesty's gracious letter. The matter, however, is not entirely in his hands, as the Council possess a veto on any grants of money: but they appear to be liberally disposed in the present instance. Lord Salisbury entirely concurs in Your Majesty's opinion that politically the Maharajah behaved very well. His private life would be more easy to criticise: and is likely to lead him into large expenses, which will probably result in a renewed application to Your Majesty's Indian Treasury. All things, however, considered the present application is not unreasonable: & he trusts may, in some form or other be entertained.[4]

As was his duty Lord Salisbury passed the Maharajah's application on to his advisers and it was considered by the

political committee, who were not all of the same opinion:
though one of the members thought that something might,
and ought to be done for him, another strongly opposed;
a third, after invoking the spirit of Lord Dalhousie, made
the point that the Maharajah was presenting himself both as
a petitioner and as a claimant and should be firmly put in his
place before the matter was proceeded with; he was of the
opinion, however, that 'the scandal of leaving the Maharajah
at the mercy of his creditors would be a very serious one'.[5]

The final version of their deliberations was embodied in a
letter which began by accusing the Maharajah of making
more unfounded claims after he had conceded a 'final settlement of the question' and ended with the suggestion that
financial help might be forthcoming as an act of grace if he
submitted to an inquiry into his management of his affairs.[6]

The Maharajah's reaction to further delay in resolving his
pressing problems and the humiliating suggestion that his
private affairs should be looked into by a public official must
have been one of impotent anger. But he was learning the
rules of the game and was diplomatic enough to disclaim his
intention of asserting any actual rights and to submit with
as good grace as he could muster to an inspection of his
accounts. On 8 April he replied:

I would take leave to point out that I do not assume that I am
personally entitled to the difference between the sum not exceeding
five lacs of rupees, named in the Terms of the 24th of March 1849,
and the sum which may have been actually expended to the present
time; but I pointed to the fact that the whole sum has not been
expended as affording a fund out of which a further sum might
fairly be allotted to me personally.

I admit that the arrangements made for me have been stated to
be final, but I have nevertheless thought that I might, without
impropriety, state my real position, and ask for further consideration at the hands of the Indian Government. I may remark that in
all the different arrangements I have been entirely in the hands of
the Indian Government, having no power to dispute any decision
at which the Government may arrive. I believe there is no other

Indian prince, in my position, who does not receive from the Indian Government an allowance largely in excess of the provision made for me.

I should not have the least objection to my accounts being submitted to the inspection of any gentleman of position nominated by the Indian Government. I should not wish to place myself in the position of having my accounts examined by a professional accountant.[7]

The 'gentleman of position' nominated by Lord Cranbrook, Lord Salisbury's successor after his transference to the Foreign Office, was Lieutenant Colonel the Hon. William Sackville-West, fifth son of Earl de La Warr and Lady Elizabeth Sackville, direct descendant of the dukes of Dorset. His instructions were received in a letter dated 24 May defining the objects of his investigation as being to ascertain: '(1) what was the real condition of the Maharajah's landed estates; (2) whether the income received by the Maharajah from Government, and from his estates, was or was not sufficient for his maintenance in England in a style befitting his position; and (3) whether His Highness's difficulties arose from causes practically beyond his own control, or whether and to what extent they were the result either of mismanagement of his estates, or of reasons under his own control.'[8]

Before learning of the appointment of his inquisitor, the Maharajah had applied for 'a small advance of even £1,000'[9] to meet necessary expenditure on farms he had been compelled to take in hand during the bad times. He was flintily informed that, 'pending receipt and consideration of Col. West's report the Secretary of State was unable to take any such step in regard to his affairs as compliance with his request would involve'.[10] If such official parsimony and such unsympathetic responses were beginning to eat into the Maharajah's soul, he greeted Sackville-West with a good spirit. They surveyed the estate together, studied bank statements and bills, and, though there appeared to be a certain lack of continuity in the Maharajah's system of accounting, his investigator was able to acquit him of personal extravagance, except for a gambling loss of £850, though it was clear that he was spending at least £2,500 a year above his income. Among the minor liabilities revealed among his papers was his personal guarantee for a £700 loan raised for his boyhood friend Tommy Scott.[11] Much of the trouble, it seemed, lay in the large capital expenditure on purchasing the estate and building and furnishing the house, on which interest had to be paid to the government. The various farms brought in insufficient rent owing to the fact that the preservation of game was the main consideration, though it was agreed that the Maharajah's splendid shoot, after the sale of game and as many as 150,000 pheasant eggs a season, cost him no more than £300 a year. Sackville-West concluded with a brief homily: 'I venture to suggest, for consideration, that should any rearrangement of His Highness's affairs be made, it is extremely desirable that it should be made a condition that his accounts should be kept and audited in such a manner as is done in most well-managed estates and households...'[12]

Sackville-West's painstaking, and on the whole vindicatory, report on the Maharajah's state of affairs was submitted on 12 August 1878. At the beginning of the month, in anticipation of its favourable reception, the Maharajah had written with studied politeness to Lord Cranbrook setting out what he hoped would be allowed him:

As Colonel West whom you very kindly appointed to investigate my affairs will shortly lay before you his report; I desire to submit to Your Lordship a statement of my hopes and wishes for a more liberal consideration than has hitherto been given me.

Without raising any claims but throwing myself entirely on the generosity of my Gracious Sovereign I beg to bring before you my following requests:

That I may be relieved from the pressure of all my present debts, that the premiums on the Policies on my life be paid out of the income of (about) £40,000 to £50,000 allotted for the support of myself, my relatives and the servants of the state; that an income be allotted to me which will properly sustain me in the position granted to me by my Sovereign at least equal to that of the great nobles of this country. That any surplus of the £40,000 to £50,000 after defraying any pensions charged thereon and the premium of my policies, be accumulated during my lifetime for my children and that a capital sum at least representing the value of only a part of my very large private property be given to me – my other property being wholly in settlement.

Should my petition be listened to thus, My Lord, myself and mine will be provided for in a handsome and liberal spirit worthy [of] the generosity of this great nation.[13]

The Maharajah was in a frustrated mood and was hardly inclined to play the bureaucratic game according to the rules for ever. He had been sensibly advised not to send forward, attached to yet another historical résumé, an audacious claim to some £480,000 worth of family jewels sold by the East India Company and supposedly distributed as prize money to the conquering army, and £1,097,000 for ancestral lands as yet undefined; for good measure he had added compound interest. But he was not to be deterred from sending a copy of his claim to the queen, with the following covering letter:

My Most Gracious Sovereign, Through Your Majesty's kind interest my pecuniary affairs will be brought before the Government of India in a few days and consequently I had prepared a statement (copy of which with that also of the letter I sent to Lord Cranbrook I humbly beg to enclose) of their treatment of me to send to the Secretary of State for India but I am advised by one or two Indian officials not to do so.

I have no friend except Your Majesty who is able to help me therefore unless your great interest is exercised on my behalf they will again treat me in as miserly a spirit as the Government of India have hitherto done. Can I therefore my Patron rely once more on Your Majesty's clemency and generosity and favour in the final settlement of my affairs?

The only plea that I put forward for thus presuming to address You is Your own never ceasing Graciousness both to me and mine My Gracious Sovereign.

I do not expect to get all I have asked for but whatever is done for me *I shall owe it entirely* to Your Majesty's *Bounty*.

I have the honour to remain Your Majesty's most loyal subject,

Duleep Singh.[14]

The queen replied:

Dear Maharajah, I have to acknowledge your letter of the 3d., with the enclosures, and have expressed my great interest in you, & yr. affairs to Lord Cranbrook, who is very well disposed towards you, & will I am sure, do what he can.

You know how deep an interest I have *ever* taken in you, and how much I feel for the trying position in which you were & are placed by circumstances over which you had no control – But as an old friend, excuse me for saying that I think you are considered a little *inclined* to extravagance which may act unfavourably on the settlement of Yr. affairs. One thing especially, I have for some time wished to mention to you, as it is unpopular in the country, and what I myself, particularly dislike, viz. the great extent to which you preserve game – It is very expensive, & is much disliked for many reasons in the Country. If you wd. reduce this, & merely keep up a moderate amount, quite enough for amusement, I am sure it would have the best effect.

I take the liveliest interest also in yr. dear children, & must ask you to let me have a Portrait taken for me of Victor? I hope he still has his beautiful hair?

With kindest remembrances to the Maharanee, ever yr. affecte friend...[15]

The queen also wrote a letter of recommendation to Cranbrook reverting to the charge of extravagance, which the Sackville-West report had not, in fact, substantiated: 'If a certain amount of unnecessary expenditure can be alleged against him, the Queen feels that great allowance should be made for his notions of oriental magnificence.'[16]

The Maharajah was anxious to refute charges of extravagance and had the Sackville-West report circulated among his friends. He also sent a copy to the queen, along with his game account books for inspection, apologizing for the ink blots. The portrait of Victor, he told her, must wait as he had already returned to Eton.

Lord Hertford, a shooting friend, who claimed to have 'some influence over him', had heard other criticisms of the Maharajah current in society and had asked Ronald Leslie-Melville to warn him to look to his reputation. The Maharajah seemed grateful for his friend's advice and wrote to Hertford:

Thank you very much for the friendly hints conveyed through Ronald Melville. Without nonsense I am exceedingly grateful to you . . . The accompanying statement will show you the state of my affairs are in and explain my apparent neglect of my wife and family.

The fact is that I cannot afford to bring them up to Town but if thru' the kindness of the Queen the Government of India treat me in a liberal spirit none of my friends will ever be able to bring against me such a charge.

It is false that I am a disbeliever in Christianity. Indeed I am quite the contrary but as I cannot act up to my convictions I disdain to lend myself to hypocrisy and do not go to church as often as some people.

With the exception of playing whist at the United Whist Club in Waterloo Place (some members of which are not of desirable character) I keep no low company – only with Lord Westbury and Captain Goldingham I am at all familiar, with the rest of the members I scarcely ever speak. All my friends are among those from the highest society in the country. I am quite willing to take my name off the list of members of the aforementioned club if my friends desire it or reform in any other way they may wish. Again thanking you for the kind interest you have taken in me . . .[17]

Hertford was persuaded to indicate to the palace that the Maharajah's little weaknesses had been moderated: 'He assures me he is leading a steady life,' he wrote to Sir Henry Ponsonby, the queen's private secretary, who had taken over the Maharajah's file, following the death of Phipps, '& has only lost £300 altogether at whist, but still thought it best to give up playing & has taken his name out of all the Whist Clubs except the Marlboro'. From all I hear I believe him to be good *au fond* but requires to be watched & taken care of . . . & that he is grateful for any interest.'[18]

It was clear to Lord Cranbrook that something would have to be done at once to rescue the Maharajah from insolvency and even a public scandal: on 8 September he authorized an advance of £10,000 pending his council's full consideration of the Sackville-West report. The result of their 'consideration' was a decision that the only sensible thing to be done was to press the Maharajah to 'sell the landed estates and invest the proceeds after paying off his debts'. As Sackville-West had valued the property at £340,000 this seemed a good accountant's solution, but it did not take into account the landlord's passionate attachment to his place. The new political secretary at the India Office, Colonel Owen Burne, recently back from India where he was described by the viceroy, Lord Lytton, as the 'most popular Private Secretary that India has known in our time', was given the delicate task of communicating the drastic proposal to the Maharajah, who left him in no doubt that such a course was not even to be considered. Burne, a charming, if conceited, gentleman, known to have got on well with the native princes in India, convinced the council that it was 'absolutely necessary'[19] to find some other solution to the problem.

Burne produced another plan which, though insisting on the sale of the estate after the Maharajah's death, did imply that the Indian government would have to find more money. Briefly the main points of the scheme were:

(i) The estates to be sold on the Maharajah's death and the proceeds to be allocated to paying off his debt to the government and to providing pensions for his family.

(ii) That if he agreed he would be advanced £40,000 to pay off his overdraft at Coutts and no longer have to pay interest, amounting to over £5,000 a year, on the various sums previously advanced.[20]

Such a makeshift settlement might well have been implemented from London, but on 11 February 1879, over a year after the Maharajah's first agitated application, the committee handling the matter decided to refer it to India for their views, and the file, including the report, was mailed off in what was described as 'a perfectly colourless dispatch' though in fact Burne, who had drafted it, had formulated the heart of the matter with some warmth:

Her Majesty's Government have ... to decide now whether they shall leave the Maharajah's affairs to follow their natural course; or whether, at the cost of an additional burden on the revenues of India which can scarcely be inconsiderable, they shall relieve His Highness from his liabilities, and furnish him with the means necessary to enable him to live on his estate, and to retain his existing position in society.

While fully alive to the paramount necessity for economy at the present time, and to the expediency on general grounds of restricting within the narrowest possible limits expenditure of so unprofitable a kind as that on political stipendiaries and pensioners, Her Majesty's Government feel it practically impossible to adopt the first of the alternatives above suggested, and to stand by while the Maharajah sinks into the position of an insolvent landed proprietor. They believe that, having regard to the history of the connection between the British Government and the Maharajah from his infancy to the present time, and to the character and general conduct of His Highness, such a result could not be permitted without discredit alike to the British Crown and nation, and to the Government of India.

... On a review of all the circumstances of the case, Her Majesty's Government are of opinion that they cannot remain indifferent to the embarrassments of the Maharajah, and they would be glad to avoid, if possible, insisting as a condition of their aid, on the immediate sale of the estate which His Highness, now arrived at middle age, has converted into a home for himself.

... Possibly your Excellency's Government may be able to suggest some method, likely to be acceptable to His Highness, by which the desired object may be attained at a smaller present cost than that above stated. I need scarcely observe that it is essential that I should be placed in possession of your views in the matter at a very early date.[21]

Despite the request for urgency, the government of India did not find time to reply until 7 July, necessitating a further advance of £3,000 to keep the Maharajah going. Their answer ran to twenty-nine paragraphs. Having recapitulated the historical background and reviewed the Sackville-West report, they finally came to the point:

... We regret that we are unable to approve the arrangement which has been suggested.

The narrative contained in this Dispatch shows that the Maharajah has been treated through a long series of years with extreme liberality, but he has been encouraged by the repeated concessions which have been made to him, to believe that he will always find in the Indian Treasury relief from all his embarrassments. We can hardly, under the circumstances, blame His Highness for such a belief, for it has undoubtedly been justified by experience; and we feel that this fact entitles His Highness, to some extent at least, to a consideration and sympathy to which he would otherwise have little claim. The motives and restraints which ordinarily ensure, on the part of honourable and intelligent men like His Highness, a reasonable economy, have in his case, been in a great measure removed by the action of the Government. He received from the public treasury the means of purchasing an estate on which, with the income previously assigned to him by the Government, he could not live, and we are now virtually asked to give from the public treasury an increase to that income to enable him to live on that estate. We sympathize with His Highness, and the more so, because we appreciate his high character and his honourable feelings, but we feel that mistaken liberality in the past is no sufficient reason for its repetition, when it can only be exercised at the cost of injustice to the people of India ...

We do not think it right that such a state of things as this should be perpetuated at the cost of the Indian tax-payers. The question is not whether His Highness the Maharajah shall be maintained at their expense in a manner befitting his historical position and his proper dignity, but whether he shall be enabled to go on enjoying the luxury of preserving his game, and rendering a great estate totally unprofitable. We should not have doubted, under any circumstances, how such a question should be answered; and at the present time it seems to us hardly necessary to discuss it, when it is certain that nothing but the ruthless reduction of most useful expenditure can avert the necessity of fresh and onerous taxation, and when it is in the highest degree doubtful whether our efforts to avert such taxation will succeed ...

So long as the Maharajah retains his present estate in its present condition, and on his present income, it will be impossible for him to avoid incurring fresh liabilities; and we concur in the opinion that the 'obviously desirable' course to adopt is the sale of the estate. We do not believe that any other remedy is possible. Even if the measures proposed in your Lordship's Dispatch were taken, and the Maharajah were to continue to live on the estate, it seems to us highly probable that he would again be involved in expenses which he could not meet, and that we should see again hereafter a renewal of those demands on the Indian Treasury which have been so repeatedly and so successfully urged in the past.

... We can now only advise that the conclusions stated in this Dispatch, be communicated to His Highness, and that he be informed that under no circumstances will any further assistance be given to him from the revenues of India. The Maharajah will naturally be unwilling to accept this decision, but we should hope that he may be persuaded to take a wiser view of the situation, when he understands that he cannot hope to obtain freedom from his embarrassments in any other way. We may add that in view of the fact that His Highness has stated his desire that his eldest son should succeed to the whole of his landed property, it seems probable that the sale of the estate after his death, which is one of the conditions of the proposal made in your Lordship's Dispatch, would be scarcely less distasteful to His Highness than its sale during his life. However this may be, we cannot agree to any plan which would involve the injustice of throwing fresh burdens on the people of India, for the purpose of relieving His Highness from embarrassments, from which he can relieve himself in a simple and honourable way, and with positive gain to his own real interests.[22]

Lord Cranbrook wasted no time in letting the Maharajah know that the news from India was bad, but he did not go so far as to state the matter had been finalized:

I regret to have to inform your Highness that, having referred for the opinion of the Government of India the various applications on the subject of your affairs, which you addressed to me in the course of last year, I have now received a Dispatch from that Government expressing views very unfavourable to your Highness's wishes.

Owing to the absence from town of many members of my Council, it will not be practicable for me to fully consider the matter, or arrive at a final decision in regard to it, until after the recess, but I think it due to your Highness that you should at once be acquainted with the tenor of the communication which has been received from the Indian Government, to whose views, as your Highness must be aware, the greatest deference is due.

I am constrained to add that your Highness must be so good as to understand that in these circumstances it will not be possible for me to entertain any further applications for temporary advances.[23]

The disappointed Maharajah, just returned to London after shooting grouse with his friend Ronald Melville at Glenferness, acknowledged the letter adding:

I cannot abandon the hope that the hardships of my position will ultimately be recognized and investigated. In the meantime I have no alternative but to raise from money-lenders, at high rates of interest, a loan sufficient to meet immediate wants, thus crippling still further my resources. The heir of Runjeet Singh, the friend and ally of England, and to whom eternal friendship was sworn, is reduced to this humiliating position, a position against which the terms of the annexation of the Punjab signed by England in 1849, seemed to afford him a perfect protection.[24]

On the same day he wrote to the queen enclosing Cranbrook's letter and his reply. All he could find to add was: 'Your Majesty will see that I am not likely to get much assistance from the government of India.'[25]

The Maharajah's lack of confidence in the generosity of the India Office did not prevent him from returning to the attack early in the following year. On 18 February 1880 he wrote to Lord Cranbrook:

I am extremely sorry to trouble your Lordship, but I have not the means of paying the accompanying enclosed large bills.

The enclosed letters from my agent and tenants will explain the state of affairs, and in order to carry on the cultivation of the farms still in hand till tenants are found for them I shall require some £3,000 as I regret to inform your Lordship that I have again met with heavy losses owing to the inclement season.

My Lord – If your Lordship is unable to help to extricate me from my pecuniary difficulties, owing to the unfavourable view taken of my petition by the Government of India, I most earnestly pray that my private landed estates illegally held in possession by that Government (as by the terms of the annexation only the State property was confiscated) may be restored to me in lieu of the stipend now paid.

I am certain that neither your Lordship nor the Council composed of honourable and just Englishmen, nor the House of Commons, nor the British Nation, which glories in doing justice to the weak, desire to deprive me of my private income of something over £100,000 per annum, not taking into account the gem Kohinoor which I feel honoured is in the possession of my most gracious sovereign and was not sold with my other jewels.[26]

Cranbrook's reply did no more than notice that the Koh-i-noor should have been introduced into the argument, though there must have been some questioning looks among his entourage.

Your Highness's affairs are at present under my consideration in Council, and pending a decision in regard to them it is impossible for me to sanction the grant to your Highness of further temporary advances.

Adverting to the concluding part of your letter, it is my duty at once to inform your Highness that, whatever course may be finally adopted in regard to your affairs generally, no claim on the part of your Highness based upon any alleged right to private estates in the Punjab or to jewels, can for one moment be entertained by the Government of India.[27]

The Maharajah may have been aware that he had overplayed his hand for he was quick to assure Cranbrook that he had only brought the matter up for tactical reasons and had not meant to be taken literally: 'I was quite aware when I wrote my last letter that the Government of India might not allow my claims to my very large private property, but

I was anxious should my affairs be brought before Parliament to stop the mouths of those self-constituted champions of India who might possibly grudge me that which your Lordship in Council might be inclined to give by showing that I might be placed in a position of great wealth without adding to taxation already existing.'[28]

In June there was a new secretary of state to contend with, Lord Hartington, who had shot several times at Elveden. Hartington was said to have a tendency 'to see every objection in a proposal before gauging its advantages',[29] but he was prepared to go into the Maharajah question with an open mind. He called for the numerous papers to be placed before him and had a long deliberation with his council. After further discussions with the Maharajah's solicitor, they came up with a new proposition:

(1) To advance your Highness a sum of £44,000 without interest, so as to enable you to discharge your debt to Messrs. Coutts & Co. and to redeem certain policies. (2) To advance you a further sum of £3,000 without interest, to defray certain debts which you deem pressing; and (3) To waive any claim to interest on the £13,000 recently advanced to you.

This offer of assistance, however, must be understood by your Highness to be made absolutely subject to two contingencies: (a) That it is eventually found to be practicable (with reference to existing settlements, &c.) to carry out the scheme in full as embodied in the enclosed memorandum; (b) That your Highness consents to, and will aid heartily, in carrying out the conditions of the scheme.

Should your Highness be ready to agree to the course herein proposed, I shall be prepared immediately to make the above-mentioned advance of £3,000 to meet pressing debts, without waiting for the result of the legal or parliamentary action required.[30]

The Maharajah accepted the proposals in principal but could hardly be expected to 'aid heartily' in supporting the government's absolute right to dispose of his estate after his death, which was one of the conditions laid down in the memorandum. He proposed that such a sale should be at the discretion of the then secretary of state rather than absolute. 'I cannot tell,' he argued, 'what the position of my eldest son may be at the time of my death but he may, by marriage or otherwise, have acquired the means of living at Elveden.'[31] Another small request he had was that he should be given an immediate advance of £5,000 rather than the £3,000 specified, on condition it was applied to paying debts rather than to farm improvements. The secretary of state was prepared to assent to the latter proposal but would not relent on the former.

That was a subject upon which the Maharajah had very strong feelings – Elveden was his, and he wanted to know that he could pass it on to his son. It was a matter which the queen might understand and sympathize with, even if Hartington would not. On the day he had his negative reply he wrote:

My most Gracious Sovereign, I have this day received the final communication from the India Office granting me a loan of £57,000 without interest during my life but on the absolute condition that my landed estates must be sold after my decease.

As the Bankers are pressing for the repayment of the advance made by them I have no alternative but to accept the accommodation thus offered – as *that* or *nothing*. Nevertheless, it breaks my heart to think my eldest son will have to turn out of his house and home and leave the place with which his earliest associations in life are connected for strangers to live in.

I implored the Government to strike out the word 'absolute' and let it remain entirely in the discretion of the Secretary of State for the time being at my death to decide whether the property should be sold or not as Victor might acquire the means by marriage or otherwise and live here as a country gentleman.

No one knows but myself, my Sovereign, the agony that I suffered when I was turned out of my home and exiled from the land of my birth and I shudder to think of the sufferings that my poor boy may undergo.

It is one thing to sell out on one's own accord which my son would always have had in his power and another to be compelled to do so without rhyme or reason.

I never have been nor can be in a position to resist the will of Your Majesty's Government my Sovereign and have always been compelled to sign any document that was required of me as no proposal has ever been made to me on any other conditions but as *that* or *nothing*.

It seems to me very unjust My Sovereign that any Government and particularly the British Government especially under the present Priminister [sic] who advocated the restoration of Ionian Islands to the Greeks should retain in possession my private estates producing an income of nearer two than one hundred thousand pounds per annum as by the document which deprives me of the sovereignty of the Punjab only 'the property of the State' is confiscated and grant me the pittance that I now crave for life.

My Gracious Sovereign – a few acres of land would not have been very much missed out of Your Majesty's vast Indian Empire and justice done to me and your loyal subjects. However as that cannot be helped I must turn to the resources placed in my hands through Your Majesty's kind interest and help myself as far as I can.

Therefore it is my resolve in future to lead a still more retired life and lay by as much as I can save out of an income at present of some £16,000 per annum so that should God prolong my life such a sum may be accumulated as would buy back Victor's home for him should he feel disposed to do so.

Imploring forgiveness for troubling Your Majesty so much with my private affairs but My Gracious Sovereign I have no one else in the world to look to and Your Majesty has proved more than a friend in name to me.

I have the distinguished honour to subscribe myself with the deepest gratitude, Your Majesty's most loyal and grateful subject . . .[32]

The queen replied:

Dear Maharajah, I have to acknowledge your letter of the 13th which has pained me so much.

You know how fond I have always been of you, and how truly I felt for you, knowing how completely innocent you were of the unfortunate circumstances which led you to leaving your own country.

I have at once written to Lord Hartington to see what can be done to ensure your own comfort and a proper position for your children.

As I once or twice mentioned to you before, I think you were thought extravagant and that that may have led to a want of confidence as regards the future.

That I shall do *what* I can for you and my godson you may be sure of.

Trusting that you and the Maharanee and your dear children are well …[33]

As promised the queen brought up the matter with Lord Hartington. After expressing her views on affairs in Afghanistan and the desirability of retaining Kandahar, she continued:

Though the Queen has asked Sir Henry Ponsonby to write to Lord Hartington more fully on the subject she cannot refrain from adding a few words and sending him this copy of a letter from the Maharajah Duleep Singh in whom she has always taken a great interest from his sad fate and natural fine qualities. He may indeed have been very extravagant, but that was almost natural for an Oriental; but he is very truthful and straightforward and loyally disposed, *rare* qualities in his race and the Queen thinks it wrong (besides being very contrary to the views of the liberals) to place a deposed Sovereign who was utterly innocent himself in a position so humiliating and painful to himself and his children. The Queen trusts that some better ultimate arrangement may be made. *We* have got his splendid kingdom and we *ought* not to let *his family* and even himself become poorer than an *English* country gentleman.[34]

The Maharajah returned again to rebut the charge of extravagance when he sent the queen a draft copy of the book he had prepared for publication of his case: reading in the papers that Hartington was staying at Balmoral, he asked that he also might study it so that he would not only see the government's view of the matter. He appended a statement showing her how he had spent the money borrowed from Coutts. It seemed to indicate that there was no more than £882 that could be attributed to personal expenditure; at the same time he claimed to be spending some £2,000 a year in restoring the church, rebuilding cottages for the poor, maintaining the village school and planting trees for the benefit of his children.[35]

The queen, in fact, discussed the whole problem of the Maharajah at some length with Hartington while he was at Balmoral and her minister's monitorial attitude seems to have modified her more maternal one. He warned her against becoming too closely involved with the Maharajah's financial problems and advised her how to reply. He seems to have sold her the government point of view. Thus her next letter somehow lacked the warm-heartedness she had hitherto demonstrated:

I have I fear been very long in answering your last letter but I at once referred the Memorandum it contained to Lord Hartington and spoke to him on the subject and expressed the hope that all that was right and just should be done as I had always taken the warmest interest in you. The answer I have only just received and it does not I fear hold out any hopes of your further claim being entertained.

I could not enter into a correspondence with you on what are affairs of State as this could only be conducted through my ministers and the Govt. of India. I think you yourself acknowledge the liberality of my Government in trying to meet your unfortunate difficulties.

If I might advise you as a friend it would be to acquiesce in the arrangements which have been proposed as I am assured they have been dictated by a sincere desire to relieve you from your present difficulties and make provision for your children, so far as the Govt. of India considers it in their power to effect these objects.

I cannot help thinking that if you were to sell Elveden Hall as you once told me you wished to do and to purchase some smaller estate and live more economically, you would then provide a house for your son which you were naturally anxious to do ...[36]

But despite the queen's apparent lack of support, the Maharajah replied like a dutiful son, saying that he had already begun to reduce his expenses and undertaking to sell his estate if he failed to make a clear £5,000 a year by the sale of game and pheasant eggs. The conclusion of his letter was less than filial: 'Your Majesty will I trust pardon my not appearing at Court for some years to come as I will now try to lay by every farthing that I can till I have saved sufficiently to provide my son with some income.'[37]

CHAPTER 9

Letters to *The Times*

✿

THE first shot at the India Office in 1881 was fired on 3 February, when the Maharajah wrote to Hartington that his increasing financial embarrassment obliged him to shut up Eleveden and establish himself in London:

It is extremely disagreeable to me to be perpetually troubling your Lordship about my pecuniary affairs, but I have no help for it.

After paying off my debts for which the money was advanced to me by your Lordship in Council, other bills have come in, and I shall have some heavy payments also to make for repairs done to farm building and cottages on my property in Suffolk, which I greatly fear (roughly speaking) will leave me some £2,000 in debt still. Therefore, it is quite obvious that this state of things cannot continue, and I must shut up my country house and reduce my establishment, as my present income is wholly insufficient to maintain me in the position I have hitherto occupied, until my farms are let and produce a fair rent.

I would let the right of sporting over my estate, were it not that I find the sale of pheasants' eggs and live game produces more money than could otherwise be obtained: and, besides, it does not annoy the few tenants I have.

I sustain a heavy loss by being obliged to cultivate four farms thrown on my hands, which, if I allowed them to go out of cultivation, would, in the event of my death, very materially affect the saleable value of my property, and my children would suffer in consequence.

Your Lordship can cause inquiries to be made of all my late tenants, whose names and addresses I will with pleasure furnish, that during their tenancy under me they suffered no damage by game, as I had given up the ground game almost entirely into their control (speaking from memory) for the last eight or nine years.

My intention is immediately to hire a house in Holland Park, at a rental of £350 per annum, to dismiss all my menservants, and reside there with my family as economically as possible, so that my children may be accustomed to a style of life which their means at my death will oblige them to occupy; a course I am sure your Lordship will commend.

But how to furnish this residence is my difficulty; therefore I earnestly request your Lordship, if you can in no other way assist me, to kindly cause the £4,000 I last borrowed from Messrs. Coutts & Co. to be paid to them out of the £44,000 due to them, so that my silver plate and other trinkets, which they hold as security for the former sum, may be set free, so that I may dispose of them, by sale or otherwise, to raise sufficient money to purchase the necessary furniture.[1]

Sir Owen Burne was deputed to find out if the Maharajah was really serious about moving to London, and on receiving assurances that he was, recommended that £4,000 should be made available on account for the purchase of furniture. Meanwhile the promised £40,000 had not yet materialized and the whole scheme was the subject of proceedings in the Chancery Court, where the master of the rolls judged that a special act of Parliament was indispensable to put it into legal effect. Impatience at the protracted processes of bureaucracy, and the realization that even when they had finally ground to a conclusion, his case would be bound for ever in the legal fetters of an act of Parliament, made the Maharajah decide to take the first evasive steps to release himself from total commitment. He had not even drawn the £4,000 when he wrote to Hartington that he was returning £3,000 because his game farm had done well and the furniture for his London house cost only £1,700; he had no wish, he said, 'to receive and retain any money that it might be considered was held under false pretences'. He ended his letter by asking 'whether the Government of India had any objections to my laying down my rank and title of Maharajah?' The reason he gave for this controversial suggestion was that as the value of his estate had decreased by 50 per cent owing to the agricultural depression, his children, 'having been brought up as princes', might have to 'descend to such poverty as the provision made for their maintenance by Your Lordship in Council will lead to'.[2] It was, effectively, his first resort to blackmail. Hartington forwarded the letter to the palace, observing to Ponsonby: 'We are rather puzzled how to deal with the Maharajah's extraordinary letter. I have answered it demi-officially to the effect that I can hardly believe his proposal to lay aside his rank and title is made seriously; but that if on reflection he perseveres in it, I will consult the Govt. of India.'[3] Ponsonby showed the correspondence to the queen, as doubtless the Maharajah had anticipated. 'This would never do,' she minuted, 'and would do much harm in India. He ought never to have done this without consulting his friend the Queen.'[4]

Hartington's cool response to the Maharajah's proposal to lay aside his title included a rejection of the offer to repay £3,000 and a refusal to discuss his financial affairs any further. Nothing more was heard on either subject until March 1882 when the Maharajah forwarded the secretary of state a cheque for £3,453 14s being the original amount plus compound interest, and declared his intention of paying more from time to time as he was able. He also reminded the secretary of state to obtain the views of the Indian government about laying aside his rank, which he threatened to do in the event of a petition he was about to present to Parliament having no result.[5]

The petition referred to was an indication that the Maharajah's desperation was outstripping his discretion: having done further homework in the British Museum, he rephrased his version of the annexation of the Punjab, describing himself as having been deprived of a kingdom producing a surplus revenue of over £1 million, of private landed estates producing an income of £120,000 a year, and of the Koh-i-noor. He stated that he had hitherto been obliged to accept whatever terms had been offered him; and concluded by praying that if his kingdom could not be returned to him, as the Transvaal had recently been to the Boers, he might be handed back some of his private estates or at least their cash equivalent.[6]

In his reply Hartington returned the cheque as being unacceptable under the rules of the Court of Chancery and added a rebuke which indicated that the Maharajah's harassing tactics were having some effect on his temper: 'I must, at the same time, express my extreme regret that, notwithstanding the unqualified assurance, given in your letter of the 13th December 1880, that it was your intention to co-operate loyally in the measures for the settlement of your affairs, which had been agreed upon after much consideration, and with an anxious desire on the part of the Home Government of India to promote your interests and those of your family, your Highness should adopt a line of procedure which I cannot but regard as inconsistent with that assurance.'[7]

The Maharajah protested, in reply, that his motives had been misunderstood and that far from wishing to set aside the pending arrangements, he was preparing to put his estates on the market as soon as he was legally entitled to do so and there was a turn for the better in agricultural economy. After dwelling on the meagre nature of the relief he was in any case likely to obtain, he concluded: 'I have again to ask of your Lordship to ascertain (if possible by telegram) whether the Indian Government have any objection to my laying aside my rank, as an opportunity has presented itself for me to go into business as a jeweller and diamond merchant, for I desire by industry and [illegible], as well as by strict economy, to add to the provision made for my children as much as I can.'[8]

Hartington did not rise to the bait. But in view of the Maharajah's gadfly persistence he coolly telegraphed the viceroy indicating that he personally could see no objection to his renouncing his rank.

On 26 June the Maharajah returned to the attack, requesting that an officer of the Indian government be appointed to take charge of the Elveden estate and 'deal with it as might be deemed best'.[9] Hartington, of course, replied that this was impossible, and the Maharajah's answer, partly pathetic and partly challenging, did little to make him change his mind; he probably thought the man was going mad:

My Lord, I beg to thank you most sincerely for so kindly promising to communicate to me the views of the Government of India regarding the laying aside of my rank as soon as your Lordship is in a position to do so, which I pray God will not be very long as the uncertainty and the consequent worry arising from it is very injurious to my health and Sir W. Gull has informed me that if I hope to live some years longer I must have no anxiety on my mind.

With reference to your Lordship's refusal to appoint someone to take charge of my estates in Suffolk, I have only to express my sorrow and to humbly beg of you to reconsider your decision.

When I came to this country after having been deprived of my Kingdom and all private property and after some years residence in England and acquaintance with its people it appeared to me best that I should under the altered circumstances of my life occupy the humble though honourable position of a Country Gentleman and with this view I asked for and was granted a sum to found a home and this my English home was the one thing on earth that I idolised.

When the agricultural depression set in and my income began to decrease I was compelled to ask the Home Government for assistance.

Col. Sir Owen Burne was sent to me with the Government's suggestion that I should sell my property in order to extricate me from my pecuniary difficulties and I cannot describe to your Lordship the pain this cruel proposition gave me coming from the Representatives of the Nation who had declared themselves my Guardians and took a paternal interest in my welfare.

When however your Lordship's ultimatum (that part of which referring to the absolute sale of my Estates at my death I at first resented) came, I began to see that there was no hope that my only wish in the world would be realised, and that my English home would be broken up and my descendants must look to some other place as their home.

Ever since then my Lord I have been tearing myself from it and have at last succeeded in bringing myself to hate the sight of it ... Therefore, my Lord, I humbly beg you either to give the means to occupy the position I have hitherto fulfilled and enable my descendants to do the same after my death, or to take these estates off my hands so that I may be able to make a better provision for my children myself, and not bring them up with such tastes as they will not be able to indulge in hereafter.

As I do not desire to trouble your Lordship with more letters than I can help I beg of you kindly to inform me on the following subjects:

1st. I presume as I am now a Naturalised Englishman there is no legal difficulty to my returning to the Punjab either to get information regarding my private landed estates &c. or to reside there altogether.

2nd. To whom is the Order of the Star of India to be returned? To your Lordship or Her Majesty?

3rd. On what grounds my claim to private property and landed Estates in the Punjab are not recognised by the Indian Government.

Surely, my Lord, as English justice acknowledges no difference between man and man ought I not to be treated on the same footing of equality with my servants who are allowed to keep their Estates?

Still trusting to your Lordship's and the Home Government's high sense of English justice and British liberality....

The Maharajah added a postscript: 'My address after the 3rd of August will be Elveden Hall as I must go there to reside for a few weeks during the time the harvest operations are carried on.'[10]

The exigences of harvest time, however, did not prevent him from continuing the battle to extract himself from the impending finality of the act of Parliament which the India Office seemed to assume was the *coup de grâce*. His first step was to get counsel's opinion as to his right to family estates in India. Mr Vaughan Hawkins of Lincoln's Inn opined, on 10 August, that 'no private estates or property were liable to be confiscated under the Treaty of Lahore, the terms of which apply to State property only'.[11] The Maharajah was quick to put the queen right on any ideas she might have had from her advisers on that subject by sending her the opinion. He also made it clear that he was going to fight:

The odds will be very much against me, My Sovereign I know, as I single-handed combat the most powerful Government in the world to obtain what I believe to be my rights for the sake of my children but trusting in the help of God I am determined to go forward whether or not I succeed or fail for no human aid is of any avail except that of Your Majesty's and that I dare not ask for as Your Majesty has most graciously already done more for me than I could ever have hoped.

How true is the saying My Sovereign that History repeats itself.

The Khedive's case at this moment in Egypt is exactly what was mine in the Punjab. His Arabi Pascha is what Moolraj was to me some thirty years ago and the British Government sent an army to put down the rebellion against me as it is being done at the present time at Alexandria but the late Marquis of Dalhousie misrepresented the whole affair and I the inocent [sic] was made to suffer with the guilty in direct controversion of the Proclamation issued by his Lordship's orders at the entrance of the British force into the aforementioned Province.

It is very hard indeed My Sovereign that I should have been classed with Your Majesty's enemies and treated as such when I never even lifted up my little finger against Your Majesty's Government.

Had I been aware my Sovereign of the true state of things the knowledge of which was carefully kept from me by the late Sir John Login – a creature of Lord Dalhousie – and all the officials were unfortunately the only friends I have had all my life except until very lately to advise me) and as well acquainted with the English law and customs as I am at present a very different provision both for the maintenance of myself and my children would have been made but even now I do not despair as having by accident discovered providentially preserved the official dispatches &c. connected with the Punjab in their entirety at the British Museum and feeling certain that Your Majesty at the head of this great nation will cause justice to be done to me some day or other.

Imploring Your Majesty to forgive me for presuming to address Your Majesty once again, I remain, my most gracious Sovereign, Your Majesty's most loyal humble subject ...[12]

While writing thus to the queen the Maharajah must all the time have been brewing his case for presentation in the form of a letter to *The Times*, which made some telling points, ably, if insidiously, rebutted in an editorial which seemed to indicate that the writer had got his facts from Sir Owen Burne, the political secretary at the India Office. The correspondence started off many arguments in the country as to the rights and wrongs of the affair.

To the Editor of *The Times*.

Sir, As the era of doing justice and restoration appears to have dawned, judging from the recent truly liberal and noble act of the present Liberal Government, headed now by the great Gladstone the Just, I am encouraged to lay before the British Nation, through the medium of *The Times*, the injustice which I have suffered, in the hope that, although generosity may not be lavished upon me to the same extent as has been bestowed upon King Cetewayo,* yet that some magnanimity might be shown towards me by this great Christian Empire.

When I succeeded to the throne of the Punjab, I was only an infant and the *Khalsa* soldiery, becoming more and more mutinous and overbearing during both my uncle's and my mother's Regencies, at last, unprovoked, crossed the Sutlej and attacked the friendly British Power, and was completely defeated and entirely routed by the English Army.

Had, at this time, my dominions been annexed to the British territories, I would have now not a word to say, for I was at that time an independent chief at the head of an independent people, and any penalty which might have been then inflicted would have been perfectly just; but that kind, true Englishman, the late Lord Hardinge, in consideration of the friendship which had existed between the British Empire and the 'Lion of the Punjab', replaced me on my throne, and the diamond Koh-i-noor on my arm, at one of the Durbars. The Council of Regency, which was then created to govern the country during my minority, finding that it was not in their power to rule the Punjab unaided, applied for assistance to the representative of the British Government, who after stipulating for absolute power to control every Government

* The conquered Zulu king, exiled in London, whose lands had been returned to him.

1 Runjit Singh   2 Rani Jindan Kour

3 Duleep Singh, aged three, with his mother in the country

4 Duleep Singh painted by
August Schoefft, Lahore
1841

5 The Second Lahore Durbar,
26 December 1846.
Maharajah Duleep Singh faces
Sir Henry Lawrence (*left*),
Lord Gough (*centre*)
and Lord Dalhousie (*right*).
Frederick Currie, translating,
sits on Duleep Singh's left.

6 Maharah Duleep Singh, painted in 1852 aged fourteen, by
George Beechey

7 The Maharajah on holiday at Mussoorie, 1853: a watercolour by
P.C. French

8 Sir Henry Lawrence

9 Dr John Login

10 A watercolour sketch
of the Maharajah by F. X.
Winterhalter, July 1854

11 The Maharajah
photographed
at Osborne, 1854

Drawings of the Maharajah by Queen Victoria from a recently
discovered Sketchbook:
12 ABOVE With Prince Leopold;   13 BELOW With Prince Arthur

OPPOSITE PAGE Sketches by Queen Victoria inserted in her *Journal*, 1854:
14 and 15 TOP, BOTTOM LEFT The Maharajah;   16 The Pundit Nehemiah Gore

17 Rani Jindan Kour, painted by George Richmond
18 The Maharajah attends 'A Drawing Room at St James's Palace'

19 Princess Victoria Gouramma of Coorg

20 The Prince of Wales arrives at Elveden Hall, near Thetford, Suffolk, an engraving from the *Illustrated London News*
21 The drawing room at Elveden Hall

22 The Maharajah at the time of his marriage

23 Maharani Bamba Duleep Singh

24 A shooting party at Elveden, 4 December 1877.
Back row (from left to right): Lord Frederick Fitzroy, Prince
of Wales (seated), Earl of Leicester, Lord Rendlesham (seated),
Duke of Atholl.

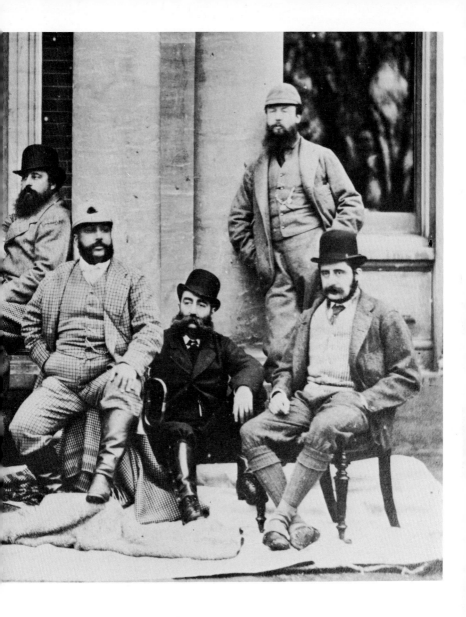

Seated: Lord Dacre (bowler hat), Lord Balfour of Burleigh, Sir Reginald Beauchamp (striped waistcoat), Maharajah Duleep Singh, Captain Goldingham, Lord Henniker (on chair, right), Viscount Holmesdale (on chair, left), Lord Westbury (wearing deer-stalker hat), Marquis of Ripon (on ground, front row, left)

25 LEFT Prince Frederick
26 Prince Victor

27 Princess Bamba, Prince
Edward, Princess Catherine,
Princess Sophia, c. 1889

28 OPPOSITE PAGE Prince
Victor painted by George
Richmond

J.W. CLARKE,   1877. Photo.

29 The Maharajah in 1877

department, entered into the Bhyrowal Treaty with me, by which it was guaranteed that I should be protected on my throne until I attained the age of sixteen years, the British also furnishing troops both for the above object and preservation of peace in the country, in consideration of a certain sum to be paid to them annually by my Durbar, for the maintenance of that force.

Thus the British nation, with open eyes, assumed my guardianship, the nature of which is clearly defined in a proclamation subsequently issued by Lord Hardinge's orders on the 20th of August, 1847, which declares that the tender age of the Maharajah Duleep Singh causes him to feel the interest of a father in the education and guardianship of the young prince. (*Vide* Panjab Papers at the British Museum).

Two English Officers carrying letters bearing my signature were despatched by the British Resident, in conjunction with my Durbar, to take possession of the fortress of Mooltan and the surrounding district in my name, but my servant Moolraj, refusing to acknowledge my authority, caused them to be put to death, whereupon both the late Sir F. Currie and the brave Sir Herbert Edwardes, most urgently requested the Commander-in-Chief of the British forces at Simla, as there were not sufficient English soldiers at Lahore at the time, to send some European troops without delay in order to crush the rebellion in the bud, as they affirmed that the consequences could not be calculated which might follow if it were allowed to spread; but the late Lord Gough, with the concurrence of the late Marquis of Dalhousie, refused to comply with their wishes, alleging the unhealthiness of the season as his reason for doing so.

My case at that time was exactly similar to what the Khedive's is at this moment: Arabi being, in his present position, to his master what Moolraj was to me – viz., a rebel.

At last, very tardily, the British Government sent troops (as has been done in Egypt) to quell the rebellion, which had by that time vastly increased in the Punjab, and who entered my territories, headed by a proclamation, issued by Lord Dalhousie's orders, to the following effect:

'Enclosure No. 8 in No. 42 – To the subjects, servants and dependants of the Lahore State, and residents of all classes and castes, whether Sikhs, Mussulmans, or others within the territories of Maharajah Duleep Singh ... Whereas certain evil-disposed persons and traitors have excited rebellion and insurrection, and have seduced portions of the population of the Punjab from their allegiance, and have raised an armed opposition to the British authority; and whereas the condign punishment of the insurgents is necessary ... therefore the British Army, under the command of the Right Hon. the Commander-in-Chief, has entered the Punjab districts. The army will not return to its cantonments until the full punishment of all insurgents has been effected, all opposition to the constituted authority put down, and obedience and order have been re-established.'

Thus it is clear from the above that the British Commander-in-Chief did not enter my dominions as a conqueror, nor the army to stay there, and, therefore, it is not correct to assert, as some do, that the Punjab was a military conquest.

'And whereas it is not the desire of the British Government that those who are innocent of the above offences, who have taken no part secretly or openly, in the disturbances, and who have remained faithful in their obedience to the Government of Maharajah Duleep Singh ... should suffer with the guilty.'

But after order was restored, and finding only a helpless child to deal with, and the temptation being so strong, Lord Dalhousie annexed the Punjab, instead of carrying out the solemn compact entered into by the British Government at Bhyrowal; sold almost all my personal, as well as all my private property, consisting of jewels, gold and silver plate, even some of my wearing apparel and household furniture and distributed the proceeds, amounting (I was told) to £250,000, as prize money among those very troops who had come to put down rebellion against my authority.

Thus I, the innocent, who never lifted up even my little finger against the British Government, was made to suffer in the same manner with my own subjects who would not acknowledge my authority, in spite of the declaration of the above quoted proclamation that it is not the desire of the British Government that the innocent should suffer with the guilty.

Lord Dalhousie, in writing to the Secret Committee of the late Court of Directors, in order to justify his unjust act, among other arguments employs the following. He says: –

'It has been objected that the present dynasty in the Punjab cannot with justice be subverted, since the Maharajah Duleep Singh, being yet a minor, can hardly be held responsible for the acts of the nation. With deference to those by whom these views have been entertained, I must dissent entirely from the soundness of the doctrine. It is, I venture to think, altogether untenable as a principle; it has been disregarded in the case of Maharajah Duleep Singh. When in 1845 the Khalsa army invaded our territories, the Maharajah was not held to be free from responsibility, nor was he exempted from the consequences of the acts of the people. On the contrary, the Government of India confiscated to itself the richest provinces of the Maharajah's kingdom, and was applauded for the moderation which had exacted no more. If the Maharajah was not exempted from responsibility on the plea of his tender years at the age of eight, he cannot on that plea be entitled to exemption from a like responsibility now that he is three years older.'

But in thus arguing, His Lordship became blind to the fact that in 1845, when the Khalsa army invaded the British territories, I was an independent chief, but after the ratification of the Bhyrowal treaty I was made the ward of the British nation; and how could I, under these circumstances, be held responsible for the neglect of my Guardians in not crushing Moolraj's rebellion at once, the necessity of doing which was clearly and repeatedly pointed out by the British Resident at Lahore?

Again, His Lordship says: 'The British Government has rigidly observed the obligation which the treaty imposed on them and fully acted up to the spirit and letter of its contract.' No doubt all this was or may have been true, except so far that neither peace was preserved in the country nor I protected on my throne till I attained the age of sixteen years; two very important stipulations of that treaty.

He further alleges: 'In return for the aid of the British troops they (my Durbar) bound themselves to pay to us a subsidy of 22 lakhs (£220,000) per annum ... from the day when that treaty was signed to the present hour, not one rupee has ever been paid.'

Now, the above statement is not correct, because of the following despatch which exists: Enclosure No. 5 in No. 23, the Acting Resident at Lahore affirms, 'The Durbar has paid into this Treasury gold to the value of Rs. 1,356,637–0–6 (£135,837–14–1, taking the value of a rupee at 2s.).'

1. Thus I have been most unjustly deprived of my kingdom, yielding, as shown by Lord Dalhousie's own computation in (I

think) 1850, a surplus revenue of some £500,000, and no doubt now vastly exceeds that sum.

2. I have also been prevented, unjustly, from receiving the rentals of my private estate (*vide* Prinsep's *History of the Sikhs*, compiled for the Government of India) in the Punjab, amounting to some £130,000 per annum, since 1849, although my private property is not confiscated by the terms of the annexation which I was compelled to sign by my guardians when I was a minor, and, therefore, I presume it is an illegal document, for I am still lawful Sovereign of the Punjab; but this is of no moment, I am quite content to be the subject of my Most Gracious Sovereign, no matter how it was brought about, for her graciousness towards me has been boundless.

3. All my personal property has also been taken from me, excepting £20,000 worth, which I was informed by the late Sir John Login was permitted to be taken with me to Futteghur when I was exiled; and the rest, amounting to some £250,000, disposed of as stated before. What is still more unjust in my case is, that most of my servants who remained faithful to me were permitted to retain all their personal and private property, and to enjoy the rentals of their landed estates (or jagheers) given to them by me and my predecessors; whereas I their master, who did not even lift up my little finger against the British nation, was not considered worthy to be treated on the same footing of equality with them, because, I suppose, my sin being that I happened to be the ward of a Christian power.

The enormous British liberality permits a life stipend of £25,000 per annum, which is reduced by charges (known to the proper authorities) to some £13,000, to be paid to me from the revenues of India.

Lately, an Act of Parliament has been passed by which, some months hence, the munificent sum of some £2,000 will be added to my above stated available income but on the absolute condition that my estates must be sold at my death, thus causing my dearly loved English home to be broken up, and compelling my descendants to seek some other asylum.

A very meagre provision, considering of what and how I have been deprived, has also been made for my successors.

If one righteous man was found in the two most wicked cities of the world, I pray God that at least one honourable, just and noble Englishman may be forthcoming out of this Christian land of liberty and justice to advocate my cause in Parliament, otherwise what chance have I of obtaining justice, considering that my despoiler, guardian, judge, advocate, and my jury is the British nation itself?

Generous and Christian Englishmen, accord me a just and liberal treatment for the sake of the fair name of your nation, of which I have now the honour to be a naturalised member, for it is more blessed to give than to take.

I have the honour to remain, Sir, your most obliged servant,

Duleep Singh.[13]

The Times' editorial on 31 August 1882:

We print elsewhere a somewhat singular letter from the Maharajah Duleep Singh. Encouraged, as it would seem, by the restoration of Cetewayo, he puts forward an impassioned plea for this consideration of his own claims. On a first glance, his letter reads as if he demanded nothing less than to be replaced on the throne of the Punjab. He professes to establish his right to that position and to waive it, magnanimously avowing that he is quite content to be the subject of his most gracious Sovereign, whose graciousness towards him has been boundless. His real object, however, is far less ambitious. It is to prefer a claim for a more generous treatment of his private affairs at the hands of the Indian Government. In lieu of the sovereignty of the Punjab, with its unbounded power and unlimited resources, 'the enormous British liberality' he complains, permits him only a life stipend of £25,000 per annum, which is reduced by certain charges to some £13,000. All that he has hitherto succeeded in obtaining from the Indian Government is an arrangement, lately sanctioned by Act of Parliament, whereby he will receive an addition of £2,000 to his annual income on condition that his estates are sold at his death in order to liquidate his liabilities, and provide for his widow and children. It is really against this arrangement that the Maharajah appeals. His argument concerning his *de jure* sovereignty of the Punjab is manifestly only intended to support his pecuniary claims. If these were settled to his satisfaction, he would doubtless be content, and more than content, to die, as he had lived, an English country gentleman, with estates swarming with game, and with an income sufficient for his needs. This is a sort of appeal to its justice and generosity with which the English public is not unfamiliar. Duleep Singh is not the first dispossessed Eastern Prince who has felt himself aggrieved by the dispositions of the Indian Government, nor is this the first occasion on which his own claims have been heard of. For a long time he preferred a claim for the Koh-i-noor, of which he alleged that he had been wrongfully despoiled. Now it is his private estates in India which he declares have been confiscated without adequate compensation. No one, of course, would wish that a prince in the Maharajah's position should be ungenerously treated. He is, as it were, the ward of the English nation, and even his extravagances might be leniently regarded. But, as the claim, now publicly preferred by the Maharajah, has been disallowed after full consideration by successive Governments both in India and this country, it may not be amiss to show that his case is by no means so strong as he still affects to consider it.

The events of the two Sikh wars, and their sequel, have probably faded out of the memory of most of our readers. They are, however, accurately stated, so far as the main facts are concerned, in the Maharajah's letter. It is not so much with these facts themselves that we are now concerned as with the Maharajah's inferences from them, and with certain other facts which he has not found it convenient to state. It is perfectly true that after the overthrow of the *Khalsa* power in the sanguinary battle of Sobraon, Lord Hardinge declined to annex the Punjab and placed the Maharajah on the throne under the Regency of his mother, the Ranee, assisted by a Council of Sirdars. This settlement, however, proved a failure, and was replaced by the arrangement under the Bhyrowal Treaty, whereby the entire control and guidance of affairs was vested in the British Resident, and the presence of British troops was guaranteed until the Maharajah should attain his majority.

The Second Sikh War, which began with the revolt of Moolraj in 1848, soon proved the futility of this arrangement also, and after the surrender of Mooltan and the battle of Gujerat, which finally broke the reviving power of the Khalsa, Lord Dalhousie, who had succeeded Lord Hardinge as Governor-General, decided that the time had come for the incorporation of the Punjab with the British Dominions in India. Duleep Singh was at this time only eleven years of age; but he had been recognized for more than three years as the Sovereign of the Punjab, and by the advice of his Durbar at Lahore, he signed the terms of settlement proposed by the British Commissioner, whereby he renounced 'for himself, his heirs, and his successors, all right, title and claim to the sovereignty of the Punjab, or to any sovereign power whatever'. By subsequent clauses of the same instrument 'all the property of the State, of whatever description and wheresoever found,' was confiscated to the East India Company; the Koh-i-noor was surrendered to the Queen of England; a pension of not less than four and not exceeding five lakhs of rupees was secured to the Maharajah, 'for the support of himself, his relatives, and the servants of the State'; and the Company undertook to treat the Maharajah with respect and honour and to allow him to retain the title of 'Maharajah Duleep Singh, Bahadoor'.

Of this instrument, the Maharajah now says that he was compelled to sign it by his guardians when he was a minor, and he argues that the political necessity which dictated it was due to the lapses of the Indian Government, which had failed to fulfil the pledges of the Bhyrowal Treaty, and had allowed the revolt of Moolraj to develop into a Sikh rebellion. In answer to these allegations, it is sufficient to quote the report of the British Commissioner, who presented the terms for signature. 'The paper,' he says, 'was then handed to the Maharajah, who immediately affixed his signature. The alacrity with which he took the papers when offered, was a matter of remark to all, and suggested the idea that possibly he had been instructed by his advisers that any show of hesitation might lead to the substitution of terms less favourable than those which he had been offered.' Moreover, the plea that the Maharajah was a minor, and, therefore, not a free agent, is fatal to his own case; he was two years younger when the Bhyrowal Treaty was signed, and younger still when the settlement of Lord Hardinge replaced him on the thrown, and restored him to the sovereignty, which he even now acknowledges might at that time have been rightly forfeited. We need not dwell on this point, however. The Maharajah himself would hardly press it. His claim of sovereignty is merely intended to cover his claim for money. He never was much more than nominal Sovereign of the Punjab, and he probably desires nothing so little at this moment as the restitution of his sovereign rights. The political question has long been closed; it only remains to consider whether the personal and financial question still remains open. The Maharajah complains that he was deprived of his personal and private property – with insignificant exceptions – and of the rentals of his landed estates. There is, however, no mention of private property in the terms of settlement accepted by the Maharajah; and a minute of Lord Dalhousie, recorded in 1855, states explicitly that at the time the Punjab was annexed, the youth had no territories, no lands, no property, to which he could succeed. The pension accorded by the East India Company was plainly intended to support the Maharajah in becoming state, and to provide for his personal dependants, and the British Government expressly reserved to itself the right of allotting only such portion as it thought fit of the 'Four Lakh Fund', as the pension was called, to the Maharajah's personal use. So long ago as 1853, Lord Dalhousie wrote a dispatch, intended to remove from the Maharajah's mind all idea that the Four Lakh Fund would ultimately revert to himself, and characterizing such an idea as 'entirely erroneous'.

The Indian Government, however, has certainly not dealt ungenerously with the Maharajah. It is true that it has not recognized his claim to certain private estates no record of which exists, still less has it listened to any of his attempts to assail the validity of the instrument whereby his sovereignty was extinguished. For some years after the annexation his personal allowance out of the Four Lakh Fund was fixed at £12,500 – a sum which was considered entirely satisfactory by the leading Ministers of the Durbar, who assented and advised the Maharajah to assent to the terms of 1849. But in 1859 this allowance was doubled, and the Maharajah himself more than once acknowledged in subsequent years the liberality of the arrangements made. The allowance of £25,000 a year has been reduced to the £13,000 mentioned by the Maharajah in his letter, not by any act of the Indian Government, but by what could well be called extravagance, though, as he is an Eastern prince, it is more generous, perhaps, to describe it as magnificence. He first bought a property in Gloucestershire, but this was sold some years ago, and his present estate at Elveden, in Suffolk, was purchased for £138,000, the money being advanced by the Government, and interest for the loan to the amount of £5,664 per annum being paid by the Maharajah. Some two or three years ago the Home Government of India proposed to release the Maharajah from payment of this annual sum provided that he would consent to the sale of the estate, either at once or at his death, for the repayment of the principal of the loans advanced. This proposal, however, was rejected by the Indian Government, which maintained, in very strong and plain language, that the Maharajah had already been treated with exceptional liberality, and that if he wanted more money he should sell his estate. The Indian Government remained inexorable, but the liberality of the Home Government was not yet exhausted; the Maharajah had built a house at Elveden, at a cost of £60,000 and had borrowed £40,000 from a London banking firm for the purpose. For this loan £2,000 interest had to be paid, and the India Office has lately sanctioned the repayment of the capital sum without making any further charge on the Maharajah. It is to this arrangement, and to the Act of Parliament which sanctions it, that the Maharajah refers with some bitterness at the close of his letter. In order to settle his affairs, and to provide for his wife and family, the Act of Parliament requires that his estate at Elveden should be sold after his death. *Hinc Illae Lacrymae.* An argument which starts from the sovereign claims of the son of the 'Lion of the Punjab', ends, somewhat ridiculously, though not without a touch of pathos, with the sorrows of the Squire of Elveden. Duleep Singh began life as a Maharajah of the Punjab, with absolute power and boundless wealth if he had only been old enough to enjoy them, and if the Khalsa would have allowed him to do so; he is not even allowed to end it as an English country gentleman, leaving an encumbered estate and an embarrassed heir. There is really a certain tragedy about the whole matter. Fate and the British power have deprived the Maharajah of the sovereignty to which he was born. He has done his best to become an English squire, and if he has lived beyond his income he may plead abundance of examples in the class to which he has attached himself; yet he is for ever to bear the consequences himself, and not to inflict them on his children and descendants, as an English squire would be able to do. The whole case is one which it is very difficult to judge upon any abstract principles. It is, no doubt, the duty of every man to live within his income, and yet if the Maharajah has failed to acquire a virtue rare indeed among Eastern princes and not too common in the class to which he belongs by adoption, there is no Englishman but would feel ashamed if he or his descendants were thereby to come to want. At the same time it is impossible for the Indian Government, which has claims on its slender resources far more urgent than those of the magnificent squire of Elveden, to guarantee him indefinitely against the consequences of his own improvidence. At any rate, it is safe to warn him against encumbering his personal claims by political pleas which are wholly inadmissible. He is very little likely to excite sympathy for his pecuniary troubles by his bold, but scarcely successful, attempt to show that if he could only come by his own, he is still the lawful Sovereign of the Punjab.

Duleep Singh's reply was published in *The Times*, 6 September 1882.

Sir, As your leading article of Thursday, the 31st ult., commenting on my letter of the 28th, which you were so good as to publish, contains many inaccuracies as to matters of fact, which no one, perhaps, can correct so precisely as myself, I trust you will allow me to do so, and to make a few observations.

(1) You say: 'All that he has hitherto succeeded in obtaining from the Indian Government is an arrangement, lately sanctioned by Act of Parliament whereby he will receive an addition of £2,000 to his annual income, on condition that his estates are sold at his death, in order to liquidate his liabilities, and provide for his widow and children. It is really against this arrangement that the Maharajah appeals.'

I do not 'really appeal' against the above arrangement, but what I do certainly think unjust in it is that I am not permitted to repay, during my life, the loan which is to be made under it – £16,000 having already been advanced to me – and that I am thus forbidden to preserve, by a personal sacrifice, their English home to my descendants. In April last I sent a cheque for £3,542 14s., representing capital and compound interest at the rate of five per cent to the India Office but it was returned to me.

My widow and children, should I leave any, were already provided for, under arrangements which existed before this Act was passed.

(2) With reference to your quotation from the British Commissioner as to my 'alacrity' in signing the terms, I have simply to say that, being then a child, I did not understand what I was signing.

(3) 'Moreover', you say, 'the plea that the Maharajah was a minor, and, therefore not a free agent, is fatal to his cause, he was two years younger when the Bhyrowal Treaty was signed,

and younger still when the settlement of Lord Hardinge replaced him on the throne, and restored to him the sovereignty which he even now acknowledges, might at that time have been rightly forfeited. We do not dwell on this point, however, the Maharajah himself would hardly press it.'

But, whether it is fatal to my case or not, I do press it, and maintain that after the ratification of the Bhyrowal Treaty, I was a ward of the British nation, and that it was unjust on the part of the guardian to deprive me of my kingdom in consequence of a failure in guardianship.

Here at Lord Hardinge's own words: 'But, in addition to these considerations of a political nature, the Governor-General is bound to be guided by the obligations which the British Government has contracted when it consented to be the guardian of the young Prince during his minority.' (*Vide* P. 49, 'Punjab Papers' 1847–49.)

(4) 'The Maharajah complains', you would say, 'that he was deprived of his personal and private property – with insignificant exceptions – and of the rentals of his landed estates. There is, however, no mention of private property in the terms of the settlement accepted by the Maharajah; and a minute of Lord Dalhousie, recorded in 1855, explicitly states that at the time the Punjab was annexed, the youth had no territories, no lands, no property to which he could have succeeded.' My reply is, that at the time of the annexation I had succeeded to territories, lands, and personal property, and was in possession, and these possessions were held in trust, and managed for me, under treaty, by the British Government.

That I had succeeded and was possessed of private estates in land, is an historical fact, and a matter of public records. Moreover, these estates had belonged to my family, one of them having been acquired by marriage, before my father attained to sovereignty. The statement in Lord Dalhousie's minute only amounts to a denial of the existence of the sun by a blind man; and there are none so blind as those who will not see.

And now with regard to my alleged extravagance, these are the facts. The life stipend of £25,000 allotted to me, has to bear the following deductions: – (1) £5,664 interest, payable to the Government of India; (2) about £3,000 as premium on policies of insurance of my life, executed in order to add to the meagre provision made for my descendants by the British Government, and as security for the loan from my bankers; (3) £1,000 per annum for two pensions of £500 per annum each to the widows of the superintendent appointed by Lord Dalhousie to take charge of me after the annexation, and of my kind friend, the late controller of my establishment, besides which there is some £300 per annum payable in pensions to old servants in India.

In order to be able to receive his Royal Highness the Prince of Wales, and to return the hospitality of men of my own position in life, and because I was advised and considered – not, I think unreasonably – that the rank granted to me by Her Majesty required it to be done, I expended some £22,000 (not £60,000 as you were informed) in the alterations and repairs to the old house on this estate; suitable furniture cost £8,000 more.

At a cost of some £3,000, I have purchased life annuities to be paid to the before mentioned widow ladies in case they should survive me.

About £8,000 more had to be borrowed from my bankers on mortgage, to complete the purchase of this estate, as the money lent to me by the Government of India was insufficient by that amount. Thus, my debts amount to something like £44,000 of which £30,000 is covered by policies of insurance, £8,000 by mortgage, and the remainder amply secured by personal assets. Therefore, instead of my estates being heavily encumbered, my heirs, were I to die at this moment, would succeed to a house and furniture which are worth much more than £30,000, without any liability, besides some £70,000 secured by insurance on my life.

I think you are bound to acquit the Squire of Elveden of extravagance.

When the agricultural depression set in, I requested the Home Government to make an allowance that would enable me to maintain my position, and they kindly, after causing all the accounts to be examined, helped me with £10,000, but did not accuse me of extravagance. Subsequently, pending the consideration of my affairs, some £6,000 or £7,000 more was advanced to pay off pressing bills, as during that time I had not completed the arrangements for reducing my establishment. Out of the above loan £10,000 was invested in live and dead stock on farms in hand, and would be forthcoming, if demanded, at a very short notice.

Thus the extravagance during my residence at Elveden is reduced to the fabulous sum of some £12,000 and I possess enough personally, beyond any question, to discharge debts to that amount, and some £6,000 more, should they exist after my death.

In common justice, therefore, Mr. Editor, I ask you to enable me to contradict, in as prominent a manner as they were brought forward in your most influential journal, the rumours as to my extravagance.

In the first paragraph of your leading article of Thursday, the 31st ult., you say, that 'the claim now publicly preferred by the Maharajah has been disallowed after full consideration by successive Govts., both in India and this country.' Yes, it is very easy to disallow a claim without hearing the real claimant.

The English law grants the accused the chance of proving himself not guilty; but I am condemned unheard; is this just?

I remain, Sir, your most obliged,

Duleep Singh.[13]

Not long after the exchange of letters in *The Times*, a small book appeared, entitled *The Annexation of the Punjab and the Maharajah Duleep Singh*. It was published by Trubner & Co. of Ludgate Hill and the author was Major Evans Bell. Evans Bell was a writer of power and lucidity, who invariably argued his causes from the native Indian point of view. He had been assistant commissioner at Nagpur but had lost his appointment for insubordination in advocating the claims of the dispossessed ruling family. His attacks on the Indian civil service had made him highly unpopular with the establishment, who could hardly appreciate being accused of 'dull mediocrity', of having an 'unconciliatory demeanour', or of the recommendation that 'no time would be lost in putting a total stop to the tide of "highly educated" young gentlemen from England'.

'Our weakest point,' he wrote, 'has been caused by the deluge of young Englishmen, whom the lust of patronage has sent forth in a stream, increasing steadily during the last quarter of a century. This has led to the establishment of the "damned nigger" system in every department, civil and military. Boys just emancipated from school, who care for nothing but beer and billiards, whose very ignorance of their

163

language and customs makes them dislike and despise their native subordinates, are placed in charge of companies of sepoys.'[14]

The Maharajah sent a copy of Evans Bell's book to the queen, who cannot have been altogether gratified by its controversial and critical interpretation of the activities of her government in India, even if it did provide confirmation of the Maharajah's argument. According to Evans Bell, the Mooltan revolt could have been put down immediately but had been allowed to spread, thus justifying more far-reaching intervention leading to annexation.

Lord Dalhousie [he summed up] might have gained the hearts of the Princes and people by a plain statement of what had been done, and what was intended to do in the Punjab. Instead of doing so, he violated treaties, abused a sacred trust, threw away the grandest opportunity ever offered to the British Government of planting solid and vital reform up to the Northern limits of India, and by an acquisition as unjust as it was imprudent, weakened our frontier, scattered our military strength, and entailed a heavy financial burden upon the Empire. That, I believe, will be the verdict of posterity and history ...[15]

Ponsonby told the queen that, according to Sir Owen Burne, 'Major Evans Bell is a professional agitator. He is a clever but entirely unscrupulous writer, & he has used his pen against us as a paid agent in every single annexation or settlement we have ever made.'[16] There was an upsetting suggestion in the Maharajah's letter accompanying the book: he again proposed entering Parliament. He gave two reasons:

1st. I am aware that there is great discontent prevailing in India and I know on the very best authority that were Russia to appear on the borders of Your Majesty's Eastern Empire there is not an Indian Prince who would not rebell [sic] and I hope by representing their grievances in Parliament to bring about such a change in the existing state of affairs as will entirely destroy the possibility of such an occurrence, and thus serve Your Majesty in a humble way.

2nd. Should the Indian Government not give heed to my appeal I hope to be able to advocate my own case in Parliament.[17]

The queen did not see why the Maharajah had to be in Parliament to get a public hearing and asked Ponsonby to look into the matter. He put the question to Sir Owen Burne, who, referring to the queen's interest in the case, replied:

The case will no doubt come on in Parliament as a result of the heavy artillery you mention, but I cannot think that the Maharajah will gain much by it. As to his private Estates we have never heard of them till lately, and we are asking the G. of I. to make further enquiries. In the meantime they have denied, as Lord Dalhousie denied after the annexation, that the M.R. had any such private estates, nor has the question, as I have said, been raised till now. The terms which Duleep Singh had to swallow at the Annexation were perhaps – after the reflection of 33 years – a little hard on him personally. But he *had* to fall because his subjects broke out in open rebellion, & it was hard on him. But in other respects the terms were fair enough & have always been so acknowledged by the M.R. until quite lately. The terms he has had to swallow *lately* in the new arrangements made with him were harder than I advocated or would have liked but the Indian Govt. forced our hands & are very angry indeed at our making any concessions at all.

For Sir Owen Burne, who liked to wear the mantle of a very perfect gentleman, such hiding under the skirts of the viceroy was to say the least hypocritical, neither could his postscript be described as gentlemanly: 'I suppose you know that Duleep Singh's mother was a very bad character, & that *he* is not Runjit Singh's son at all, but the son of a Bhistee, or water carrier, a favourite at her Court.'[18]

It was not until November that the queen, still at Balmoral, put her mind once again to the matter of her Maharajah: 'The Queen is anxious to answer the Maharajah without delay, having been so long without answering him . . . She feels very sorry for him – & wishes something cd. be done,' she wrote in a memorandum to Ponsonby. Ponsonby must have passed on Burne's story of the Maharajah's questionable descent, for the queen added tartly, if illogically: 'The story – of his not being Runjeet Singh's real son – is nonsense as he was acknowledged as such & placed on the throne *by Ld. Hardinge*. The Queen reads the books also.'[19] It might be thought that her advisers were trying to discredit her protégé in her eyes, as they were to do ten years later in the case of another Indian friend, the munshi.

The queen's letter, drafted by Ponsonby, avoided all the controversial suggestions put forward by the Maharajah in former correspondence and referred him back to Lord Hartington, who she was sure 'would not be party to any injustice'. She reproved him for his letters to *The Times*. 'If I might advise you – it would be better not to write in the papers. It is beneath you to do so. Is there no one on whose wise & impartial opinion you could rely & whose advice in these difficult questions would be of use to you?'[20]

CHAPTER 10

Arguments with the India Office

✿

AFTER the passing of the Maharajah Duleep Singh Estates
Act in 1882, the Maharajah began to feel that his fortunes and
his future had taken an unacceptable turn for the worse. Not
only was he unable to leave Elveden to his eldest son, but
his position in society was rapidly becoming untenable
through lack of funds.

He had never been one to accept the meaning of 'final
settlement', especially when settled under duress, and was not
long deterred by the apparently awesome act. Accordingly,
on 1 March 1883, he wrote to Lord Kimberley, Hartington's
successor, giving 53 Holland Park as his address as an indication that he could no longer afford to live at Elveden:

> I have the honour to lay before your Lordship a statement of
> my wishes in the confident hope that my Case will be reconsidered
> and such a provision made as will enable me to maintain the high
> rank confirmed to me by my Gracious Sovereign during my life
> and by my Children after my death, worthy of the magnanimity
> of this great just and civilised Nation.
>
> 1st. I would venture humbly to request that if no greater
> generosity can be bestowed upon me at least my present life
> stipend of £25,000 per annum be continued to my male heirs at
> my death.
>
> 2ndly. That the £138,000 in which I am indebted to the Indian
> Government together with £105,000 given to me for the purchase
> of an Estate in this Country may be considered as a full compensa-
> tion for the loss of gold and silver plate and Palace jewels, thus
> relieving my stipend of the heavy charge of interest deducted from
> it.

3rdly. That the Premiums on the Policies of Life Insurance effected for the benefit of my younger children and widow paid by me out of my life stipend of £25,000 per annum be discharged from the surplus arising out of the unexpected balance of the sum allotted for the maintenance of myself my relatives and servants of state at the Annexation.

My Lord, I feel very deeply the hardship to which my children will be subjected, viz., being brought up in the position which I occupy in this Country through the graciousness of my Sovereign on being compelled to relinquish it at my death for a lower sphere of life ...[1]

These moving proposals, mainly on behalf of his children, did not seem inordinately demanding, yet Lord Kimberley's reply, received three weeks later, was cruelly negative, even if he signed himself 'Your Highness's Sincere friend and well-wisher': 'I regret to be under the necessity of informing Your Highness that I am entirely unable to entertain the request which you now put forward, and that, so far as the Indian Government is concerned the arrangements embodied in the Act of Parliament which received the Royal Assent on 10th August last must be considered absolutely final.'[2]

When the queen saw a copy of the letter she was sufficiently agitated to scrawl an immediate memo to her private secretary Henry Ponsonby which indicated her strong feelings in the matter: 'The Queen will write later abt. the Maharajah, but thinks Ld. Kimberley *most* heartless and unkind. She feels something *must* and *shd.* be done and as *she* and the Pce. always took a *real personal* interest in him she wishes that a personal appeal should be made to him. Could Sir Henry go to him! He has been very hardly used – and it is potentially *bad* for *us* if he goes back impoverished and full of grievances. Sir O. Burne (his enemy) was a *child* when the Maharajah came over here and was treated as an exiled deposed Sovereign. The Queen feels *very* strongly on this subject.'[3]

Strength of feeling was one matter, but being able positively to override the decisions of the India Office was quite another and *that* the queen, as a constitutional monarch, should not, and in this case would not, do: the Maharajah's money was hardly a matter on which she could bring about the resignation of her minister.

At the queen's request Ponsonby approached Sir Owen Burne to see if anything could be done. His reply indicated a hardening of official attitudes which did not promise well for the future. 'We are very *determined* at the India Office – and so are they in India. We find that the matter admits of no compromise, and that if we commence upsetting Acts of Parliament immediately after they have received the Queen's sanction we shall get into a slough of despond.' Burne added a drop of acid for the royal ear: 'The Indian Council are inclined to have less sympathy with the M.R. by some apparently well founded rumours that he has settled £2,000 a year on a Miss Ash whom he has taken into his keeping.'[4]

If the queen-empress could not influence an adamant India Office, the Maharajah advertised that he had no recourse but to leave the country and go and live in India, where life was cheaper. He emphasized his intention by announcing that he had no option but to sell some of his possessions, which should raise £20,000, so that he could at least live there as a person of importance.

Lord Hertford was quick to register concern about what seemed to be the Maharajah's first positive action in following a course that had hitherto been only a threat. 'Having taken an interest in the case of Duleep Singh I am much concerned to see that he is actually selling his Plate & Jewels for the purpose of going to India!' Hertford wrote to Ponsonby. 'Surely this is not only suicidal for himself, but may be productive of immense mischief to England ...'[5] When the queen learned of the Maharajah's intemperate action she scribbled a note to Ponsonby: 'Could not Ld. Hertford see the Maharajah & persuade him to pause? He cd. do so out of friendliness. Where the Queen finds herself in difficulty is that she repeatedly told the Maharajah to come to her or write to her if he was in difficulties. As his best friend she *cannot* let him think she deserts him.'[6]

Hertford could do nothing. The sale was to start on 23 July 1883 at the rooms of Messrs Phillips, Son & Neale, of New Bond Street, and to bring the point home, Ponsonby and Hertford were invited to attend the private view. An article in *The Times* on 20 July was sympathetic, and encouraged the idea that authority might be persuaded to bow to popular opinion.

The news of His Highness being compelled to sell his jewels and other valuables will excite a deep feeling of sympathy among all who are acquainted with the history of the 'Lion of the Punjab' ... There is very good reason for the complaint on his part that he has practically been deprived unfairly of a large share of the income which was guaranteed to him ...

Although the Government, from a purely business point of view might be justified in believing that the Maharajah has 'partly brought his pecuniary difficulties upon himself', it could be said in extenuation that the ways of Oriental potentates are not as those of modern English Princes, where the nation was not under the same obligations as it is under towards His Highness the Maharajah ... A golden bridge might, with generosity and dignity, be built for retreat from a position which is embarrassing for both parties.

According to *The Times*, the most striking item in the sale was the silver and gilt plate, of which there were twenty-four breakfast services – 'teapot, sugar basin, cream ewer, toast and egg frame, etc.' – alone. But the pièce de resistance must surely have been Lot 150: 'A magnificent centre piece, 39 inches high, composed of a large and finely modelled figure of an elephant carrying the Maharajah of the Punjab, surrounded by several equestrian groups etc....' There were also cashmere shawls and 'rare Indian carpets' up for auction, whilst the third day's sale was given over to 'elegant and fashionable Indian jewellery'. Items included enamelled bracelets and necklaces set with diamonds and pearls, pendants and bracelets set with *cabochon* emeralds, pearls and

Sale No. 0401.

A CATALOGUE

OF

25,000 Oz. of Chased Plate,

VALUABLE

CASKET OF JEWELS,

AND

RARE INDIAN CARPETS,

EMBROIDERIES, &c.,

THE PROPERTY OF

HIS HIGHNESS THE MAHARAJAH OF LAHORE

DULEEP SINGH, G.C.S.I.,

Preparatory to his leaving England for India.

Which will be Sold by Auction,

BY MESSRS.

PHILLIPS, SON & NEALE,

At their great Rooms, 73, New Bond Street,

On Monday, 23rd July, 1883, and Two following Days,

AT ONE O'CLOCK PRECISELY EACH DAY.

May be Viewed the Friday and Saturday preceding the Sale, and Catalogues had at Messrs. PHILLIPS, SON & NEALE'S Great Rooms and Offices,

Telephone No. 3670.   73, New Bond Street, London, W.

DRYDEN PRESS: J. DAVY AND SONS, 137, LONG ACRE, LONDON.

diamonds, as well as some of the Maharajah's celebrated pearl necklaces and earrings, one of which had fifty-two large graduated pearls. The Maharajah's best pieces, it was said, were not included in the sale. Of the pearls, *The Times* said: 'There is a certain modest native beauty of tint, rich yet subdued in the natural pearl ... singularly beautiful in their natural hue, like the veiled beauties of Lahore and Cashmere.'

The interest generated by the sale caused a question to be asked in the House of Commons by Mr Mitchell Henry, Home Rule member for Galway and therefore not a spokesman for either of the parties responsible for the state of affairs, who asked the secretary of state for India, Mr Cross, 'whether the Maharajah Duleep Singh and his family had ever received the £45,000 a year guaranteed by the Treaty of Lahore, or whether, on the contrary, the Maharajah's income had been so diminished by the Government that for many years he had not had more than about £13,000 a year to live on'. He ended by requesting the government to present for inspection by the House a full account of their financial dealings with the Maharajah and his family since the annexation of the Punjab.

In his reply Cross quoted the terms of the Lahore treaty and concluded that Her Majesty's government did not think it necessary to produce the information in question. Mitchell Henry got to his feet again and gave notice that he would also move that the whole dealings of the Maharajah with the government should be referred to a select committee. There were shouts of 'order' as Mitchell Henry asked whether 'the Government had not induced the Maharajah to settle as an English gentleman in this country and to purchase with the money guaranteed by the Treaty an estate which only paid three percent interest, while the Government charged the Maharajah between four and five percent for the money they had lent him'. There were further cries of 'Order' before Henry continued with a supplementary question. Was the government aware that 'the Maharajah was returning to India a disappointed man in consequence of the treatment of the Government in order to live in a private station in life'?

Cross did not attempt to answer these telling questions, and dismissed them with offhand brevity: 'If the Honourable Member had read all the papers he would have come to a different conclusion.'[7]

Despite Cross's arrogant dismissal of his claims the Maharajah was determined to establish the equity of his position. He had his case carefully drafted in copperplate and a copy went off to the queen, 'as a last resort before quitting this country'.[8] The last two paragraphs read:

Your humble Petitioner's Prime Minister after the annexation was permitted to enjoy an income of £15,000 per annum during his life and yet his Sovereign, the Son of the Lion of the Punjab to whom was sworn everlasting friendship by the British Nation, and the Ward of that Nation has £2,000 a year less than his former Minister and is compelled to sell live game and pheasant eggs in order to add to his income as he receives hardly any rents from his landed estates owing to the present agricultural distress.

Therefore your Humble Petitioner after throwing himself entirely upon the Christian charity and generosity of the British Nation implores that some more equitable and just arrangement be entered into with him. He had been hitherto obliged to accept whatsoever terms have been offered as that or nothing and if the Transvaal has been restored to Boers because it was considered bare justice and the Island of Corfu to the Greeks may he not hope that if his kingdom cannot be restored his landed estate or a portion thereof may be handed back to him or a fair and reasonable sum be paid to him in respect of his estates and loss of private property and thus justice will be done to one of Her Majesty's most Loyal and grateful subjects.[9]

The reply came:

It has given the Queen much pain to read the Memorandum which Your Highness has forwarded, for Her Majesty fears that whether well or ill founded Your Highness is suffering under a sense of injustice. This deeply distresses the Queen whose earnest hope was that your difficulties had been met and that her Secretary of State was always ready to listen to any appeal made by Your

Highness... The Queen cannot help expressing a doubt whether it would be desirable in Your own interests to visit India at present, but Her Majesty has no desire to restrict the freedom of Your movements if you think a voyage to the East would be conducive to your amusement, health and comfort.[10]

It is likely that the Maharajah saw through the queen's homely placebo that she did not want to restrict his movements. He knew only too well that the government did, and for good reason, and he must have seen that she was doing no more than offering a salve to their relentless scourging. There is no doubt that the India Office was worried that he might go, especially in his present mood. Memories of the mutiny hung heavily on the minds of many, and though the Indian nationalist movement was still in embryo, there was mounting feeling among Indian intellectuals that they should have more say in the running of the administration. Lord Ripon, the viceroy, may not have been too worried, but Ronald Melville, who had recently been in India, found that the Sikhs had shown 'the greatest possible interest and enthusiasm in the Maharajah, although they knew he had turned Christian'.[11] Kimberley was not sure what to think and sought the viceroy's views on what to do if the Maharajah actually did go to India. Ripon replied that he would simply restrict his travel by forbidding him to go north of Allahabad, or visit any state ruled by an independent prince,[12] of which there were at that time five hundred and fifty. Kimberley decided not to aggravate the Maharajah with Ripon's decision: he was of the opinion that the whole idea of going to India was in any case nothing but a bluff.

Ronald Melville did not believe that limiting the Maharajah's movements would affect his declared intention, but he maintained that his friend had no more sinister a motive in returning to his homeland than a desire to marry off his daughters to suitable Indians, and to be able to live within his means. Having known him for thirty years he was certain the Maharajah would have mentioned anything questionable, Melville thought, as he had been in the habit of talking quite 'freely' with him. His good friend, Lord Hertford, was not so sure, but they were both agreed that it would be better in every way if the Maharajah remained in England. One possible solution that occurred to them was that he might be given some responsible job that would enhance his self-esteem; the only office he had held to date was as a local justice of the peace. Some more responsible job, say with the Indian Council, would serve to make him an ally instead of an enemy of the Indian government. Ronald Melville saw it all clearly – 'With his knowledge of Native character, his devotion to the Queen, his love of England, and his natural abilities, coupled with the feeling of his countrymen towards him, he ought to be a source of strength rather than a trouble to our Indian rule.'[13] Hertford added: 'Of course, if he were so placed, the Maharajah's decisions would be subject to a veto from experienced Englishmen.'[14]

There was still the matter of the Maharajah's private estates, which had been for so long outstanding. 'The Queen cannot understand the difficulty about settling the question of fact as to whether the private estates in the Punjab exist or not,'[15] she wrote to Kimberley. If they did, they might form the basis of a claim. She also asked Gladstone for his opinion and intervention. The prime minister's opinion was that he did not consider the Maharajah had a case 'as of strict right', but, as he verbosely phrased it, 'Mr Gladstone shares what he understands to be Your Majesty's feeling, that a great dilapidation of the fortune of a fallen Indian Prince may be a cause of pain and scandal, irrespectively of the wisdom or unwisdom of his conduct, and that some effort should be made to get rid of that pain and scandal may be proper.' His intervention consisted of a talk with Kimberley who, Gladstone informed the queen, had told him that the problem would have to be settled by the Indian government. 'The matter has thus been put in train for consideration,' he concluded lamely, 'but of course the result cannot at present be forecast.'[16]

From painstaking searches in village records by the Maharajah's agents, it seems that Runjit Singh had indeed privately possessed a considerable amount of land, as well as several revenue-producing salt mines, which was confirmed by a London lawyer commissioned to investigate. The Maharajah, encouraged by the India Office, had been to a great deal of trouble and expense to establish their existence, but the India Office had long ago decided that even if acceptable evidence were produced, it could in no way be admitted so long after the event. Two years were to pass, however, before they officially dismissed his claim.

Nevertheless, by the end of October there was a break in the ranks of the Indian establishment. Kimberley was in touch with Ripon again in an effort to come to some arrangement for the Maharajah's financial betterment. No doubt motivated by a desire to please the queen, Kimberley seemed to be doing his best: thinking he had found a way round he let it be known through Ponsonby that the Maharajah should send in a 'respectable' letter asking for an increased pension specifically on account of the agricultural depression, and *not* based on a re-interpretation of the Lahore treaty. Kimberley made the position clear: '... if he repeats any of his unfounded claims and pretensions he will get nothing.' Neither should he mention, he discreetly advised, anything about a proposed visit to India, which might be construed as a threat.[17]

But the Maharajah would have none of these face-saving devices, and he positively rejected any grant made under such conditions. All he wanted, he had now decided, was an independent inquiry into the justice of his claim, not a tentative handout under false pretences. He made his new approach clear in a letter to Kimberley, firmly stating that he refused to be regarded as a suppliant, 'dependent on its merciful bounty or compassion'.[18] To the palace he sent a heartfelt plea: 'Oh! that it were possible to obtain an impartial hearing into what I ought to have had under the Treaty and whether I have ever realised what that treaty was to secure to me. This is all I ask for!' His pride had been injured, his sense of justice mocked. The aggravated Maharajah explained his attitude to the queen:

The India Office clearly feels itself in a difficulty – gross injustice has been committed, and it is equally embarrassing to persevere or to acknowledge the error. The latter is however the safe and honourable course.

After sad experience I have come to the conclusion that my appeal to the personal consideration of the Government would, like former appeals, merely serve the Government as an excuse for withholding justice ...

I have never desired more than justice. I would scorn to bring my pecuniary difficulties before the officials, if I did not feel that I was merely demanding my own.

From childhood I have been absolutely in the hands of the Government without a will or independent action of my own – trusting implicitly to their good faith.

Now there appears to have been a deliberate intention from the first, merely to do what least might suffice to answer my urgent demands and leave my children and family to gradually sink in the world, believing that they need no longer be regarded as objects of apprehension or of service to the British Nation.[19]

From the beginning of 1884 the Maharajah was in a state of great despondency, even if a reassuring letter from the queen had calmed him down. Nevertheless, he was still taking a belligerent line: though he gave out that he was making his claim on behalf of his children's future, it is clear that his personal pride was at stake and that what had been an argument was developing into a vendetta.

His strategy was to hit the Indian government where they were most sensitive – the questionable annexation, his unjust deposition, their unwillingness to accept arbitration, and their illiberal interpretation of the financial clauses of the treaty. After all, that 'discrowned debauchee' the King of Oudh, who had actually refused to sign a treaty, had been allowed an income of £100,000 a year.[20] The Maharajah's best card was the queen, and he played her strongly against successive secretaries of state. The opening bid in his play that year was his warning that in addition to his private estates and salt mines, he would also be claiming the value of his jewels, questionably confiscated to pay the costs of war. He included the Koh-i-noor for good measure, but did not seem to realize that those additional jewels from his father's treasury were even then in the Tower of London. He also gave notice that he would be asking for the 'just, honourable and only possible interpretation to be put upon the Treaty of 1846'.[21] He was prepared to put his case to arbitration. And in the background was the threat of going to India and stirring up the pot.

In July, the Maharajah sent Queen Victoria, and a number of other influential people, a copy of his 'little book', which had been compiled at his request by a barrister of Lincoln's Inn. This volume, nicely printed and bound in leather, was also intended to inform the Maharajah's personal friends of the leading features of his case, even if they did not already know it by heart. Some copies were circulated in India.

By the next post, the Maharajah sent an extraordinary letter to Ponsonby:

May I beg of you kindly to lay at the feet of my Sovereign the accompanying paper knife the handle of which I ordered specially to be manufactured for Her Majesty when I was on a visit to Naples with my two sons last Spring. On the reverse is the emblem of my fealty. My father was an ally of England all his life. I also as such have had the honour conjointly with my Sovereign of having a salute fired before the fortress of Mooltan and as I have been a most loyal subject of the Crown for the last 35 years I shall not therefore now turn traitor although I may re-embrace the faith of my ancestors and eventually take up my residence in India, but I will not take the latter step without laying before Her Majesty my reasons for doing so.

There is a terrible storm gathering in India and I hope to render such service as to compel the principal ministers of the Crown to recognise my just claims which perhaps under the present circumstances they may be disinclined to admit. I know that the advent of Russia is hailed with intense joy both by the people and Princes of India in their secret hearts whatever they may outwardly say and they are all prepared to rebel as soon as that Power advances a little nearer.[22]

It might have been deduced from that letter that the paper knife was more symbolic of a stab in the back: a change in his religion might disappoint the conscience of the queen and would certainly affect hopes of Christianizing the subcontinent, but the reference to Russia, though it could not exactly be construed as a threat, indicated a certain dangerous drift in his thinking. Ponsonby sent the letter to his opposite number with the Prince of Wales, Sir Francis Knollys, who replied from Sandringham in what sounded like the gruff voice of his master: 'I am afraid the Maharajah has retained all the bad qualities of the Eastern without gaining any of the good qualities of the European. He is a bad lot, I fear. My own impression is that not 1 in 500 (not 1 in 1,000 I may say) converts to Christianity are improved by their conversion.'[23]

However startled the queen may have been by the tenor of the Maharajah's letter, the reference to it in her response was more in sorrow than in anger, as if she was not prepared to notice the menace in its composition, and in her blandest manner was trying to calm the storm that she felt raging in his breast.

Dear Maharajah, You were so much attached to my dear Leopold* from his earliest childhood, that I thought you would like to possess a recollection of him, and therefore send you an enamelled photograph of him. I likewise send you *my* last book.

In your last letter (to Sir Henry Ponsonby I *think* it was) you made use of some expressions which *pained* me and which I would wish to refer to. You mentioned the possibility of returning to your *own* old *faith*. Now, considering what a fine and fervent Christian you were for between 30 and 40 years, I *cannot believe* you would forsake the blessings of that pure Religion – for one which offers none of its comforts and blessings. I say this without doubting the least that there are many good and excellent Hindoos, but the faith is one the principles of which cannot be admired. Forgive me

* Prince Leopold, duke of Albany, died in the spring of 1884.

saying this – but I have known you, taken too warm an interest in you for so long, not to speak out plainly. I am sure the Maharani (to whom I wish to be kindly remembered) and your children would feel the same.

Believe me always, your affectionate and faithful friend,

Victoria R.I.[24]

The tempest was not stilled. The Maharajah's reply to the queen's gentle request for his views about religion led to an outbrust that must have made her realize that she was now dealing with a deranged and possibly a dangerous mind:

My Sovereign, Your Majesty's most gracious letter and the gifts which accompany it have duly reached me and I humbly beg of your Majesty to accept my heart's sincere gratitude for this further mark of your continued graciousness and remembrance.

Like a dog participates in the joys as well as sorrows of his master so do I humbly share whatever affects your Majesty.

What all the British cannon, though they can blow me to pieces, could not make me say now that I know my true position, viz., I yield, your Majesty's boundless graciousness towards me has entirely accomplished – and I hope always to remain as I am at this moment your Majesty's most loyal subject unless the persecution of the Government will compel me to seek asylum beyond the bounds of your Majesty's Dominions on my return to India.

As your Majesty is the only true and disinterested friend I possess in the world I did not like that you my Sovereign should hear from any other source in the first instance but myself of the possibility of my re-embracing the faith of my ancestors, though I mentioned it to Sir Henry Ponsonby.

I have since sent for a Bhaee or Brother to come with a copy of the Holy Book of the Sikhs to teach me to read it.

My Sovereign the Faith of Nanuk and the Hindoo religion of the present day are very different from each other. The former is a pure Deism containing many tenets apparently of Christianity whereas the latter is mere idol worship which can not commend itself to any reasoning mind.

My Sovereign when lots were cast before the Holy Book of the Sikhs for the purpose of selecting a name for me Dleep came up, which was afterwards corrupted by my English and Persian tutors into Duleep.

Shortly after I ascended the throne of the Punjab it was found written in a book of Sikh prophecies called Sakheean that a man of my name would be born who, after becoming entirely dispossessed of all he inherited and residing alone for a long period in a foreign country, would return to be the eleventh gooroo or Teacher of the Khalsa or the Pure and that his prosperity then would far exceed that of his ancestors. He would also establish a new faith.

I suppose from the similarity of the two names and what has taken place regarding me this prophecy is believed in by millions of Punjabees who have been long looking forward to its fulfilment and wonder if I am the right man why I do not return.

I myself was told of it when only six or seven years of age and so much did I believe at the time that I was the person to whom the above prophecy was applicable that I had purposely a cage constructed and placed every night near me to carry away in it a favourite pair of pigions [sic] which as a child I prized beyond all the contents of my Treasury, for I was to leave my residence suddenly and however strange it may appear, I left my Palace on less than a week's notice.

I did not remember until last year when I was about to leave England against my will all this apparent nonsense, nor think of the almost prophetic words uttered a short time before her death by my mother when on one occasion while discussing the above prophecy with her I jeeringly remarked 'but mother, how can all this come to pass if I do not return to India at all.' She replied, 'Mark my words my child, perhaps I may not live to see the day but whenever the right moment arrives circumstances will so shape themselves that thou wilt be compelled to quit England against thy will,' and your Majesty perhaps recollects how nearly this was brought about by the action of the India Council and may yet be fulfilled.

Under all these rather curious circumstances I hope your Majesty will pardon me, if I have begun to believe in the force of destiny. I do not believe and indeed my Sovereign I do not now particularly care that justice will ever be done to me, but I do believe that my destiny whatever that may be will be fulfilled.

My Sovereign in my humble opinion only that religion is of

God which influences the actions of its professors. I embraced Christianity because those by whom I was surrounded at the time happened to be so consistent in their conduct.

We Sikhs though savages by nature implicitly act up to the (such as it is) morality of our faith. We do not profess one thing and do the other.

Your Majesty is now fully acquainted with the treatment I have received from the Christians who spend vast sums of money annually to teach the heathen to do justice, love mercy and walk humbly with God as well as defraud no man and to do to others as you would wish them to do to you.

I know two members of the India Council to be eminently pious yet they persist in doing me injustice although they fully hope to sit among the God's elect hereafter. Also, Lord Dalhousie wrote in a Bible he present[ed] me with the following inscription '... This Holy Book in which he has been led by God's grace to find an inheritance richer by far than all earthly kingdoms is presented with sincere respect and regard by his faithful friend' (?) ... or in other words having deprived me of my inheritance which was in his power to let alone, he hoped as my friend (!!!) that I may acquire another which was not in his power to bestow.

My Sovereign, such vile hypocrisy of the Christians as the above has made me wish to revert to the faith of my forefathers which is simple trust and belief in the great architect of the Universe whom to praise and glorify should be the all-absorbing duty of His worshippers. Thus believing and worshipping God, like my ancestors, I now desire to pass the rest of my life and die.

My wife who begs me to present her humble duties and gratitude to your Majesty for graciously remembering her, does not, like your Majesty, believe in my turning a Sikh again – but she will be undeceived should I be compelled to go to India.

Imploring your Majesty's forgiveness for troubling your Majesty with such a long letter ... and pleading your own graciousness as my excuse for doing so ... I have the honour to remain My Sovereign's humble and most loyal Subject...[25]

The queen, who described the letter as 'extraordinary and half cracky',[26] must by now have realized that she was getting into deep waters, and was unusually stern in her reply, but even if she hid behind her ministers sometimes, she could truly claim that she was doing her best for the Maharajah and though she could not go much further than she had already done in pressing his claim directly, she had by no means given up hope of seeing him satisfied.

Balmoral, Sept. 29th.

My dear Maharajah, Though your letter was an answer to mine I cannot leave yours unanswered as there are observations in it which I must much regret.

In the first place you know that I cannot interfere in your claims; they must be decided by my responsible advisers. But secondly as your friend, and perhaps the truest you have, I would most strongly warn you against those who would lead you to do what would inevitably bring you into trouble without doing you any good. Do not use threats or abusive language, for it will not be the means of obtaining that impartial hearing of your claims which you desire. Above all I most earnestly warn you against going to India where you will find yourself far less independent and far less at your ease than here.

Ever your affectionate friend, V.R.I.[27]

The Maharajah replied by return of post with a plea that, though contentious, must have impressed upon the queen the profound distress he was suffering:

My Sovereign . . . how shall I express the gratitude which I feel at Your Majesty's condescension in giving me such advice which shall be acted upon by me to the last letter.

All that I desire, my Sovereign, is an impartial enquiry into and a hearing of my claims, and I feel very, very happy to leave myself in Your Majesty's hands whatever may be mine ultimate fate.

With reference to my going out to India to reside I humbly beg to inform Your Majesty that I had determined on, should it ever be my destiny to do so, seeking this property and settling the proceeds (which I have the power to do) on my wife and children and after resigning the stipend paid to me by the Indian Government and thus terminating the treaty of 1849 to proceed to my native land as a Sikh Fakeer leaving my family in England.

Your Majesty may not be aware perhaps that liberty to a recluse is of no use as he can devote himself to the contemplation of the Deity anywhere and the more persecution he suffers the more

sanctity he acquires in the sight of the Indians. Besides, My
Sovereign, the 45,000 Punjabee soldiers in Your Majesty's Indian
Army who assisted in re-establishing Your Majesty's Eastern
Empire during the Mutiny of 1857 might petition for the release
from prison of their chief as the reward of their services rendered
on that occasion which the Indian Government might find difficult
to refuse. But I do not for a moment fear any such treatment at
the hands of the India officials because my unwavering loyalty to
the British Crown for upwards of 35 years is known both to them
and my country ... My Sovereign I humbly beg to be pardoned
for causing Your Majesty pain by anything I said in my last letter
but my history, My Sovereign, is such a painful one that whatever
I quote from it must cause pain to a just and generous mind like
Your Majesty's, besides I feel bitterly the unjust acts of the India
Government. I often ask myself am I in my right senses or am I
mad ...[28]

By the spring of 1885, the Maharajah was considering
putting Elveden up for auction. There had been no reaction
from India nor in England. The politicians were being totally
inflexible. Money was running out and he could see no end
to the affair. In desperation he sank his pride and begged for
cash, say £5,000, to keep him afloat until the answer came
from India. If he were forced to go ahead and sell his estate,
he told Ponsonby, no offer would compensate for its loss –
'for if once my English home passes into other hands though
the India Office may then offer to pay me 2 million a year I
shall not be able to reside in this country'.[29]
     At the end of March there was talk of trouble with the
Russians on the Afghan border. Here was a chance, the
Maharajah thought, to affirm his devotion and loyalty to the
queen and perhaps win favour with an establishment which
was beginning to question his soundness. He wrote to Ponsonby offering his services in India:

Should serious news respecting the breaking out of hostilities on
the Afghan frontier ... unhappily prove to be true I beg of you
kindly to implore my Sovereign graciously to cause me to be
appointed an Aide-de-Camp to HRH the Duke of Connaught's

staff in India. Two of my former subjects, viz., the Maharajah of Cashmere and Sirdar Kot Singh as well as many Indian Princes have the honour of possessing rank in the British Army and therefore may I humbly implore that the same distinction may be conferred on me also? I do not possess an army and therefore cannot offer to lead it against the enemies of my Sovereign but I do possess my life which I am willing to sacrifice in Her service. If my loyalty is in doubt my family may be held as hostages in England for my good behaviour. It is possible that I might raise a regiment of volunteers in India in that case my Sovereign will hear that I was not unworthy of the confidence she was graciously pleased to place in me and prove how grateful I am for her boundless graciousness towards me.[30]

The reply came via Ponsonby from Aix-les-Bains: '... I can assure your Highness that the Queen was very much gratified by the loyal feelings evinced by your Highness in offering your services at this important crisis. H.M. hopes and believes that there will be no rupture of our amicable relations with Russia, still at the same time the Queen commands me to thank you for your devotion and to add that she has enquired of Lord Kimberley whether you could be in any way employed should the necessity unfortunately arise.'[31] In a scribbled memo, Ponsonby noted: 'The Queen thought if he went it wd. pacify him. I cdnt. explain how he cd. volunteer. The offer surprised her.'[32]

From India, in response to Kimberley's request to keep the Maharajah 'in good humour',[33] came a reply that could only have been drafted by the new viceroy, Lord Dufferin: 'Government of India is very sensible of the loyalty of the Maharajah in offering services on present occasion, but it has been our object to conduct our preparations for a home emergency in such a manner as to prevent excitement in minds of public, or lead the people of India to consider that our normal resources are not sufficient to deal with the present crisis. The arrival in India of His Highness for object he proposes would, I fear, lead to our imperfectly informed subjects to imagine that the condition of affairs was far more unsatisfactory than it is. Under the circumstances Government of India does not consider it necessary for His Highness to make the sacrifice he contemplates.'[34]

To the son of Runjit Singh, who was apparently offering himself body and soul, to fight for the queen, his rejection was discouraging. But probably his suggestion had in any case been no more than a gesture, and his next move indicated that his underlying intention had been to embarrass the Indian government. If he could not be a staff officer he would join the British army as a volunteer! 'Should war unfortunately break out between England and Russia,' he wrote to Kimberley, 'I plan to proceed from Bombay via Karachi and through Belochistan to Afghanistan, thus entirely avoiding passing through the Punjab.' The provocation came in the next paragraph – 'I am determined not to be deterred from this resolve (unless physical force is employed by the Indian Government).'[35]

When Kimberley communicated the Maharajah's latest intention to volunteer to the viceroy, Lord Dufferin telegraphed back: 'We think it undesirable he should visit India, and we could not let him join the Army.'[36] On her copy of the message the queen pencilled in purple a note of surprise: 'Why? He really is loyal to the Empress, only very much vexed and disappointed.'[37]

The wayward Maharajah, meanwhile, decided to play host again at Elveden. A grand shooting party took place, just as though nothing had changed: several thousand head of game were killed, and all was reported in the press, much to Kimberley's annoyance, who remarked that it did not help matters for the public to read that this 'distressed Prince' could entertain as of old.

CHAPTER II
'The Eleventh Future Guru'

❧

A DARKER element in the many-sided story of the Maharajah was now to appear, ready to catalyse the dangerous thoughts that had been forming in the back of his mind. The recent death of his comptroller and friend, Colonel Oliphant, who had for so long been the anchor of his household and counsellor and censor in his dealings with the India Office, had broken another of the personal links he had forged with Englishmen. Neither was Bamba of much help to him at that time; she seemed to have turned in on herself and to be incapable of coping even with the simplest of problems. In May 1885 a cousin called Thakur Singh arrived from India, together with another cousin and a small band of followers, who were to undermine even further his sense of identification with his country of adoption.

Thakur Singh was described by the police, who had been keeping an eye on him in India, as 'of an intriguing disposition and not without a certain sort of capacity'.[1] The Maharajah had been in communication with his impoverished cousin for some time, and had used him to obtain information about his considerable family property in India, which Thakur Singh had described as 'enormous'.[2] Suffolk locals reported unusual comings and goings from the station of turbaned Indians and there were deep discussions in the library at Elveden as the visitors tried to persuade the Maharajah to come to India. Now that they knew he was returning to their religion, all the Sikhs, they assured him, were devoted to him and, in accordance with prophecy, were urgently looking forward to a revolution and his restoration on the throne of the

Punjab. The other cousin, described by the police as 'of a profligate and indifferent character', would read him the Granth, the sacred book of the Sikhs, which contained the writings of Nanuk, the Hindu founder of their faith. Nanuk had been succeeded by nine Gurus, or teachers, the last of whom, Govind, died in 1703. Govind had proclaimed the *Khalsa*, the sacred commonwealth of Sikhs, and decreed that devotees should receive the *pahul*, or initiatory rite, wear their unshorn locks beneath a special turban, and assume the surname of 'Singh', meaning lion. Govind ended the succession proclaimed by Nanuk; but, according to the story, he had made a prophecy, that when retailed in full to the Maharajah amplified certain unsettling propositions which he had already heard, in essence, from his mother.

Being asked upon an occasion by his disciples whether he would ever again visit the world, Gooroo Govind Singh replied in the affirmative adding that he would be born again in the household of a Sikh who would marry a Mohammedan wife, and that his name would be Deep Singh. After being dispossessed of all he had inherited this Deep Singh would reside for a long time alone in a foreign land and would return to correct the errors in which the Sikhs had fallen in their worship of God and the neglect of the Gooroo's tenets. Before the latter would come to pass Deep Singh would suffer much persecution and be reduced to absolute poverty. The Gooroo further predicts that Deep Singh will marry a Christian wife, and his children by her the Gooroo, in the prophecy, calls Englishmen ... The Gooroo foretells that there will be a war between the two dogs, the bear and the bulldog, Boochoo and Dultoo, in which Deep Singh will take part, but that he will be defeated and will take refuge at a certain village and when there self-knowledge will be revealed to him ... About that time 'The English after selling the country will quit the land. Then will thunder my snakes (young followers) ...' It is further predicted that Deep Singh and his descendants will reign for three generations over the land lying between Calcutta and the Indus.[3]

It was not difficult to persuade the Maharajah to accept what he already half-believed, that he, Duleep, was indeed Deep Singh. Had not his father, the great Runjit Singh, been one of the few Sikhs who had been through the marriage ceremony with a Muslim woman? And were not Russia and England, the bear and the bulldog, already at each other's throats? The rest of the prophecy spoke for itself – the reincarnation of Govind stood before them.

The Maharajah, perhaps to show his importance to his cousins, wanted them presented at court, and wrote to Ponsonby asking him to arrange things so that they would have a chance of meeting the queen: '... My cousins who are to be presented at Court tomorrow are very anxious that they may not miss seeing their Empress of whose graciousness they have heard so much from me, and perhaps you will kindly cause instructions to be given for them to be sent forward before Her Majesty retires. They are extremely poor for their station in life and hence their appearing before H.M. in their present costumes. It is most painful to me to think what these blood relatives of the Lion of the Punjab have, and my children will, come down to, but who can resist the force of destiny?'[4] Thus, the following day, the queen empress met the Maharajah's secret agents at her reception at Buckingham Palace.

Thakur Singh and his party soon returned to India with instructions to prepare the people for their Maharajah's return. He himself, it was agreed, could regard himself as the future prime minister of the Punjab.

It was soon to come to the queen's ears that certain 'evil-disposed persons',[5] meaning Thakur Singh and his associates, had influenced the Maharajah for the worse, and were leading him to India to act against British interests. It is likely that the queen's intervention on this occasion was not so much to save the Maharajah as to safeguard the security of her empire. On 15 August 1885 Ponsonby wrote to Lord Randolph Churchill, yet another secretary of state for India called upon to investigate the Maharajah's affairs. 'The Queen commands me to inform you that she fears the financial difficulties of the Maharajah Duleep Singh are rendering him desperate, that he is consequently susceptible to the intrigues of evil counsellors in India, who are calling upon him to come to the Punjab, and that she fears if not relieved from his pressing necessities he may take some step which may lead to serious consequences.'[6]

Having spent the best part of a day looking through the voluminous file, Lord Randolph was quick to reply:

I have arrived at the conclusion that I cannot recommend to the Govt. of India to undertake any further burdens on account of H.H. the Maharajah, and moreover that even if the Govt. of India was willing to be liable for further expenditure on H.H.'s account and were to make proposals to me in such a sense, I should be unable to agree to such proposals, on the grounds that such a course of action on my part would be surely attacked in the House of Commons in a manner and by arguments to which I would be unable satisfactorily to make an answer ...

The Maharajah's claim to the ownership of private estates in the Punjab cannot really be seriously considered. They were never advanced until 1880, and Lord Cranbrook most emphatically refused to entertain them. Perhaps you are not aware that the Maharajah claims compensation for the loss of the Koh-i-noor.

Every single one of the other statements of the Maharajah contained in the book which he has circulated and which seems to have made so much impression upon the Duke of Grafton, Lord Henniker and others, is utterly misleading, inaccurate and at variance with history and will not bear one moment's real investigation.

I shall be prepared to lay all the official records in the possession of the India Office before Parliament if necessity should arise; though they are not to the credit of the department as far as careful business management is concerned, they show beyond refutation that the treatment of H.H. the Maharajah by successive Secretaries of State has been indulgent and generous to a fault.

H.H. the Maharajah is at liberty to visit India whenever he pleases, but when he lands in that country he will have to conform to the orders of the Governor General, and reside wherever the G.G. shall desire, and to travel in India only with the Governor General's permission.[7]

After making several other negative points, Lord Randolph Churchill concluded by stating that 'after careful consideration of the facts of the case' he could not assume any responsibility to increase the 'ample, liberal and generous' allowance 'in any degree'. He made no reference at all to possible 'serious consequences'.

When Ponsonby showed Henniker the uncompromising reply, Henniker thought it painfully 'blunt' and that it should not be shown to the Maharajah unless he was there 'to soften it to him'.[8]

Rejection hardly needed rubbing in, yet A.W.Moore, Lord Randolph's secretary at the India Office, took it upon himself to write to Ponsonby and put salt upon the wound. In 1879, when acting in the same position for Lord Cranbrook, Moore had taken a more indulgent attitude towards the Maharajah's problems, but now a strong note of moral disapproval can be detected – gambling, womanizing, extravagance are spectres at the civil servant's elbow: 'Since that [Lord Cranbrook's] time the Maharajah has deteriorated in more ways than one. The plain truth is – and you will do a public service if you can bring it home to the Queen, painful as it may be for Her to realise – the Maharajah is unworthy of the Royal favour which he has received, and must be left to take his own course. Even if he were bolstered up for a year or two more, the end would be the same, the scandal only postponed.'[9]

Whatever Moore may have thought about the Maharajah's way of life, his friends were not prepared to give him up, even if each one of them – Henniker, Grafton, Hertford and Leicester – were men of the highest rectitude. But it was difficult to get him to agree to a firm line of action. 'He never remains in one mind 24 hours,' Grafton complained. 'Excited to a degree, one day firmly believing he is the man who is alluded to in some wonderful prophecy (which was probably concocted last year but which he believes was made years before he was born) & the next sitting down broken hearted and saying he could not leave Elveden. I believe he has a cousin, whose dupe he is, encouraging him to go out and do wonders.'[10] If the Maharajah's friends were concerned about his deterioration, they were also concerned about his estates. 'Everything', according to St George Walker, rector of Elveden, 'is at a standstill, if not in a state of collapse.' The rector put the situation directly to the under-secretary of state:

His Highness the Maharajah Duleep Singh has lately declared to us his intention of at once giving up to the Government his Estates here in England and forthwith proceeding to India. Notices to this effect have been sent to servants and the tenantry generally and directions given for all labour to cease and an immediate sale of stock etc. to take place. The consequence is that numbers have already been thrown out of employment and others are preparing to quit their cottages. As a matter of course the able-bodied portion in the parish will be compelled to seek for employment elsewhere – but what will become of the afflicted, the aged and the extreme poor I know not – for the schools, clubs, and charities, hitherto entirely supported by His Highness, will be supported by him no longer. We in this neighbourhood are indeed sorry and in a measure surprised at the very serious turn which affairs have taken, it being generally supposed that His Highness, having proved the justice of his claims, the Government would at once redress his grievances and so prevent the deplorable troubles & privations which now threaten this and the surrounding parishes.[11]

The rector's letter gave the first official notice that positive steps were being taken to leave England. The Maharajah confirmed this intention in a letter to the queen a few days later. 'My Sovereign ... that no justice should be rendered to me I entirely attribute to destiny, but what I greatly grieve at is that I should be prevented by action of the Government from paying my last homage to Your Majesty before my departure for India on the 11th of December next and be thus banished, dishonoured, and disgraced from Your presence the only Friend I thought God had raised up for me in the world.' He ended: 'I have the honour to remain, my Sovereign, Until death (provided the Government do not make my life intolerable in India), before God Your Majesty's most loyal and humble Subject.'[12]

Lord Randolph Churchill's dismissal of the problem had an almost unchallengeable authority about it but it did not stop the Maharajah's friends from petitioning the queen, nor the Maharajah from sending her protestations and veiled threats: 'This is hardly the treatment I expected to receive when because I had nothing else to offer I volunteered to spill my last drop of blood in Your Majesty's service ... Your Majesty's Government are making a most grievous political blunder in thus trying to crush a loyal heart, and if I mistake not, Your Majesty will be, bye and bye, of the same opinion when time has disclosed the result, but God's will be done.'[13] The loyal-hearted Maharajah was even then engaged in earnest intrigues in the Punjab.

On 2 November 1885, on learning that if he went to India he would be confined to the small hill station in southern India at Ootacamund, which, though an agreeable spot, was as far from the Punjab as possible, the maddened Maharajah wrote a highly provocative letter to Lord Randolph Churchill:

I cannot tell your Lordship how pleased I am to learn that the Govt. have definitely determined on pursuing the very course which I have all along desired should be followed towards me on my arrival in India in order to help forward my destiny. I welcome therefore the Official persecution which awaits me in India. For it has been foretold by the last Sikh Gooroo or Teacher (who died about 1725) that I shall suffer in this manner and that when I shall have been reduced to absolute poverty then my prosperity is to commence.

It also flatters my vanity that the All Powerful British Government should think me worthy of its notice and desire to make a martyr of me in the eyes of my countrymen and now co-religionists instead of treating me as I expected with contempt and leaving me to my own devices until I had committed some act of disloyalty towards the Crown.

I feel very proud indeed of the fact that the buzzing of a wretched little gnat should have disturbed the repose of the Mighty British Lion, and in consequence the India Government should think it necessary as it were to 'set out to seek a flea'.[14]

QUEEN VICTORIA'S MAHARAJAH

To indicate that his intention of leaving for India was in earnest, the Maharajah informed Lord Randolph that he would be sailing with his family on 16 December. As the time for departure drew near, the Maharajah became more aggressive. He had been told yet again that on reaching India he would be debarred, if necessary by force, from entering the Punjab, but he insisted that he would make his way from Bombay to Delhi. If they wanted to arrest him they could! On being told repeatedly that he would be required to live at Ootacamund or at some other place in the Madras Presidency, the Maharajah flatly refuted Dufferin's well-Lord Dufferin – order, and reasserted his intention of going to Delhi, southern gateway to the Punjab, and a suitable base for political manœuvrings. 'His Excellency the Viceroy has only to put me under arrest and sent to any part of India that he may think proper to do so. For I am quite prepared to suffer any persecution from the most immoral and unjust British Government which, because it is incapable of doing justice, prefers to bully the weak, rather than disgorge what it had acquired in a most unscrupulous manner.'[15]

When the queen saw the letter she scribbled on it, 'The Maharajah is outrageous.'[16] 'Outrageous' he might be but he was still a threat both to her peace of mind and the security of the empire; as time drew near for departure, frantic messages were sent from the palace to the India Office, the prime minister and the Maharajah's friends. The Maharajah meanwhile waited at the Carlton Club – on hand should something move the government to come to satisfactory terms. Henniker and Grafton were working hard behind the scenes.

...Henniker and myself have drawn up a Petition to the Queen, asking Her Majesty to use Her influence in obtaining a fair and equitable adjustment of the affairs of the Maharajah Duleep Singh. We have not touched upon claims, but merely on what we feel are the rights of every Englishman and every right feeling person.
If Her Majesty will read it privately and at all entertains our view and feels that it should be further enquired into, our object is that

it should be calmly considered by *Lord Salisbury*, that he should obtain the highest legal opinion and if the result should be favourable that an equitable arrangement should be brought about which should be satisfactory to the Maharajah and the Country. We think the following are arrangements that should be made clearing His Highness from present debts; leaving the Elveden Estates entailed on his sons, and the payment of the *full pension* of 4 lacs, settled by the Treaty, minus the pensions still being paid to Family and adherents, until they fall in (as by Treaty undoubtedly settled) by death or otherwise, and an investigation as to whether arrears should not be paid also. All this should be accompanied by a friendly acknowledgement of a long mistaken cause, (which is far more to his heart than all the money) ...[17]

A friendly acknowledgement of past mistakes was one thing the government was not prepared to offer and to some extent it was the Maharajah's intransigence in requiring it that was behind their present attitude. His letter to Randolph Churchill, described by Sir Owen Burne at the India Office as 'breathing of the malice and vexation of impotent rage', had alienated officialdom to such an extent that Lord Salisbury, now prime minister, flatly refused to consider the Grafton–Henniker petition, though it had come forward from the queen herself.

Grafton and Henniker needed more time. So did the Maharajah. They had no difficulty in persuading him to defer his sailing, while they engaged in yet another round with the India Office. The new approach, it was agreed, would be based on the Maharajah's request for arbitration, which, to fair-minded Englishmen such as they were, seemed the best way to settle the matter once and for all.

CHAPTER 12

The India Office Adamant

A T the beginning of 1886 the argument with the India Office had entered its most critical phase. On the one hand the Maharajah was crudely threatening to renounce Christianity and immediately set off for India; on the other he was putting forward financial claims which he knew were unacceptable, or demanding arbitration which he had been told was politically impossible. His inflammatory letter to Lord Randolph Churchill indicated that he was in the grip of passions he could not control – pride, mental excitation and a superstitious belief in dubious prophecies.

The Maharajah had been taught by his mentors, from Login onwards, that in correspondence with officials, especially the high-minded mandarins at the India Office who had such corrosive power over him, losing one's temper never paid and even the most unpalatable statement must be couched in terms of extreme urbanity; a show of anger, however righteous, could weaken whatever goodwill there might be and provide cover for a bureaucratic withdrawal. No one was more aware of this than the patient Ponsonby, who dealt with even the most trying correspondence with restrained courtesy. In a memorandum to the queen, he reported that he proposed asking Lord Henniker, who was coming to see him to discuss the Maharajah's vexatious affairs, to encourage his friend and neighbour to 'use more conciliatory language to the Indian Secretary and Council'. In the same note Ponsonby, appreciating that the queen was the last hope of influencing her wilful subject to resolve a dangerous situation, asked if he might 'hold out a hope that

Your Majesty would receive the Maharajah after returning to Windsor'.[1] To which request the queen tersely minuted 'Certainly'.

That meeting, however, was not to take place. The Maharajah told Grafton that he thought it would be very 'uncomfortable', and implored him to dissuade her from ordering it.[2] But even without the queen's mollifying influence, he was persuaded by Grafton and Henniker to adopt a less aggressive, if strategically more deceptive, approach towards the new secretary of state, Lord Kimberley, who was back in office following the fall of the Conservative government. After bringing him up to date with his case, the Maharajah ended with an apology for, and an offer to withdraw, 'any expression of disrespect ever employed intentionally or otherwise by me towards Her Majesty's Indian Government'.[3]

The Maharajah must have had a good idea why the government was adamant in its refusal to allow an inquiry into his affairs, which would expose them to precedent and possible humiliation, and bring up any number of embarrassing questions that had long been shelved in the India Office archives, but at least he was prepared to let Grafton and Henniker continue their efforts in that direction in the knowledge that an official refusal would gain him a point. If the case was put to arbitration, Henniker assured Ponsonby in a vain effort to influence affairs, the Maharajah would then 'put aside prophecies and letters written in a heated tone' and accept the outcome in 'a fine manly way'.[4] The Duke of Grafton added his weight, complaining to Ponsonby, in a manner less than urbane, that 'to refuse a simple request ... is not a very high or dignified line; but to refuse him everything, even an *inquiry*, is surely a great injustice. The truth is, they have spent the money and have no funds to fall back on and so *fear* an investigation.'[5]

Grafton's sincerity was apparent when he guaranteed his friend's good behaviour: 'I can only say this about him that since I first enquired into his affairs & saw so much more of him his whole conduct has altered that he is not like the same man, he is never excited now, is amenable in every way to advice given and sees *now* that however foolish may have been some of his assertions & acts, he would be far happier if taken by the hand, *prevented* from going to India & a friendly arrangement made. He is like a child now longing to be led and only too grateful for a word of kindness.'[6] Grafton had sufficient influence over the Maharajah to persuade him to postpone the date of his departure in the hope that the India Office might yield to any last-minute pressure that could be applied.

'There are very grave objections to such an arbitration as he demands,'[7] Lord Kimberley wrote to Ponsonby, though he did not go so far as to spell them out. The queen, who must have regretted that the Duke of Wellington was no longer there to solve the problem, instructed Ponsonby to refer the matter once again to Mr Gladstone. The prime minister's reply, dated 25 February 1886, did little more than Lord Salisbury's to gratify:

I think five years have elapsed since I went into the case of the Maharajah, with a strong compassionate presumption in regard to his unfortunate condition. At that time, Hartington went fully into the matter with me, and I am sorry to say convinced me (if I remember right) that the Indian Dept. & Govt. had done very much on his behalf, and that his difficulties were due to his unfortunate errors of judgement on his own part. I have conversed with Lord Kimberley on your note. I think with him there is a good deal of difficulty, on the point of principle, in the introduction of arbitration. On the other hand one will feel that in the case of a man like the Maharajah, 'fallen from his high estate', the scales ought not to be too nicely poised in his prejudice. So I am glad that the Viceroy has been asked whether further concession can be made and to what extent.[8]

Despite his Liberal affiliations, Mr Gladstone refrained from stating that one 'point of principle' on which arbitration was so 'difficult' was the fact that it would bring into a public forum, bruited about also in India, the whole dubious question of the original annexation of the Punjab, and other territories on the subcontinent besides.

The palace was not then privy to the correspondence that passed earlier in the year between the viceroy and the then secretary of state, Lord Randolph Churchill, on the subject of 'further concessions'. On 16 January a telegram from India had indicated that they were seriously worried about the effects of the Maharajah's arrival and were prepared to buy him off:

Have you any further information about Duleep Singh? Is it certain that he really intends coming to India? If so, we think he should be informed that persistence on his part in attempting to disregard our express wishes will, under Article 5 of the Terms granted to him in 1849, absolve us from any existing obligation regarding his pension. At the same time we think Duleep Singh's arrival in India so undesirable that, if he abandons his intention and enters into formal undertaking not to leave England in future, we should be prepared to examine present state of affairs with view to ameliorating his position.[9]

The last sentence had originally read 'to a final & liberal settlement' but Dufferin, the viceroy, personally sent out urgent instructions to all departments to amend their copies for the record.

Could the Maharajah be bought off? And, if so, for how much? Sir Owen Burne was given the job of testing the market. At their first meeting on 25 January, Sir Owen was in a hurry to catch a train, so, after an exchange of politenesses, the Maharajah left a memorandum of his claims for study and returned the following day. A record of the subsequent interview was presented by Burne to his master in the form of a dialogue:

Sir O. Burne: Well, Maharajah, I have read your Memorial to Lord Salisbury. There is nothing in it which has not been already dealt with in past correspondence, so that I will not attempt to argue your case with you. This, in your present frame of mind, will, I see, be labour thrown away. I will merely, therefore, speak of your claims as they strike me personally, as one who is a true friend to you. They are preposterous. I cannot comprehend how a person in your position can court rebuff by demands which no Government in its senses can even consider, much less satisfy.

Maharajah: I like your frankness, and appreciate it. But I can assure you that nothing short of their recognition by Government, and adequate compensation, will satisfy me. I want, at any rate, a full inquiry on them. If the case is given against me I shall be satisfied. Why cannot the Privy Council, or the House of Lords, adjudicate on my case?

Sir O. Burne: That is impossible. It is a question which has often been raised and settled in the negative, and you will never get any Government to agree to so direct an interference with the powers of the Government of India, in its dealings with Native Princes and their pensions. Moreover, you refer to transactions of nearly half a century ago, which, if reopened as you desire, would reopen every act of State of the British Government in India from the rise of the East India Company till now.

Maharajah: True. I see it, and other people have told me the same thing. I give it up. But will not the Government of India give me this full inquiry? They have treated me like an animal; they are now trying to goad me to desperation; they forget I am a king; they have offended a man once loyal to them, and only too anxious now to show his loyalty, if he be given, what high legal authorities and others tell him are his just dues.

Sir O. Burne: All this, Maharajah, is beside the mark. You have got wind in the head, and have lost your ordinary good sense. Now let us view this matter in a business-like way. You, on your part, signed away your kingdom with alacrity; you could say nothing at the time against the justice then dealt out to you; you have since then thankfully accepted from year to year, until lately, all that the Government of India have done for you. Finally, you agreed to an Act of Parliament which you now want to upset, by claims which it is impossible for any Government to admit.

Maharajah: I acknowledge all this. I now see, however, that I have been a fool. It is only lately that I have learnt to realize my position as a king.

Sir O. Burne: But suppose now I were a most benevolent Secretary of State, filled with pity for you, and with every desire to meet your views, what would satisfy you? Suppose I were to say, for instance, that you shall have £25,000 a year, clear of all charges, would that do so?

Maharajah: Certainly not. I want an inquiry into my claims, and reasonable compensation for money unjustly withheld from me.

Sir O. Burne: Suppose, then, I were to offer you an increased allowance for your eldest son on your death, and buy a moderate estate for him as a gift, would that satisfy you?

Maharajah: Certainly not. I am a king. My son ought to have what I have and an estate befitting a prince. This you will not give. No. The Government of India want to get rid of me and my family, that we may sink into oblivion.

Sir O. Burne: Well, Maharajah, I see that benevolence won't do. Picture me, therefore, an austere Secretary of State. Suppose I were to say to you, 'You are disobeying our distinct wishes by going to India. You will therefore be seized when you get there, you will be deprived of your stipends, and be made to reside in some spot selected by the Government of India.' What then?

Maharajah: I should laugh at you. This is just what I want. You must at any rate clothe and feed me and my family, and my income will be then more than made up by subscriptions from every ryot in the Punjab, and from every part of India. Moreover, I know that no Government would dare resort to such a step in view of English public opinion, and the consequences of it in India.

Sir O. Burne: Well then, Maharajah, I see that, from your point of view, neither benevolence nor austerity will meet your case. What on earth are you going to India for? I cannot quite understand why a nobleman like you, who has embraced Christianity, who, whatever you may say to the contrary, has had a comfortable home in this country, and has been treated with consideration, should want to go to India, where you will certainly not be comfortable, and may risk the loss of all you have got.

Maharajah: I have already taken the first step to abjure Christianity, because I no longer believe in 'so-called' Christian Governments.

I am resolved to go to India, in order to settle at Delhi, where I can resume my native habits, bring up my children to a livelihood there, get my hawking and shooting &c. The Government of India should let me do this. If they touch me, it will shake the Punjab, if not now, at any rate later on. I am determined to go. I have fixed the 17th February, but I may delay a week. My friends advise me to stay on, to see if I can get an inquiry, and, moreover, there is now a change of Government, and I think Lord Kimberley will befriend me.

After a few more words the Maharajah left. Throughout our conversation we were both perfectly good tempered, my sole object all the time being to endeavour to ascertain *what* would satisfy his so-called claims. On leaving he repeated his wish for an inquiry, he thanked me for receiving and listening to him, and left an impression on my mind that he really intends to go to India as a last venture, and that his so-called claims necessitate some very large concession if they are listened to. It is only fair to add, however, that the Maharajah emphatically repeated, 'If I am granted an inquiry, and adjudged to receive nothing, after a fair examination of my claims, I shall be satisfied.'[10]

What exactly *did* the Maharajah hope for? Did he really expect a very large cash handout to meet all his claims? Did he really expect an inquiry when he had been told so many times that it was impossible? Did he really want to leave his sport and his friends and go to India and become a Sikh guru? He was like a man in a maze, uncertain how to emerge.

Following his receipt of Burne's memorandum, Kimberley, who had placed the problem firmly in the lap of the viceroy, telegraphed Dufferin on 2 February: 'Recent interview with Burne confirms opinion that no reasonable concession would be accepted. Still, it might be useful to know the maximum limit of pecuniary concession you would recommend.'[11]

This significant question was not to be answered for several weeks, meanwhile the Maharajah asked for an interview with Lord Kimberley. Kimberley, though reluctant to involve himself personally in the matter, agreed to an appointment as 'otherwise he would have represented me as unwilling even to hear what he had to say'.[12] All the Maharajah had to say was a polite reiteration of his position and an assurance of his loyalty. But he wanted an inquiry – 'Pray understand', Kimberley reported him saying, 'that nothing like an offer of £5,000 or £10,000 a year to my income would satisfy me. I want an inquiry into my claims.' Kimberley thought his demands 'preposterous' and gave little hope that they would even be considered. On leaving, the disappointed Maharajah, who had at least expected a more sympathetic attitude from a Liberal minister, could say no more than: 'I see it is all of no use, but I shall wait a few days to see whether I get any satisfaction, and if not, I shall go broken hearted to India.'[13]

So the Maharajah, it appeared, was staking all his cards on arbitration. It is possible, however, that he was still playing a cunning game of bluff in the knowledge that this was a course which the India Office had rejected on a matter of principle, and 'principle' was for them, once invoked, likely to be as immovable as a mountain. But pressure on that weak point might lead to their yielding to his financial demands, sufficiently at least to enable him to restore his position and assuage his pride. At the same time there was the beckoning finger of fate that led to India and the glorious destiny of the eleventh guru.

Meanwhile, despite the Maharajah's statement to Kimberley that his sole object in going to India was domestic, and his undertaking to stay at Ootacamund with 'loyalty and obedience', the authorities there were all the time uncovering native plottings in his name and by no means desired his presence even under the most stringent supervision. 'Has Duleep Singh started for India?' Dufferin cabled on 18 March, 'if not, what are his present intentions?'[14] 'Duleep Singh intends leaving on the 31st in *Verona*' was the reply.[15]

Kimberley was now down to his last card – a cash offer. 'Can you now reply to mine of the 2nd of February?' he cabled urgently. But the viceroy seemed in no hurry and did not answer until 20 March:

Duleep Singh question was considered by Council during my absence, and I have now seen their opinion. We are willing to afford the Maharajah such relief as can be obtained by maximum grant of £50,000. This sum, or a small sum which you think sufficient, could be applied, first, to payment of any debts due to persons other than Government, second, to decreasing of debt due to Government, so as to make reasonable addition to Maharajah's income. Money would be given on understanding that Maharajah abandoned all claim to mines or other private estate, that he gives acquittance in full, and effectual undertaking never to return to India, and that no further payment will be made hereafter on any ground. Grant would preclude all future claim regarding five lacs fund and provision for family.[16]

So £50,000 was the price they put on the Maharajah's total surrender. Little more than enough to pay off his overdraft at Coutts!

It fell to Sir Owen Burne to impart Kimberley's ultimatum based on the viceroy's offer. It was to be part stick invoking the stringent Regulation 111 of 1818, which gave the Indian government power to detain without trial, and part very small carrot of a cash settlement. On 24 March the Maharajah and Sir Owen faced each other once again. After preliminary politenesses Burne read out the minister's statement:

The Secretary of State has received with satisfaction the repeated assurance which the Maharajah has given of his unshaken loyalty and devotedness to Her Majesty, and it need scarcely be said that it would give Her Majesty's Government the greatest pain if anything should occur to disappoint the expectations, which they trust they may confidently entertain, as to His Highness' conduct in India.

In view, however, of the communications received from the Maharajah, specially those letters which relate to a certain Sikh prophecy and to His Highness' announced intention on arriving in India to be re-baptised into the Sikh faith, the Secretary of State thinks that, before the Maharajah proceeds to India, it is due to His Highness that he should be reminded that, independently of the right under the Terms of Lahore of 1849 to withdraw his pension if he does not remain obedient to the British Government and reside in such places as the Governor General of India may select, he will, whilst in India, come under the provision of Regulation III, of 1818, by which the Governor General in Council is empowered, for reasons of State, to place under personal restraint individuals against whom it may not be deemed proper to take judicial proceedings; those reasons being the due maintenance of the alliances of the British Government with foreign Powers, the preservation of tranquillity in the territories of Native Princes entitled to its protection, and the security of the British dominions from foreign hostility and internal commotion.

The Secretary of State further desires to make known to the Maharajah that the Viceroy, having had His Highness' various applications under his consideration, has recently informed the Secretary of State that the Government of India would be willing to grant His Highness a sum not exceeding £50,000, to be applied, first, to payment of any debts due by him to persons other than the Government; and, secondly, to decreasing the debt due by him to Government, on condition that His Highness enters into a formal engagement to desist from all claims whatsoever on the Government and never to return to India ...

Sir Owen went on to describe the Maharajah's strange reaction:

The Maharajah listened attentively to the first portion of the Note, and, on my asking him if he clearly understood it, replied in the affirmative, saying that he had considered the whole matter, and was quite aware that the Government of India had the powers of which I had reminded him. I then proceeded to read the second portion of the Note, upon which he observed, with vehemence, that nothing would induce him to accept the 'paltry sum' offered; that his claims to private estates alone reached £400,000 a year; that he was not in debt, and wanted no money; that he was resolved to go to India, and that on no account whatever would he sign any paper either in renunciation of his claims or binding him never to return to his own country.

I deemed it my duty to assure the Maharajah that the communication I had now made to him had been inspired solely by feelings of consideration towards himself, and to save him, if possible, from blindly pursuing a course of conduct which exchanged a life of certainty for one of uncertainty, and which could only end in misery to himself and his family. His Highness replied that he was not unmindful of this, and not ungrateful for the kind intentions of Government towards him. He then entered into a somewhat rambling statement, assuring me, in the first place, of his loyalty, and warning Government, in the second place, of the risk they would run if they imprisoned him in India. That step would exactly fulfil one part of the Sikh prophecy; then to find himself in some, as yet unknown, Sikh village, to be supernaturally elected as Prophet and to lead the Sikh nation; there was then to be a great war between England and Russia, in which he was to have a part, although it was not yet known which side he was to take; that he was now to be a fakir, and that he cared no longer for his position or property in England. After warning the Maharajah that all this was merely dreaming, as to which he might some day have a sad awakening, I took my leave, His Highness reassuring me that nothing would induce him to accept the grant of money offered to him, and that he had made all arrangements to leave for India on the 31st instant. He was firm and quiet in his manner during the interview, and thanked me very warmly at the end of it for what he called my courtesy towards him.[17]

Immediately on his return to Holland Park the Maharajah put his uncompromising position in writing:

With reference to the communication you were directed to make to me by the Secretary of State for India this afternoon, I think it only right to state, for his information, in this letter that not even for five hundred thousand pounds (£500,000) were it offered to me, would I either give quittance for my just claims on the British Government, or bind myself never again to go to India.

The offer of fifty thousand pounds (£50,000) made to me by you for the above purpose this afternoon would have been treated by me with the greatest contempt, were it not that it came from a Minister of Her Majesty's Government for whom I have sincere respect.

My position on re-embracing the faith of my ancestors will become, in fulfilment of the prophecy, that of a Sikh Gooroo, and should the Indian Government be so ill advised as to imprison me, I dare not predict the serious consequences that will follow sooner or later. For it will be believed by the Sikhs, of whom a considerable number are in the British Army, that I suffered degradation not in consequence of any disloyalty on my part towards the Government, but on account of my having renounced Christianity and embraced Sikhism.

It is extremely distasteful to me to say anything with reference to the above subject, but as a loyal subject I must do my duty, however painful, and warn Her Majesty's Government against the blind and suicidal policy intended to be followed towards [me] in India, who am the son of the old ally of England.

I must confess that, thinking over what passed at our interview this afternoon, I have become convinced that the prophecy regarding myself will be literally fulfilled, and that I shall really be the Gooroo of the Sikhs after all, through the misguided policy of the Viceroy. But I do not care what happens to me, for my trust now is in the God of my ancestors, and in my destiny.

Farewell, Sir Owen. May the blessings of the God of Baba Nanuk rest upon you.[18]

To make his intentions perfectly clear, the contents of Elveden were sent to the sale room and thousands of catalogues at a shilling each were dispatched to interested buyers. There was a vast amount of furniture listed, much of it in amboyna wood, and sandalwood inlaid with ivory. The sale was scheduled to run from 27 April to 5 May by which time the Maharajah had firmly determined to be out of the country. On 25 March he released to the press the text of a letter to his fellow countrymen that indicated he was about to take the first step in the evolution of the Sikh prophecy:

London, 25th March 1886.
My beloved Countrymen, It was not my intention ever to return to India, but Sutgooroo, who governs all destiny, and is more powerful than I, his erring creature, has caused circumstances to be so brought about, that, against my will, I am compelled to quit England, in order to occupy a humble sphere in India. I submit to his will, being persuaded that whatever is for the best will happen.

I now, therefore, beg forgiveness of you, Khalsa Jee, or the Pure, for having forsaken the faith of my ancestors for a foreign religion; but I was very young when I embraced Christianity.

It is my fond desire on reaching Bombay to take the Pahul again,

QUEEN VICTORIA'S MAHARAJAH

and I sincerely hope for your prayers to the Sutgooroo on that solemn occasion. But in returning to the faith of my ancestors, you must clearly understand, Khalsa Jee, that I have no intention of conforming to the errors introduced into Sikhism by those who were not true Sikhs – such, for instance, as wretched caste observances or abstinence from meats and drinks, which Sutgooroo has ordained should be received with thankfulness by all mankind – but to worship the pure and beautiful tenets of Babu Nanuk and obey the commands of Gooroo Govind Singh.

I am compelled to write this to you because I am not permitted to visit you in the Punjab, as I had much hoped to do. Truly a noble reward for my unwavering loyalty to the Empress of India. But Sutgooroo's will be done.

With Wah Gooroo jee de Futteh,* I remain, my beloeved Countrymen. Your own flesh and blood,

Duleep Singh.[19]

The effect of such a proclamation on the security of India can hardly have been shattering. As an editorial in *The Pioneer*, the widely read newspaper published in India, commented: 'In brief it means that his Highness has no intention of giving up either beefsteak or brandy pawnee. What effect the manifesto will produce remains to be seen. If Duleep Singh makes himself troublesome he will have to face the consequences. He may have reason to conclude before long that the position of a well-to-do English country gentleman is more comfortable than an Oriental pretender.'[20] But the peculiar proclamation was shocking enough to Kimberley who read it in *The Standard* and deputed Sir Owen Burne to ascertain its authenticity. Sir Owen sent round a messenger who returned with the Maharajah's answer: 'The letter is perfectly genuine, and therefore I do not desire to repudiate it. We leave here at about ten this evening, and sleep at the Great Eastern Hotel in Liverpool Street, so as to be ready to quit England tomorrow morning.'[21]

That day the queen saw her foreign secretary Lord Rosebery at Windsor and, according to the journal, after talk 'of the

* Blessed be the name of our glorious guru!

Greeks & the French who behaved ill; of trouble with Pce Bismarck about Zanzibar', she brought up the subject of 'the poor M. D-S, who is becoming very violent & threatens open defiance, & his going to India to raise the Sikhs! All this is perfect madness, & Ld Rosebery thinks he had not been well managed & that money should be given him, to prevent him going to India.'[22]

But there was nothing to be done about it. The following morning the Maharajah's party, consisting of himself, the reluctant maharani, his six children, a Sikh attendant, a native servant, a European nurse and an *ayah*, embarked on the P & O *Verona* bound for Bombay. His last letter, written on board before sailing, was to the queen:

My Sovereign, Before quitting England I humbly venture to address Your Majesty in order to convey to Your Majesty the inexpressible gratitude I feel for all Your Majesty's graciousness both to me and mine during my stay in this country now extending over some 30 years.

So long as I live I shall never forget all Your Majesty endeavoured to do on my behalf with Your Majesty's ministers.

I could not face the pain that such an event would cause me if I ventured to take my leave of Your Majesty in person and therefore I humbly implore Your Majesty's forgiveness for not paying my last homage before starting for India.

That God may bless Your Majesty and grant you a long life and every happiness both in this and the world to come is the humble but fervent prayer of Your Majesty's Heartbroken subject,

Duleep Singh.[23]

His last telegrams, however, were to Thakur Singh and three other co-conspirators in India. They contained the single word 'Started'.[24] The messages were intercepted by the authorities in India and the recipients duly put under close observation.

CHAPTER 13

Arrested at Aden!

IN India rumours of the return of the former Maharajah of the Punjab were circulating in the bazaars. The time was ripe: it was a period of developing nationalism; the wounds of the Mutiny had not entirely healed; the vernacular press was influencing the newly educated classes to regard the British as oppressive. Colonel Hennessy, commanding the 15th Sikhs, asked by Government House for his opinion, asserted that:

... the gravest discontent prevails, and has long prevailed ... and on that point I am positively certain ... It is the law courts that are driving these simple minded people to distraction. They are very good for lawyers of every degree, but are draining the life drops of the unfortunate population. It embraces the entire system of the internal Government of the country. This being the case it is extremely probable that the people would not object to a change of rulers, although I firmly believe they would prefer to be ruled by Englishmen if only the laws were remodelled to suit their own views and ideas. In regard to Dalip Singh's influence over the Sikhs he would indeed be a bold man who could say he had no fear of it in his own regiment. I most devoutly trust the subject will not be put to the test in my day. The spirit of the Sikhs is not dead, and they are full of national fire. I should tremble in my shoes were that gentleman to arrive at our borders with the Russians! The British Government should hold him fast and secure in England in my opinion.[1]

The 'Abstract of Political Intelligence, Punjab Police No. 11' of 20 March 1886 and 'No. 16' of 4 April summarized the current situation:

The Maharajah Duleep Singh is expected to arrive in India in April. People in Delhi are speculating as to where he will reside.

Anxious enquiries are being made about His Highness in Hoshiar-pur and wild rumours are current regarding the powers that will be conferred on him. Thakur Singh Sandhanwalia is said to have sent letters announcing that the Maharajah has re-embraced the Sikh religion in England, and has betrothed both his daughters to the Buriya Sirdars in the Ambala district. The Sikhs are elated and declare that they will pay their respects to His Highness, if per-mitted to do so by Government. The Hindus, on the other hand, pray that Duleep Singh and the Sikhs may never come into power again, but are of the opinion that the Nihangs and Kukas* may be foolish enough to join in any demonstration got up in his favour. The Maharajah, they say, will lose his pension, and Sirdar Thakur Singh will get into trouble before long, as he is of an intriguing and grasping disposition.

The question of whether Sikhs will be permitted to visit Dhulip Singh after his arrival in India is a good deal talked about. The Sikhs are in favour of his being allowed to embrace the Sikh reli-gion if he desires to do so. Jamiat Rai ... came to Gurdapur on the 14th April with the intention of proceeding to Bombay, whither, he said, he had been summoned by the Maharajah Dhulip Singh by telegraph. He gave out that, on Dhulip Singh's arrival at Delhi, he would interview all the Sikh Sirdars (evidently careless remarks). The Russian Government, he added, are friendly to the Maharajah and have a secret understanding with him. He expressed hope that before long Dhulip Singh will be placed in power and position as a ruler.[2]

The viceroy had confirmation of the untoward departure in a telegram from Kimberley dated 31 March. The message continued with information that gave him more cause for anxiety than had been suggested by the Maharajah's earlier bland communications about his acceptance of a place of resi-dence and his intention to abide by the viceroy's orders:

In recent communications with Political Secretary he has used language of menacing character, referring to eventual troubles in India, war with Russia, and part he may take as head of Sikh nation. An address from him to Sikhs, stated to have been sent to India, just published in newspapers here and since acknowledged by

* Nihangs and Kukas: doctrinaire Sikh sects.

Maharajah to be genuine. It announces his intention to be rebaptized into Sikh faith, with view to take his place as Gooroo of nation. Maharajah lays stress on text of alleged prophecy announcing successive steps by which he is to be restored to power. He no doubt intends to circulate this in India. Affairs, if neglected, might possibly give serious trouble, but I have no doubt you will take whatever measures you may deem necessary to prevent any dangerous feeling being excited amongst the Sikhs. Duleep Singh's communications should be carefully watched. He is now in a state of mind which seems to border on monomania.[3]

The monitory wording of the telegram, with its misleading summary of the Maharajah's proclamation, caused some show of nervousness at Simla, the hot season seat of government, and the legislative department set themselves to investigate the legality of cutting his progress short before he reached India. The only legal expert not then on leave was bold enough to maintain that as Aden came under the jurisdiction of the Indian government he should be arrested there, and a warrant was accordingly made out on the grounds that it was necessary 'for the security of the British dominions from internal commotion'.[4] Thus the order for arrest was issued under the all-embracing Regulation III of 1818, which was hardly designed to apply to British citizens such as the Maharajah could reasonably claim to be, and it was suggested that it might be as well to consult the highest legal authority in India, the advocate general, as to its validity. Sir Courteney Ilbert, the council member who was personally handling the affair, rode over the proposal with an evasive minute: 'I do not think it worthwhile to do this. It is necessary for reasons of State, that Dhulip Singh and his party should be detained, and we must run the risk of the legality of our proceedings being questioned. So far as I can see, we have done our best to conform to the law.'[5]

On 15 April the order went out from Simla to Aden:

Maharajah Duleep Singh with Maharanee, six children, and servants is passenger by Peninsular and Oriental *Verona* from London. Please require whole party to land and detain them under sur-

veillance at Aden until further orders. You can inform Maharajah
that the address which has been issued by His Highness renders his
return to India undesirable. Should His Highness on this announcement express a desire to go back to England, he may be allowed
to do so in an English ship, on giving you a solemn pledge in writing that, in consideration of his release from his present detention,
he will not renew his attempt to return to India and will abstain
from all treasonable practices.

Keep me informed by telegraph of the result of your proceedings.[6]

On the same day the viceroy reported his questionable
action to London:

In consideration of fact noted in your telegram of 31st March,
that Duleep Singh has issued an address to Sikhs, which he acknowledges to be genuine, and in which he announces intention of
assuming authority over Sikh nation, and which, at the same time,
indicates steps by which he is to be restored to power, and in view
of communication made by him to Political Secretary at India
Office of a menacing character in reference to eventual trouble in
India and war with Russia, we have thought it desirable to issue
warrant for detention of Maharajah and party at Aden. Orders to
this effect have been sent by telegraph to Aden authorities.[7]

On the day following, the gentlemen in Simla were
embarrassed to read a transcript of the Maharajah's proclamation in *The Pioneer*,[8] the text of which was confirmed by
'communications' just arrived in the mail from England.
Where was there mention of 'assuming authority'? Where
was there reference to prophecy? Ilbert admitted that 'the
case against the Maharajah is less strong than the telegram
led me to suppose', but held 'that the Council orders of April
15th were justified by that telegram'.[9]

There was some argument about whether the family
should be named on the warrant. 'What are the ages of the
children?' it was asked. 'We must not court ridicule by serving warrants on babies.' It was finally decided to name only
the Maharajah and, if possible, to avoid producing the warrant at all.

213

The viceroy's follow-up message to London dated the six-teenth, did not mention the discrepancies, presumably because newspapers and dispatches had not yet been perused, and referred to the proclamation as 'disloyal'.

We have instructed Resident at Aden to inform Maharajah that the issue of his disloyal Proclamation appears to render his return to India undesirable, but that he will be at liberty to go back to England in an English vessel, should he so desire. We are now dis-patching to Aden trustworthy Political Officer who will be in-structed to enter into communication with Duleep Singh, in case he refuses to embark for England, with the view of ascertaining whether it is possible to obtain from him such security for future good conduct as may be necessary. It is needless for us to point out great inconveniences which would arise were His Highness allowed to take up his abode in India with the avowed object of exciting revolt in the Punjab, without Government of India taking every precaution to render abortive so mischievous a design.[10]

For the information of Queen Victoria, Kimberley sent Ponsonby the telegrams ordering the Maharajah's detention, personally disassociating himself from the action and placing responsibility firmly on the shoulders of the Indian govern-ment. In his covering letter, he wrote: 'This is a matter which is eminently the province of the Viceroy to deal with, as it is impossible for any one not on the spot to appreciate what danger may arise from such proceedings as those of the Maharajah. We may hear at any moment of his arrest as the ship should arrive at Aden today.'[11]

The queen was 'rather startled' when she heard the news, but did not exactly disapprove. 'This is rather sharp practice,' she scribbled on the message, 'but better than if he went to India. He has brought it on himself.'

The *Verona*, delayed by headwinds, reached Aden on 21 April. The Maharajah, who had donned his Sikh costume at Suez, had been the cause of much discussion among the passengers, most of whom had had to listen to his tale of woe – one of them described him as 'very loquacious'. Victor and

Freddy were particularly popular on board, the former openly saying that he objected to his father's proceedings and referring to him as 'my idiotic parent'.[12]

On arrival, the Resident, Brigadier General Hogg, came on board, and under the interested eyes of the passengers informed the Maharajah that by order of the government of India he could not be allowed to proceed any further. Though Hogg had the warrant in his pocket he discreetly retained it and took care to avoid the word 'arrest'. The Maharajah, however, refused to leave the ship before he was officially 'arrested', and it was necessary for the brigadier to tap him symbolically on the shoulder, after which he protested vehemently and invited the attention of all present to the fact that he was not leaving the ship willingly, declaring that there would be a 'great State trial' as the outcome of the action they were witnessing. Passengers and crew gave a loud and sympathetic cheer as he and his family filed down the gangplank into 'captivity'.[13]

The brigadier general had the viceroy's order: 'It is desirable that His Highness should be treated with all due personal consideration, and that his comfort should be provided for at Government expense as far as circumstances permit. Most important that the health of the party should not suffer. Maharajah should not be permitted to communicate with the outside world.'[14]

Back at the Residency, Hogg did his best to make his visitors feel they were guests rather than detainees. Though it was made clear to the Maharajah that he could return to England when he wanted to, he was unwilling to do so and thought at first of going to Egypt with Bamba and the children, but he decided to stand his ground and take the opportunity of exploiting his arrest to his own advantage. Having sent his family back to England, he would try some arm-twisting on his own account. His bold proposition was embodied in a telegram sent by the Resident to the viceroy:

Maharajah states his reason for not wishing to return to England is that he cannot face ridicule, but His Highness will agree to return to England and sign any protocol, provided Government promise a full judicial investigation of all his claims by Law Lords of the House of Lords, with a view to granting him only a reasonably equitable redress within six months, and provided Government pay him immediately, on reaching London, the sum of two hundred and fifty thousand pounds sterling as compensation for the sacrifice of his liberty, which, as a loyal subject, he is asked to make, in binding himself not to visit India without permission of Government.[15]

The Maharajah was insistent upon making it clear that even though he had been charged with issuing a 'disloyal address' he still regarded himself as a 'loyal subject'. He was anxious to give no justification for being considered 'disloyal', a status that would have put him in bad grace with the queen and the British public and justified his arrest by the Indian government. On learning that his actions had been so described on the warrant, based on the wording of a proclamation that had in fact been passed by his lawyer, he was anxious to make that point clear to the viceroy, with whom he now had permission to communicate: 'I desire your Excellency clearly to understand that whatever instructions you give, provided the word "disloyal" is not employed with them, or I am requested *not* to return to India, will be loyally carried out by me. If it is desired to detain me here for any length of time, I request that I may be permitted to correspond with friends in England, and also that my 17 servants awaiting my arrival at Bombay be sent on here, the Government paying all their expenses.'[16]

Dufferin's patronizing reply was designed to pour oil on troubled waters. There was only the most oblique reference to the loyalty issue, and it cannot have offered much consolation to the frustrated Maharajah, cooped up in the stuffy Residency, uncertain which way to turn to strike at his intangible enemies:

I desire to thank your Highness for your telegram, and to assure you that it is my desire that your Highness should be treated with every possible respect and consideration. I deeply regret the unhappy circumstances which have occasioned your Highness's detention at Aden, especially as I had taken some pains to arrange for your Highness's comfortable establishment in this country; but, if your Highness will forgive the expression, the ill-advised documents which have been put into circulation by your Highness have imposed upon the Government the necessity of asking your Highness to abandon your idea of coming to India.

I this morning telegraphed to the Secretary of State the circumstances connected with your Highness's detention at Aden, and as soon as I shall have received His Lordship's reply, I will communicate at greater length with your Highness. I am very sensible of the courteous manner in which your Highness expresses your willingness to comply with any suggestions which may be made to you from hence, and your Highness may rest assured that no expression shall be used calculated to wound your Highness's feelings.[17]

It was perhaps as well that the Maharajah had changed his mind about going to Egypt. The viceroy had taken the precaution of checking with the all-powerful high commissioner in Cairo, Sir Evelyn Baring, who had no wish to see trouble stirred up in his own recently settled fiefdom, and encyphered his negative response: 'It is most undesirable that Dhuleep Singh should come to Egypt. He is sure to fall into the hands of those who are hostile to us and he will probably exercise a bad influence on the Khedive and the Pacha clique as well as on the Mukhtars and on national opinion generally by distorted accounts of British policy in India especially as regards native princes. Nubar Pacha, whom I consulted very confidentially, is much opposed to his coming.'[18]

Having packed his family off to England, the Maharajah's next tactical move was to fall back on the hope that the viceroy personally might improve on cash offers already put forward in London. On 29 April he telegraphed: 'One object I had in view in going to India was personally to lay my claims on the British nation before your Excellency, as I had gathered hopes from different sources that whatever recommendations your Excellency made to the Home Government would be acquiesced in, but now that I am prevented from proceeding there, what steps am I to take in the matter?'[19]

In reply Dufferin maintained his friendly tone but was not to rise to the lure:

In reply to your Highness's telegram of the 29th, I beg to say that your Highness's representations had been very carefully considered by the Government of India, and the communication which was made to you before leaving England embodied its view of the case. Should your Highness on returning to England be inclined to address me privately as a friend, it would always be a pleasure to me to give you the best advice in my power.

In conclusion, allow me to express my deep personal regret at having been the cause of exposing your Highness and your Highness's family to inconvenience in the discharge of my public duties.[20]

On finding this approach firmly blocked the Maharajah, who told Hogg that 'his expectations were shattered'[21] was now determined to make himself as much of a nuisance as possible. The telegraphic charade continued with the Maharajah's apparently amiable but ultimately embarrassing reply: 'Return heartfelt thanks. Will gladly address your Excellency as a friend should occasion arise. On further reflection, determined on sending family to England at my own cost for education. I remain here prisoner at your Excellency's pleasure. Request that Government pay expenses of and send 17 servants from Bombay. Addressed letter last mail to your Excellency.'[22]

The letter referred to enabled the Maharajah to express at greater length than the telegraph would allow, the ideas that had been churning in his mind. He was determined to reestablish himself as a loyal, if mis-used citizen. That point having been accepted, he may have hoped that the viceroy, with his plenipotentiary power, might settle affairs to his advantage both as a paternal friend and a forestaller of further trouble.

As I desire to remove the erroneous impression which appears to have been caused on your Excellency's mind regarding the publication of the documents alluded to in your Excellency's kind and considerate telegram of 22nd April, in reply to mine of same date, I venture to address your Excellency on the subject.

The document I submitted to Lord Salisbury setting forth my claims and his reply have been published both in English and Indian journals, with the view of laying my case fully before the public, and with the intention of appealing both to my brother Princes and people of India for pecuniary aid on behalf of my unfortunate children shortly after reaching India, as the Government do not appear to care to grant me any adequate redress for the great injustice I consider I have suffered at the hands of the British nation, who, if the Blue Book speaks the truth, were my guardians, and are even now my trustees, but for no other or disloyal reason.

The address to my co-religionists has been published from no disloyal motives whatever, but simply as my public renunciation of Christianity, and to lay before my countrymen my bitter complaint against restrictions put upon my movements in India and thus classing me with the disloyal. For, your Excellency, it is incomprehensible to me, and appears extremely hard on me, that, whereas the Maharajahs Sindia and Holkar, as well as the Nizam and others, who all possess great wealth and armies that might cause some anxiety to the Government, are permitted liberty of movement, poor I, who have but only some score of servants in all and a very limited income, am about to be entirely banished from setting foot in my native land, where I had hoped, by strict economy (which is not possible in England), to have laid something by from my stipend during my life for the benefit of my unfortunate children, should the aforesaid appeal on their behalf have failed.

Your Excellency, the late Marquis of Dalhousie, immediately after the annexation, when many of the old Sikh Sardars and soldiers were still living, did not think it dangerous to the stability of the English rule to appoint Fatehgarh as a permanent residence for me, but now, after a lapse of some 35 years, during which period the British Raj has been now firmly established in the Punjab, my mere setting foot in India is about to be prohibited, because I have published some documents for reasons already explained, and am placed under arrest here under false, and to me *most hateful*, accusation of issuing a disloyal address.

Your Excellency, I dearly loved my English home, where I

would fain have ended my life and which it has broken my heart to leave.[23]

The viceroy was still not prepared to enter into arguments about the loyalty issue, nor did his reply seem to indicate that 'all possible consideration' amounted to more than admonition. But in a letter to the queen, of whose special interest he was all too aware, informing her of the story of the arrest, he ended with a strong indication that he was of a mind to make a cash offer:

... Lord Dufferin has received a very kind and considerate letter from the Duke of Grafton who seems to have taken great pains to go into the Maharajah's affairs & to have shown him an extraordinary amount of personal kindness. It seems to be the Duke's opinion that there is one point in the case where perhaps His Highness may have a certain amount of right on his side. This point it is Lord Dufferin's intention to have most carefully examined and if fair grounds can be established for any further concession he will be very glad to take advantage of them but it has of course to be remembered that any further relief which may be given to the Maharajah must of necessity come out of the pockets of the Indian Tax payers, & therefore that it would not be just or right to indulge His Highness, except a fair justification can be made out for doing so.

No sooner had Dufferin completed his promising letter than he received the message that the Maharajah intended to remain at Aden. The viceroy reacted to the aggravating information in a postscript:

Lord Dufferin is sorry to say that since writing the above he has received a most provoking telegram from the Maharajah saying that he has changed his mind, and that he intends constituting himself a prisoner at Aden, while sending his wife and children to England – Lord Dufferin has told His Highness in reply that he is very much surprised that he should have changed thus suddenly his mind, that there is no question of his being a prisoner as all Europe not to say Africa is open to him but that of course if he chooses to remain at Aden he is at liberty to do so, under certain conditions.[24]

The queen's reaction from Balmoral no doubt caused eyebrows to be raised among the hard-headed members of the viceregal entourage.

The Queen Empress thanks the Viceroy for his last kind letter of the 5th May about the poor Maharajah Duleep Singh. He was so charming & good for so many years, that she feels deeply grieved at the bad hands he has fallen into and the way in which he has been led astray, & the Queen thinks it will have a very bad effect in India if he is ill-used & rather severely punished & especially if the Maharanee (an excellent pious woman) & their six children especially the two boys, quite Englishmen, are in poverty or discomfort. In the Maharajah's present state of excitement nothing can be done but he is sure to quiet down & then the Queen is ready herself to speak to him. Some money should be settled on his wife & children & a good man of business be placed about him & enough given him to enable him to live as a nobleman in England. The Queen wishes he or his son could be made a Peer & then they could live as any other nobleman's family. It is most important that his Indian advisers & relatives should be kept from him for they are those that have brought him to this pass.[25]

The queen was not aware that one of his scheming Indian relatives had in fact arrived in Aden; Thakur Singh★ had hoped to meet him in Bombay but hearing of his arrest had taken the first boat west. 'I desire to take advantage of my cousin's presence here to be re-initiated into Sikhism,' the Maharajah wired the viceroy. 'Kindly telegraph Resident, saying I may go through the ceremony in his presence.'[26] The viceroy referred the matter to his man on the spot, the lieutenant governor of the Punjab, who advised that 'refusal would be misunderstood and might cause irritation as interference with freedom of religious convictions; it would also magnify his importance. So long as he does not return to

---

★ There was some confusion in India as to whether this was the Thakur Singh of the Sandhanwalia family who had visited the Maharajah in England, and who was thought to be in Delhi at the time, or another cousin of the same name from the Wagah branch of the family. It appears to have been the latter.

India or Punjab, consent will do little if any harm. A few persons might make capital out of conversion, but most of the intelligent and loyal Sikhs understand situation and are comparatively indifferent. Intended baptism long rumoured. I would not advise that Resident be present.'[27] This advice was translated into a telegram from the viceroy to the Resident: 'You can allow the ceremony to be performed, but it is not desirable that you yourself should be present, or that any of our officials should have the look of countenancing the proceedings. On the other hand, if you can manage it, it would be well to prevent any private communication between the Maharajah and the Punjab gentlemen. I dare say your tact and skill will enable you to arrange the business in a desirable manner.'[28]

The ceremony by which the Maharajah returned to the religion of his ancestors took place in the morning of 25 May. Five Sikh witnesses were prescribed, and it was necessary to borrow two from a ship in the harbour. In accordance with his parole, given as 'a Prince and a Gentleman', he made no effort to converse with his initiators who were packed off to India by the next boat. The previous night, in honour of the queen's birthday, the Resident had given a large dinner party and the Maharajah had attended sporting his diamonds. The weather was even hotter than usual and he had complained of feeling 'very queer in the head'. Doctors Jackson and Hay reported 'weak action of the heart'.[29]

The government of India would be placed in a most embarrassing position should their charge become seriously ill or even die while under questionably legal detention at Aden. Apart from the queen, he had powerful friends in England and only the day before his initiation into Sikhism, Mr Hanbury, in the House of Commons, had raised the question of his detention, and in view of the under-secretary for India's unsatisfactory reply had given notice of his 'intention to take an early opportunity of calling the attention of the House to the general treatment of the Maharajah'.[30] The Indians, however, seemed less concerned about the fate of their compatriot, though the *Shamshar Akhabar*, a vernacular paper published in Madras, carried a long article about him claiming that he had been harshly treated and confined to a desert island, and that his detention was a mad act on the part of Lord Dufferin.[31]

Four days after the doctors' diagnosis the Maharajah's health had sufficiently improved for him to return again to the attack. On 28 May he telegraphed the viceroy: '... I demand both as a domiciled Englishman and a loyal British subject to be publicly tried for any disloyal act I am accused of having committed against my most Gracious Sovereign's Government, and to be punished, if found guilty, or set at liberty if otherwise.'[32] The Indian government had by now realized that they were in a weak position over the loyalty issue and certain changes were made in the records at Government House. 'His Excellency has directed me to strike out the word disloyal in the first telegram,' the viceroy's private secretary wrote to the political secretary, and on the papers being forwarded to Sir Owen Burne in London, H.M. Durand, the India government foreign secretary, remarked that some of the enclosures 'were somewhat altered from their original shape in order to avoid the publication of some possibly inconvenient passages'.[33] Fully aware that he had placed the viceroy in an embarrassing position, the Maharajah pressed the attack with a demand that he be promised an investigation into his claims to property in India and implied that he would not move from Aden until his demands were met. In a minute that laid bare the heart of the matter, Mortimer Durand, the foreign secretary, advised the viceroy what he already knew – that such a course was not admissible: 'I think there is nothing to be gained and much to be lost by such an investigation as is proposed in this telegram, and I would not agree to it. The result would be to keep the case very much before the public and to open up a number of political questions which are better left alone. I would reply that I had no power to make the required promise, and that I do not think such an investigation could be of any advantage.'[34] This advice was tersely communicated to the Maharajah as 'Government of India has no power to make any promise of the kind.'[35]

Though he must have expected such an answer, the desperate Maharajah was straining for a way out of his predicament. The previous day, by way of further embarrassing the viceroy, he had asked if he could telegraph the queen appealing for a public trial on the loyalty issue. An admission by the viceroy that the original charge had been removed from the record might have enabled the Maharajah to claim substantial damages for wrongful arrest, and Dufferin may have felt some anxiety that his handling of the case would be unfavourably criticized. But he could hardly refuse the Maharajah permission to communicate with the queen and accordingly, on 1 June, he telegraphed: 'Having been arrested on charge of publishing an Address alleged disloyal, I have demanded a public trial of the Viceroy in order to refute the accusation, therefore appealing to the proclamation issued when Your Majesty assumed the title of Empress of India that justice shall be rendered to all your subjects, I pray Your Majesty to cause my demand to be granted. [signed] Maharajah.'[36]

It was Ponsonby who phrased the royal reply: 'I have gladly received your denial of having issued a disloyal proclamation and I have desired my Secretary of State to enquire into the matter. General Ponsonby will see Lord Kimberley tomorrow.'[37]

Back in the lap of the India Office! The confused Maharajah, his stance at Aden shown to be in vain, responded with a last desperate manœuvre to obtain a public hearing. Unaware that Dufferin had doctored the telegram that had originally charged him, he telegraphed the queen: 'I do not deny having issued the alleged disloyal address, but implore that a public trial be granted me either to prove my innocence or guilt and punishment.'[38] If he was to be hanged for a sheep, he wanted to be tried for a sheep. There was no reply from the palace. What was there to say when the secretary of state, who considered the Maharajah 'quite off his head',[39] had so unsympathetically explained to the queen that one of the main purposes of the regulation under which he had been arrested had been to keep such cases out of court?

At the same time as the troublesome telegrams were passing to and fro, the viceroy decided to take positive action to have the Maharajah removed from Aden. Apart from the fact that he might die on them, whether he wished it or no, the Resident was becoming bored with his house guest and was anxious to go off on a trip to the Somali coast; there was the added problem of the Maharajah's request for a household establishment of twenty-five Indians to administer his needs now that he was a Sikh. Accordingly on 1 June Dufferin instructed Hogg: 'If medical officers inform you in writing that further stay on the part of the Maharajah at Aden will endanger his life, you may consider yourself as under orders from Government of India to require him to proceed on board first P. & O. vessel bound for Suez. You must remember that we have no legal power to take this step, but under the circumstances I consider it will be justifiable.' Hogg was also advised to tell the Maharajah 'in as gentle terms as possible' that should he come to India they would be forced to take 'very decided steps'.[40]

The Maharajah realized that the Aden game was up. The next boat out was the French mail steamer on its way to Marseilles. That at least would be less humiliating than travelling P. & O. to England. 'I return to Europe, from 1st July next. I resign stipend paid to me under Treaty of Annexation, thus laying aside that iniquitous document. Perhaps Government may care to continue payment of 500 pounds sterling per annum to each of the widows of my late Superintendent and Comptroller Oliphant respectively,' he telegraphed the viceroy.[41] To Ponsonby he sent the defiant message: 'I return to Paris being unable to obtain justice. Resigned stipend thus ending Annexation Treaty and getting rid of all dealings with the most tyrannical Government in the world, Indian Administration.'[42] He did not mention that he had told his lawyer that he had no objection to his allowance being paid to his wife.

On 3 June, the Maharajah sailed on the s.s. *Natal* bound for Marseilles. The queen, still at Balmoral, learned of his departure the following day. Her erring subject was on the loose, out of touch with her and away from the control of her ministers. She was angry with Lord Kimberley for his apparently hard-hearted treatment and annoyed that her expressed wishes should have such little effect. What would her Maharajah get up to next? What was to be done?

'Some kind and firm person,' she ventured in a scrawled memorandum, 'shd. meet him at Paris & set him straight – pacify him & prevent his ruining his Children. The Queen's godson she must see shd. not be ruined by his poor, she is still convinced, good-hearted but utterly deluded father's follies. The Queen is gtly. grieved abt. it as she was so fond of him and for many years he went on *so well*.'[43] When Kimberley deputed Sir Owen Burne to look after Bamba, the queen noted: 'Not a vy. good person to choose as he is ill-disposed towards the Maharajah.'[44]

On reaching Suez, forlorn yet defiant, the Maharajah posted off to *The Times of India* a letter that indicated that there might be some truth in Kimberley's assertion that he was going 'quite off his head'.

Sir, Will you permit me, through the medium of your influential journal, to narrate a few events in connection with myself, in the hope that they may prove interesting to the general public. Although I am a naturalised Englishman, yet I was arrested at Aden without a warrant, one having been issued since. I re-embraced Sikhism while staying at Aden. Before quitting England the Indian Government, in great trepidation, offered me £50,000 in full settlement of all my claims upon it, provided I promised never to return to India. But I declined this offer, as I would not accept £500,000 and give a receipt in full. My health having broken down through residence at Aden, I am now travelling on my way back to Europe, in order to drink the German waters.

Although the Indian Government succeeded in preventing me

from reaching Bombay lately, yet they are not able to close all the roads that there are to India. For when I return, I can either land at Goa or Pondicherry, or, if I fancy an overland route, then I can enter the Punjab through Russia. In that event I suppose the whole of the British army in India would be sent out, as well as the assistance of 'our ally' the Amir invoked, to resist the coming of a single individual, viz., myself. What a wonderful spectacle!

The taxpayer of India, no doubt, will be glad to hear that I have resigned the miserable stipend paid to me under that iniquitous treaty of annexation, which was extorted from me by my guardian when I was a minor, thus setting aside that illegal document entirely. As soon as restored to health, I hope to appeal for pecuniary aid to the oriental liberality of both my brother princes as well as the people of India. Should, however, the Government place its veto upon their generous impulse, then I shall have no alternative but to transfer my allegiance to some other European Power, who, I daresay, will provide for my maintenance. I find it very difficult to collect my thoughts at present owing to bad weather.

Yours, &c.,

s.s. *Natal*, Suez.   Duleep Singh.[45]
7th June 1886.

CHAPTER 14

'A Rebel Now in Earnest'

THE Maharajah did not in fact go to 'drink the German waters' as he had indicated was his intention; he established himself in Paris and immediately began the next round in his struggle with what had by now become virtually the entire power structure of the British empire. He must have felt that even the queen had forgotten him: she did not write: his friends Grafton and Henniker had suggested to her that it was 'better to leave him alone till he has calmed down'. They assumed that as he 'could not afford to give up his allowance, he would probably come to reason when he required money again'.[1]

The Maharajah was by no means 'calming down', and the raging of his mind is revealed in a letter he sent to un-offending old Sir Robert Montgomery at the India Office, who was only trying to help, begging that no communication should be addressed to him from there. 'I neither respect such a tyrannical and unjust administration, nor am I any longer loyal to the British crown (having offered my services to Russia)' he continued. 'I seek nothing from you gentlemen as I have been refused justice and my loyalty insulted. I have only one prayer now, that God may, before I die, enable me to have revenge on the Indian administration and humiliate that Government, and to cause the expenditure of many more millions of poor John Bull's money than the £3,000,000 I should have asked for the loss of my private property, out of which I have been so piously swindled by the Christian British nation.' He signed himself 'a rebel now in earnest'.[2]

The Maharajah had already been in touch with the Russian ambassador. That he was indeed in earnest in transferring his allegiance was conveyed to Grafton in a letter from Paris: 'I wrote yesterday to the Russian Ambassador offering my services to the Emperor and requested a passport which as soon as I receive I shall go to St. Petersburg. If I am well received by the Emperor I shall go to the border of India. If not I shall go to Pondicherry and be a thorn in the side of Lord Dufferin.'[3]

When the queen saw a copy of the letter, which Grafton, as was no doubt intended by the sender, forwarded to the palace, she must have realized for the first time that the Maharajah was really beginning to run amok, and she tried with all her powers of persuasion to still the passions apparently affecting his mind. First he had forsaken the faith of which she was the Defender and now he talked about going over to those hateful Russians, whom she was shortly to refer to as 'fiends'.[4] She wrote from Windsor on 6 July 1886:

I hear extraordinary reports of your resigning your allowance, & of your intending to transfer your allegiance to Russia. I cannot believe this of you who professed such loyalty & devotion towards me – who you know has always been your true friend & who I may say took a maternal interest in you from the time when now 32 years ago you came to England as a beautiful & charming boy. In earlier years, your life with its interests & thoughts, your home with your aimiable wife & five [sic] children, was a pattern to all Indian Princes. But after the death of your really true & devoted friend Col. Oliphant, bad & false friends have surrounded you & put things into your head & heart. Let me appeal to all that is good & noble in you to abandon wild ideas & plans wh. can only plunge you into deeper difficulties & lead to disastrous consequences.

Think of me as your best friend & the Godmother of your son. Trusting you may be able to give me assurances that the reports are untrue. Believe me always, your true friend . . .[5]

Grafton, who was shown the queen's letter, wrote to Ponsonby: 'He must be far gone if he resists such friendship.

His readiness to give up his religion is a very bad sign for you would have been astonished (the Prince of Wales was at Euston & heard him) at the wonderful sermon, one may call it, he gave us after dinner at Euston some years back (Dorchester having *professed* to know *more* of his former religion than he did himself) when he explained all the Religions he had studied & finally said "that he found no comfort in any until he understood Christianity & *then* he found *hope in a Future*".'[6]

The Maharajah's reply cannot be said entirely to have 'resisted the Queen's friendship', and though on one level it seemed to be totally intransigent, on another there was the implication that he had not yet committed himself to the Russians but would return to the fold if he was given satisfaction:

Gracious Sovereign, I am highly honored by the receipt this day of Your Majesty's most gracious letter and return my heartfelt thanks for this mark of great condescension.

It greatly pains me to inform Your Majesty that it is no longer in my power either to contradict the current reports or to give the assurance which you so graciously demand. For Your Majesty's Government having branded me disloyal when God knows I was most loyal and devoted to Your Majesty I had no other course left open to me except either to turn traitor or continue to submit to the insults repeatedly offered to me by the Administration of India. Unfortunately however my nature proving too proud to follow the latter course I offered my services to Russia but as yet have received no definite reply and I would willing[ly] return to my former allegiance if full justice were rendered me.

I am not responsible most Gracious Sovereign but it is the Council of India and Lord Dufferin together are responsible for driving me away from my allegiance to Your Majesty.

I have most Gracious Sovereign not only resigned my stipend but have also set aside and annulled that wicked Treaty of the Annexation of the Punjab which was extorted from me and my ministers by the late Marquis of Dalhousie when I was of tender age and the ward of Your Majesty's Government. For I do not see why the weak is bound to observe the stipulation it contains and not the strong?

It deeply pains me and also Your Majesty can not but be much displeased that I am compelled to make such a reply to so gracious a letter as Your Majesty has honoured me with but I must speak the truth no matter what the consequences might be.

Your Majesty I implore you to pardon me when I say that I am a proud Sikh although I may and most likely will break yet by the help of God, I will never bend however disastrous the consequences of my own acts might prove but will cheerfully lie on the bed I have made for myself.

Most Gracious Sovereign believe me when I say that neither a friend nor a foe 'has put these notions into my head and heart'. It is the study of the records of the wicked deeds of my guardians as preserved in the Blue Books of 1848–9 and the subsequent refusal both on the part of the Council of India and the Home Government to render me some measure of justice added to that very recent degradation inflicted on me at Aden that has embittered my feelings.

I am deeply sensible and to the day of my death will never forget Your Majesty's boundless graciousness to me and mine but history teaches us that it is the sense of injustice and suffered wrong, the cruel coercion, and infliction of tyrannical oppression that has driven many men to desperate deeds and I also am human.

Imploring your forgiveness most Gracious Sovereign for thus freely giving vent to my feelings and for any expressions or word that might appear disrespectful towards Your Majesty as well as for this badly written letter but being much out of health I am not able to write any better.

I most humbly implore to be permitted to subscribe myself, Your Majesty's most devoted humble faithful servant ...[7]

In his letter to the Russian ambassador in Paris the Maharajah had asked for an interview and must have felt that in view of the imperialistic rivalries between the two powers in the East he would be warmly received and given all possible support. It was, in fact, a period of *rapprochement*, with teams to establish an acceptable boundary in Afghanistan already in the field; in any case the Russians were giving priority to their expansion towards the Mediterranean rather than towards India.

From the report of the Russian ambassador, Kotzbue, marked 'secret' and 'personal', to his master, the foreign minister, de Giers, it is apparent that the Maharajah's approach was lacking in subtlety, nor was the production of the queen's letter likely to further his cause even if it did establish his bona fides as a man with good connections:

Monsieur le Ministre, Maharajah Daleep Singh has come to see me to show me and make me read an autograph letter which he had just received from Queen Victoria, I should have liked to take a copy of it but he did not consent.

The Queen has written to him in affectionate, even maternal terms reminding him of the care that she had bestowed on him in his childhood, her position as God-mother to his child and her hopes that he would become a 'pattern' for all Indian Princes. She requests him to abandon the path he has taken under the influence of bad counsellors and she asks him if she should believe the rumour that has reached her that he has offered his services to Russia.

'From where does the Queen know that you came to the Embassy?' I asked him. He seems not to know.

While questioning him again about his intentions and the results that he expects from his contact with Russia, I have come to know that he hopes to extract a large sum of money from the English Government.

Hence, it is to be feared that the offers which the oriental Prince makes us are only a means of blackmail. He thinks he will be able to frighten the English and make them pay by threatening them with the prestige that he would gain by placing himself under our protection.

The Maharajah says that he would accept the money that he might obtain because he is poor but all the same he will not return to England. He says that he insists, whatever may happen, on placing himself under the protection of the Imperial Government.

On my observing that it would not be right *vis-à-vis* England and that the English would not be so simple as to give him money without making sure of his loyalty, he said that they are so afraid of the difficulties he could raise for them in India, that they would make any sacrifice only in return for the hope of preventing him from it. He hopes to extract out of them up to three million pounds sterling.

Whatever may be the future chances of the Maharajah, at present it is apparent that it is not through strict honesty that he reckons to distinguish himself.

Kindly accept Monsieur le Ministre, the homage of my most respectful and profound devotion.

Kotzbue.[8]

While privately not discouraging military adventurism in Central Asia, de Giers was not anxious to be caught out making trouble with the western powers for no useful purpose. It was in that spirit that Kotzbue also informed him: 'Not wishing to go to his house in the likelihood that Duleep Singh is watched by British agents, and thinking that a verbal communication is more subject to fantastic misinterpretation than a letter, I have therefore written him.... This is the only written material from the Imperial Embassy in his hands. The Maharajah has not replied and has not been to see me again.'[9]

There was indeed little the Maharajah could have said on receipt of the Russian response, worded, perhaps, to be read by other eyes:

Highness, The Imperial Government protects peace. It wants it and maintains it in its own vast possessions; it desires it in those of the other powers and feels that the Governments are jointly responsible in their effort of guaranteeing among the peoples the benefactions of security and stability of institutions. Far from it, hence, the thought of favouring or provoking troubles in India.

No reason impels it and Your Highness would not find the means necessary to realise plans of insurrection or of vengeance.

I am authorised to affirm this to you in consequence of what you were good enough to say to me in the course of our interview.

Kindly accept etc. Kotzbue.[10]

The Maharajah was in a position he described to Grafton as 'desperate', still uncertain whether to hope for arbitration and thus be able to return to England and his family with some degree of honour, or whether to proceed further along the road to rebellion, which was already turning out to be stony. As the India Office seemed to be ignoring him totally, the Maharajah tried out his new weapon to gain their attention – the proclamation. For a start, he sent copies of the first announcement he proposed to make to his countrymen to his lawyer, and his instructions to let Grafton look at it might indicate that he expected it to be passed on. Grafton indeed was quick to send it on to Ponsonby at the palace:

I have received a copy in *strictest* confidence of a letter addressed to the Sikhs which the Maharajah intends (if not sent already) sending to all the Indian papers asking them to insert it. It is so wrong a letter and so seditious that one cannot believe the journals will insert it: but if not certain, I do not know what Dufferin may feel about such a Circular, but I think he should be warned of such a letter & perhaps he has power to prevent its insertion. All I can say is, privately, that if anything the Maharajah can do can cause trouble this Circular is meant to do all the mischief he can. He sent two copies over and told Mr Lawrence *no* one was to see it except myself 'if he thought it wd. not make me too unhappy'. If I could propose anything to save him from his folly I would, but I see no way and unfortunately Lord Salisbury is more against him than any minister I have communicated with last year & this. I should think the Maharajah's last act was not to be ignored completely.[11]

'No. 1   *Dated Paris, the 15th July, 1886.*

By the grace of Sri Sat Guru Ji we Maharajah Dalip Singh, the lawful sovereign of the Sikh nation, under the Treaty of Bhyrowal entered into without coercion between ourselves and our Durbar on the one part and Great Britain on the other, do from hereby in consequence of the insults and indignities repeatedly offered us – of which the recent imprisonment inflicted on us at Aden is a proof as well as an account of no fulfilment with us of the stipulations of the Treaty of annexation of the Punjab by the Indian administration, set aside and annul that iniquitous and illegal document, the so called 'Terms granted', which was extorted from us in 1849 by our wicked Guardian, the Christian British nation, when we were an infant of only 11 years of age, and by the above first mentioned covenant, under the protection of England.

Wah Guru Jee de Fateh.

Sd. Dalip Singh,
Maharaja of Sikhs under Treaty of Bhyrowal 1846.'[12]

The proclamation was in essence no more than a personal renunciation of the Treaty of Lahore, but the queen was sufficiently alarmed to ask the viceroy what he thought might result from its publication in India. Dufferin replied that he had consulted his colleagues and the lieutenant governor of the Punjab and concluded that it would have no 'appreciable effect' and that 'it would not be advisable to take action in reference to Duleep (and his claim?) (or proclamation?)'.[13]

The Maharajah was holding back the publication of the proclamation; Grafton thought that 'in his heart he longs to be out of this mess'.[14] But time was passing and his plottings were coming to a head. On 7 September he sent Grafton a confused statement of his position, which showed that he still wanted to be made to change his mind:

I am constrained to address you a few lines again as time is passing away & the sympathy I have created for myself among my countrymen will die away unless I keep myself constantly before them in one way or another.

A lawyer gave me a hint some time back that you were most kindly corresponding with Sir H. [Ponsonby] & trying to have a Court of Arbitration apptd. & Henniker was also of the opinion that by patience the present Govt. might be induced to follow such a course. I have kept back the publication of my two proclamations.

I shall not be satisfied with anything less than Court appt. to investigate into & arbitrate on whole question....

I earnestly implore you and Henniker not to expose yourselves to a refusal on my behalf...the wretched treaty which thank God I have torn up.

P.S. I am under a Solemn Compact to my country not to accept less than £3 million or the award of the Court of Arbitration. This time led by me the Sikhs shall fight for their rights.[15]

Grafton sent the letter to Henniker, and Henniker sent it on to the palace. In his covering letter to Ponsonby Henniker wrote: 'If the Govt. would accede to what the Duke of Grafton & I proposed in our Petition to the Queen *at once*, I hope it might be accepted, & to end a difficult & disagreeable business. Of course, if it goes much further there will be no retreat from either side.'[16]

As far as the India Office was concerned there was no intention whatever of a retreat. The secretary of state, Lord Cross, stated unequivocally that arbitration was 'impossible' and that 'as far as the Maharajah was concerned nothing further could be done'.[17] It was clear that their policy was simply to ignore him.

Neither was there any sign of a retreat from the Maharajah. Though he denied having authorized it, two of his 'proclamations' appeared in the newspapers and various stories were published about his plans to co-opt the Russians. Grafton realized that events were moving rapidly and that the Maharajah had lost no time 'for fear', as Grafton expressed it, in a letter to Ponsonby, 'of being pressed to relinquish his folly'. He continued: 'At all events he has done for himself, but is he to do this and England support his wife & family. I do not know with whom I find most fault; the Government who behaved ill to him, ignored him, & drove him to folly, or the Maharajah for his folly – but I see nothing but a mess, I only hope *ignoring* him may not turn out a real mistake & bring trouble on us. It is easy to judge *after* events, but it now seems Dufferin was wrong; he ought to have let the M. go to India & *then* if he did *anything* shut him up; now he is at large & mischievous – I really believe he is off his head.'[18]

The Maharajah at this time made another approach to the Russians, duly reported to de Giers at St Petersburg by his Paris ambassador.

Maharajah Daleep Sing has come again to see me. He tells me that proclamations have been published in the Punjab calling upon the people to revolt in his name and with the assurance that it would be supported by Russia. He affirms that this has come about without his giving the order, even without his knowledge. But he thinks that a rising in the Punjab would perhaps be opportune today in view of the political events which are brewing. He has again offered his services to the Imperial Government, in spite of our reply which had rejected his first overtures. Moreover, he thanks us for having clearly declared that he cannot count on us. If he continues to have hopes, it is because he is convinced that a war between Russia and England is imminent.

I have told him that he should not have illusions, that the reply he had received was final.

'Then so as not to expose my poor people, I shall send the order to my adherents to suspend all action.'

'That is what is best for you to do.'

He wished to remain in Paris for about two months more and then will try to go to Pondicherry to settle down there.

While leaving me, he again repeated to me that the war with England is inevitable and that notwithstanding our present refusals, we shall see him serving our cause because of his hatred against the power which had despoiled him and because of his thirst for vengeance.

He congratulates himself that we shall find in his people a very useful ally, considering that it lives at the borders of the frontiers of Afghanistan and its warlike qualities surpass those of the other Indian peoples.[19]

It is clear that the Russians did not entirely dismiss the Maharajah's approaches: the correspondence was passed to the Tsar Alexander III, who wrote on the above letter in his own hand, 'maybe sometime it will be useful'.

On 10 October the Maharajah seemed to have made up his mind. 'I write to say that it is now too late', he informed Henniker. 'I start very shortly for the East. I could not recede even if I wished (which I do not except on my own conditions). There was not a more loyal subject than I was before my recent arrest. It was foolish on political grounds to refuse me a Court of Arbitration such as I demand ... There are 45,000 Sikhs in the British Army. To expect such a thing as devotion from a conquered people towards their conqueror is against human nature. It is true they have been loyal – but they have no leader. I am now with them.'[20]

Henniker sent the letter on to Ponsonby, who observed that the Maharajah's 'language and conduct' had 'alienated the Queen's friendship for him', and that now she only felt anxious that the maharani 'should not suffer for her husband's folly'.[21]

The Maharajah's dramatic statement that it was 'too late' and that he was shortly to start for 'the East' was still un-implemented by December. The feverish state of his mind at that period is revealed in his correspondence with Robert Watson, an associate from Mulgrave days, who had been helpful in his obtaining support in his plans to contest Whitby. It was Watson who had been responsible for getting Hanbury to ask his question in the House and was now press-ing him to force an inquiry into the whole matter. The Maharajah's reply to Watson's encouraging letter shows something of the tortured processes of his mind during this period:

I thank you very much for your letter which shows me that there are still some right minded Englishmen in England.

It is most kind of Mr Hanbury to think of bringing my case before Parliament, but I am persuaded that he would be disappointed with the result were he to do so. For he is not likely to succeed where the sovereign herself has failed. Lord Salisbury has already refused to grant a Court of Arbitration composed of Law Lords of the House of Peers, and he is not likely to permit a discussion of my claims in the House of Commons. It is very easy always for the Government of the day to cause the House to be counted out whenever a member desires to force a discussion of a disagreeable topic and my tale would reveal to the British public that Russia is not the only unjust, unscrupulous, and immoral nation in the world. England appears at this moment to be much interested about the liberties of Bulgaria, because Russia is meddling with their free-dom, yet Great Britain herself hesitated not to depose me, her ward, from the throne she had guaranteed me by the Treaty of Bhyrowal in 1846 and deprived the aspiring Sikh nation – those eighty millions of people – of their own nationality when it suited her own purpose. Yes! 'People that live in glass houses should not throw stones at others.' Yes! India groans under the Christian injustice of England, but out of loyalty to the Empress I remained willingly blind to the misery of my countrymen until I suffered the degradation of an arrest at Aden last spring when my loyalty ended. I, a naturalised Englishman and (before God I declare) a most loyal subject of England apprehended, without a warrant, and prevented from exercising my liberty as such to reside in any part of the British Empire. A public trial not even having been granted me to refute the charge of disloyalty brought against me by the administration of India, because I happened to supply a common form of salutation current among the Sikhs, viz. Wah Guru jee de Fatteh as a victory to the teachers, in a proclamation which I issued to my countrymen before quitting England on religious matters is a treatment that no man of honour would for a moment submit to, far less I, the proud son of the Lion of the Punjab.

No, Watson! I have done with the British Government for ever and by the help of the God of my fathers, I will for once at least overthrow the tyrannical, immoral and unscrupulous administration of India.

Let Russia give me only 10,000 men to appear on the North-West frontier of India, and the thing is done. For there are some 45,000 of the Punjabis, my former subjects, in the British army at this moment, who would come over to me at once, and when other British troops would be sent to oppose me then the whole of the Punjab would rise in their rear. Also all Native Princes would make common cause with me, for they have suffered injustice like myself from our present rulers.

In endeavouring to bring this about, I do not seek any advantage to myself. I shall do it purely out of revenge for the wrongs I have suffered at the hands of my guardians, the British Government, who pretended to regulate their acts by the tenets of Christianity. Vile Hypocrites!

I enclose copies of two proclamations which will shortly be issued. Hitherto no proclamation has been issued either by my knowledge or sanction in the Punjab.

Good bye Watson! May God bless you.

(sd.) Dalip Singh,
The Lawful Sovereign of the Sikh Nation under the Treaty of
Bhyrowal with Great Britain, 1846.[22]

Stripped of its vainglory, the second proclamation was little more than a plea to the people of India to provide funds:

Brother Princes and Nobles and the people of beloved Hindustan.

By the grace of Almighty God, the Creator of the Universe, the most merciful and gracious, and of Sri Govind Singh ji, We Maharaja Dalip Singh, the lawful sovereign of the Sikh Nation, have set aside and annulled that treaty of annexation of the Punjab, which, to the disgrace of Great Britain, be it said, was extorted from us and our Durbar, when we were of tender age, and ward of Christian England under the treaty of Bhyrowal 1846 (in order to lay his wicked hands on our dominations) by the late Unscrupulous Marquis of Dalhousie.

But the moral (?) British nation is no respector of 'Solemn covenants' and treaties when its own interests are at variance with the interests of the weaker contracting parties thereto; as most of you as well as ourselves know by experience.

No doubt, your mighty rulers will call upon you to refute the above assertion, but dare they deny that it is not in their hearts what the leading journal in England *The Times* not very long since (in spite of the proclamation issued when it suited the purposes of Great Britain in the name of the Empress of India immediately after the suppression of the mutiny of 1857, to the effect that the internal administration of your respective dominions would not be interfered with by Her Majesty's representatives in Hindustan) advocated, viz., the abolition of your armies, the maintenance of which is dearer to you than life itself. But fortunately for your friends, just about that time a storm commenced to gather on the north-west frontier of India, in the presence of which your mighty rulers did not feel themselves sufficiently strong to carry out such high-handed measures and you escaped therefore the fate intended for you.

However, let us hope now that evil day may never dawn upon you, for the poor old British lion is becoming so treppid [sic] indeed as to show the 'white feather' at the mere buzzing of a gnat, but that, however, is not to be wondered at, because the Sikh is the son of the renowned Lion of the Punjab as well as the lawful sovereign of the Sikh nation, and like his people, who by their valour saved the British empire in Hindustan in 1857 from utter annihilation, at least, fears no odds that might be opposed to him.

The poet spoke truly when he said, 'It is conscience that makes cowards.'

Yes, the Government of India are conscious of the wickedness practised by them towards us, the ward of the righteous British nation, and tremble lest we should come and avenge the wrong inflicted upon us by our guardian. For in great trepidation, they offered us £50,000 in full satisfaction of our just claims provided we signed a protocol never to return to Hindustan without their permission.

But their Christian immorality knows no bound, for rather than render justice, the Government have preferred to commit another and still greater wrong so as to try to cover the first by refusing us a court composed of Law Lords of the House of Peers to enquire into and arbitrate these (admitted by Lord Salisbury to be so) 'controverted matters' on the miserable plea that they had not the power to appoint such a tribunal. The Government of Great Britain powerless to grant a court of arbitration!!!! Ah! what mockery! What falsehood!!! On our part, however, we should have cheerfully accepted the verdict of such a court as final had it awarded us but a single pice in damages.

We, therefore, appeal to your oriental generosity, Brother Princes and Nobles and the people of Hindustan, as we vastly prefer to suffer the greatest degradation, humiliation and shame of Bheck Manga or begging our bread from you beloved countrymen, to being under any pecuniary obligation to such a most iniquitously unjust, tyrannical and foreign Government, who, though professing code of high morality, piously swindled us out of our Kingdom, and defrauded us of all our private property, both of which the British Nation as our guardian under the Treaty of Bhyrowal 1846 had taken upon itself to protect during our minority, and is bound in honour either to restore the whole or give equitable compensation for the same, but Jesus Christ, by whose tenets these Christians profess to regulate their morals, has not said in vain that we do not gather grapes of thorns nor figs of thistles; therefore, not even in England is justice to be had.

In the glorious days of yore, it used to be the pride of your ancestors to defend the weak who sought their protection as we seek yours this day against the strong, though they might lose all

241

they possessed in doing so. Therefore, if that spirit of noble chivalry is not quite dead among you, then aid a brother Prince and countryman in adversity.

The Government of India out of spite may indeed put its veto upon the generous impulse of your hearts, but if you all unite, it will be powerless to harm you as you cannot all be deposed or sent to the Kala Pance for not paying any heed to the arbitrary behest of such a timorous administration as it has now become. For see, that notwithstanding all its boasted vast resources how it dreads the return to India of a Sikh who unlike you does not even possess a single soldier.

Therefore, be not cowards but be brave and worthy of your great forefathers.

(sd.) Dalip Singh,
The Lawful Sovereign of the Sikh Nation[23]

The most rousing proclamation, presumably for release at a later date when the Maharajah appeared with troops on Indian soil, read:

Courage! Courage! Courage!

We your own flesh and blood, tell you, lift up your bowed down heads and drooping hearts 'for your redemption draweth near' and by the help of the Almighty, Aryavarta shall once more be free and the rising 'Young India' shall enjoy both liberty and self-government.

Yes, beloved countrymen, an avenger of our common great wrongs is indeed about to appear, and the just God of the Universe will shortly cause your wicked rulers to be crushed under his feet. But you must have a little more patience yet, so as to allow us to work out your salvation most effectually.

The iniquitously unjust and unscrupulous administration of India have succeeded at last by their arbitrary acts in driving us away from our (we declare before God) most loyal allegiance to the Empress of Hindustan, but by the aid of Providence they rue the day on which they dared to insult us by causing our arrest at Aden. For although we were naturalised Englishmen, yet we were placed under arrest without a warrant having been previously obtained for our apprehension.

The British Government dared not have treated a born Englishman as thus, but because we were not such, we were neither allowed a public trial nor were sufficient pecuniary means placed at our disposal (though we requested both) so as to enable us to procure legal advice in order to refute effectually the foul and revolting charge of disloyalty preferred against us towards our then Most Gracious Sovereign.

Behold then, countrymen, that there exists one law for the Englishmen and another for the hated Indian, though he might even be a Christian as we were previous to our arrest at Aden notwithstanding all the avowals to the contrary of the pious British Government.

If we, who were once heart and soul as one with England, and who would cheerfully have spilt the last drop of blood in the service of the Empress of Hindustan as an inadequate return for all her personal boundless graciousness towards us have been denied justice and even a hearing before a competent court of arbitration and branded disloyal when on the contrary we were most loyal. Then, what chance have you, brother Princes of India, for preventing the immoral administration of India – whenever it should suit their purpose – from ignoring the rights they have hypocritically guaranteed to you by so-called solemn treaties with England.

Therefore, believe our word when we tell you that you sit on your thrones only until a convenient opportunity presents itself to your so-called just rulers for your deposition. For look at what has lately taken place in Burma. In spite of the declarations of the Queen's proclamation of 1858 to the contrary, does it appear to you that the days of annexation have come to an end as yet?

Therefore, friends, if you have not yet entirely degenerated into cowards and become effeminates, nor turned into mere puppets in the hands of your deadly enemies, then rise up and make common cause with us and share with us also in the glory of liberating our mother country. But although we thus invite you to take part in this grand both work and duty, do not for a moment suppose that we shall seek any aid from you, for God has otherwise made us strong who were once so feeble.

Sri Khalsa ji, you by your far renowned great valour saved the British Empire in India in 1857 and you did well then to act so for we ourselves at that time were most loyal to England. Besides owing to our absence from India at that period, you had no leader appointed by Sri Sat Guru Ji of your own nation to instruct you as to the part that you should have taken in the warfare that was then going on, but now in the coming struggle sovereign both by the will of Sri Sat Guru Ji as well as in the virtue of the Treaty of Bhyrowal 1846 with Great Britain (under which Christian England assumed our guardianship, though by a most pious act shortly after they swindled us out of our Kingdom), we command you to prepare for our advance into the Punjab.

We command also such as of our loyal subjects as may then be serving in the British army, and who may be left behind, to attack the British forces sent against us in their rear and those who may be in the troops opposing us to come over to our side. But let our enemies and disloyal subjects beware for we intend to annihilate them utterly.

Sri Khalsa ji, we exhort you to study the Sakheean and learn therein your glorious destiny as predicted by Daswan Padshah Sri Guru Govind Singh Ji.

Wah Guru ji de Fateh   (sd.) Dalip Singh,
(February, 1887)   Sovereign of the Sikh Nation.[24]

Such warlike enclosures seem to have had a spine-chilling effect on the Yorkshire worthy, who replied in agitated tone almost oriental in style:

Your Highness, Your letter and enclosures duly to hand and have filled my heart with dismay. Would to God that I could see my way clear to avert the calamity which I see coming to you! For I am confident, my prince and dear old Master, that nothing but disaster and ruin await you if Your Highness will persist in the course you have laid out; rest assured that Russia will only aid you in so far as it would favour their future purpose. Then let me beseech you, my dear Old Master, by the mercies of Almighty God, whether the God on Whom I trust, or the God of your fathers, to hesitate before precipitating such a castrophe; and Englishman that I am, I should hate to see the accounts of triumphs of my own countrymen over you. No! My Prince, I refuse to believe but that some way is yet open for a reconciliation between my beloved Sovereign and your Highness. It is the fact of my knowledge of Your Highness's loyalty to the Empress of India that has been the greatest puzzle to me throughout all this business, and by the help of God I will not rest a day or night to avert your utter ruin. My deep love and attachment to you is equal to my own life and may the Father of lights be my guide and may I be the humble instrument, in his hands to assist you in your difficulties is the prayer of

Your humble & Faithful servant,
Robert D. Watson.[25]

Watson was so upset that he took what for him must have been entirely uncharacteristic action. Without telling the Maharajah he forwarded the letter and proclamations direct to the queen with the drastic suggestion, here made for the first time, that she should personally force the government to take action:

I most humbly desire to approach Your Majesty on behalf of dear Old Master, the Maharajah Dhulip Singh, and to implore Your Majesty to use every effort to avert a catastrophe which I am satisfied will be disastrous and bring ruin to him, and bring no credit to our own country.

My first duty as a loyal subject is to Your Majesty, and secondly to do my utmost to try and avert the utter ruin of one to whom I am deeply attached. With this object I enclose the copy of a letter I have just received from the prince, bearing date 7th, and I beg most humbly to implore Your Majesty to bring pressure to bear on Your Ministry to at once do justice and avert a calamity.

I have only to add that I should wish this communication to be held strictly private, the intended proclamation I should only be willing to place in the hands of Your Majesty's Private Secretary, and not in the hands of any of your ministers and unless Your Majesty asserts your authority as the head of this realm I can see nothing but danger ahead.

I also enclose a reply I have sent to my Dear Old Master.

I am, Most Gracious Sovereign, Your True and Loyal Subject,
Robert D. Watson.

P.S.
Madam, I see only two courses open. One to force as head of the nation, Your Government to do an act of common justice, or secondly to command the Prince to Your Majesty's court at Windsor, and to exercise that influence over him which I know Your Majesty to possess.[26]

The Maharajah may have thought that Watson's urgent response represented the anxieties of the British public as a whole and even of those in authority, for his reply indicated that he was still under the impression that he had some cards to play and some threats to make that would shake the India Office from its complacency. His offer to yield his position in exchange for £3 million and his restoration to the throne of the Punjab, indicated a thinking that was both wishful and tumultuous:

> Believe me, Watson, I have it in my power either to save or destroy the British Empire of India and I will either have £3,000,000 or my revenge. Let the British Government ask (some) 45,000 Punjabi soldiers employed in the Anglo-Indian army whether they will or will not fight against me if sent to oppose my advance with forces of Russia and convince themselves of the truth of my assertion that their loyalty would replace me on the throne of the Punjab and make use of my unique position for strengthening their empire.
>
> For I will guarantee that Russia or any other power in the world would never trouble them in India. They would thus have some 8,000,000 of the most brave people of India heart and soul with them, instead of not possessing the loyalty of a single Indian. But they have been dead to their own interest in suspecting me of disloyalty and not reposing implicit confidence in me.

27th December, 1886.   (sd.) Dalip Singh,
                                    Sovereign of the Sikh nation

If he thought he had gone too far in expecting to be restored to the throne of the Punjab, the Maharajah in a postscript had an alternative proposition:

> I might just as well tell you as this letter is not likely to be published in the newspapers that since I wrote you, I am assured of pecuniary aid up to one million pounds sterling (£1,000,000) and therefore, I am not likely to accept any proposal that the British Government are likely to make. As I only at present require £10,000, this sum will be placed in my hands within six weeks by which time the political events in Europe will have developed themselves more decidedly. The British Government if they do not

like to try the experiment of replacing me on the throne then let them only restore my estates, in the Punjab, giving me at the same time a peerage as well as an honorary seat both in the Council of India in London and the Council in Calcutta and publish abroad that I am appointed to enquire into and amend the petty grievances of the natives of India, which believe me, are like thousands of little fires ready to be blown into a great conflagration at any moment by the merest accident, and I shall be more than content to serve England loyally and undertake to establish Her Empire on the sure foundation of justice without which it will never stand. No one (though I say it of myself) knows so well as I do both the English and the Indians by the peculiar circumstances of my life.[27]

Poor Watson did not get much satisfaction from his correspondence with the seats of power. Having no response to his presumptuous suggestion that the queen should force her government's hand he asked Ponsonby to forward the correspondence to Cross, now a viscount, at the India Office. Lord Cross did not reply and the offended Watson wrote threatening to withdraw his work as a Conservative agent.[28] The secretary of state coldly replied that 'no useful purpose would be served in entering into correspondence on the subject'.[29]

The Maharajah's last pathetic communication with authority was to Sir Robert Montgomery, on 28 January 1887. He was still in Paris, but all his plans were made to leave:

Kind and good Sir Robert, might I beg of you to cause a receipt to be sent to my solicitors, Messrs. Farrer & Co., for the 'Star of India' which they forwarded at my request to the India Office some time ago, and which I am anxious to possess before my departure (which may now take place any day) from Paris.

Doubtless you will be surprised to hear that I have received promise of pecuniary aid up to £1,000,000, on certain conditions, and, from India, of assurance of loyalty of the entire Punjab and allegiance of some 45,000 Punjabis in the British army. Lord Dufferin has gained nothing, you see, by arresting me at Aden. After all, what he did not wish should happen (viz., that my countrymen be not in a position to show me sympathy) has happened. The trodden-down worm at last has been enabled through the mercy of God to lift up his bowed down heart and head in order to avenge the injustice and the insults (as the only reward for his loyalty) showered down upon him for the last 36 years.

I enclose also three proclamations, two of which will be published here in a few days, the 3rd a little later on. None are genuine that do not bear my signatures.

May the Almighty bless both you and your kind hearted good lady. Once more farewell.

Your most grateful,   (sd.) Dalip Singh,
Both Sovereign and Guru of the Sikh nation.[30]

Knowing his vacillating nature and still claiming to have some influence over him, Henniker and Grafton continued working for the Maharajah's rehabilitation. They were still intent on setting up an inquiry, apparently his minimum condition for giving up his dangerous plans, which Russian rejection did not seem to have dampened. The India Office, however, seemed determined to refrain from conciliation or even communication, though they were prepared to make some sort of a financial arrangement for the now deserted family. This concession was mainly due to the influence of the queen who had seen Lord Cross when she was at Holyrood and spoken to him, according to the journal, 'about the unfortunate M. D-S's wife and sons, who will have to be provided for if he throws up everything & goes quite wrong in his passionate excitement & irritation, having been misled by wrong-headed Indians and relations'.[31]

It was decided that out of the Maharajah's rejected stipend, £6,300 a year should be allowed the maharani and £2,000 a year to the eldest sons. The two eldest boys were more able to look after themselves: 'The young men in their tastes are thorough Englishmen,' Lord Dufferin wrote. He was less than altruistic when he went on to say, 'The more completely they can be induced to regard England as their home the better, as the appearance of even a grandson of

Runjit Singh in the Punjab might have inconvenient consequences.'[32] Victor was at Sandhurst and Freddy would
soon be leaving Eton to go to Cambridge. Henniker was
wondering what would be the best regiment for Victor to
join. 'Surely he would be better in a good regiment like the
Scots Greys,' he wrote to Ponsonby, 'than in the Grenadier
Guards, where he would practically be his own master ...
The Blues or any other Household regiment will bully
him ... We want him to be under a good Colonel, in a
good regiment, which does *not* go to India.'[33] With the
queen's approval they settled on the Royal Dragoon Guards,
the Royals.

The main problem was the younger children – Bamba
had for some years been virtually an invalid and totally
neglected their education; Oliphant had attributed what
he called her 'strange habits' to the fact that some eight years
ago she had fallen on the ice; Kimberley had the story that
'whether from despair or being neglected she had taken to
drinking alcohol to an injurious extent'.[34] But according to Dr
Lawson, of the American mission in Cairo, who had come
over to comfort his former charge, 'there was nothing wrong
with her at all.'[35] Because of Bamba's inability to cope
with the situation Henniker undertook to become the
children's legal guardian, and Arthur Oliphant, son of the
Maharajah's late comptroller, took over the task of actually
bringing them up. 'It is all a sad sad story,' Arthur Oliphant
wrote, 'and I feel most thankful that my dear old Father was
not spared to know him [the Maharajah] as he is.'[36] He
moved them all to his house at Folkestone where he and his
wife effectively became foster-parents to four confused young
Indians. Oliphant recalled their old nanny, Miss Dale, who
had left when Bamba became difficult, and gone to Russia
to look after Princess Gortschakoff's children. She would, it
seemed, have a hard job ahead, for Oliphant reported that
the girls, 'did not know how to walk like young ladies' and
'the poor Maharni was also going to give them lessons in
callisthenics, and always going to take them to church, but

these intentions, as indeed all others, were never carried out'.[37]

Despite the efforts of well-wishers in England, the Maharajah was proceeding with his seditious plans. He described some of them in letters to Thakur Singh in India: 'I am glad you have come down to Pondicherry. Stay there and continue intriguing with the Sikhs and the Native Princes ... Please be careful in your goings, for if you act openly the English, who are at present on friendly terms with the French, will get you turned out of Pondicherry ... Send me some money as soon as you can. Without it I cannot proceed any further. The Russian Minister at Paris has asked me for £1,000,000 without which he will not allow me to do anything with his government ... I have offered 3½ million as tribute to Russia. You should now try and ascertain from Nizam, Baroda, Holkar and C [Cashmere] whether they will join me in paying this sum and thus driving away the English from India. But, as far as I am aware, they are puppets in the hands of the English and I cannot expect much from them. Tell them Russia cares very little for India and the Indians. She cares only for money ... I want to have a monarchical government. I will rule India something like Germany by which the Native Chiefs will be independent kings. I will never allow any other nation with the exception of Indians to take part in the administration of the country ... I have appointed you my Prime Minister and you are at liberty to negotiate with the Native States in my name.'[38]

The Maharajah was consorting with any anti-British element in Paris who cared to contact him, particularly the Irish Fenians, committed with American aid to the freeing of Ireland from English rule. The Fenians had been staging acts of terrorism for the past twenty years, culminating in the Phoenix Park murders in 1882. In the following year they had tried to blow up the public buildings in Whitehall which very nearly wrecked Sir Owen Burne's room at the India Office. For their various acts of terrorism, five of the 'Invincibles' had been hanged; a number were on the run in

Paris. Among the Irish expatriates were two brothers, Patrick and James Casey, fine examples of Irish revolutionaries who, when drunk enough, could command an inspiring flow of rhetoric. They wrote poetry for the Irish papers and supplied the English press with alarming tales of Irish conspiracies. They took the Maharajah under their wing, printed his manifestos, and encouraged him in the more fanciful aspects of his projects.

It was through Patrick Casey that the Maharajah came into communication with the great Russian journalist, Katkoff, editor of the *Moscow Gazette*. Katkoff's family connection with members of the imperial court enabled him to express opinions in opposition to official policy: if England was giving aid and comfort to Russian revolutionaries, he would do the same for enemies of England, particularly if they could further the cause of Russian territorial expansion. Katkoff was interested in the Maharajah and his case even if his government appeared not to be. He invited him to Moscow and promised the support of his newspaper.

During those heady days in Paris, the Maharajah had developed a romantic relationship with an eighteen-year-old English girl called Ada Wetherill. Her father was said to be a major general and her mother his housekeeper. She called herself an actress and was by no means what Lady Logan would have described as a lady. When the Maharajah decided to go to Russia she was sufficiently attached to follow him and his fortune wherever the road might lead.

CHAPTER 15

'England's Proud Implacable Foe'

THE Maharajah, as usual, had difficulty in making up his mind which course to adopt. Should he go straight to Russia? – the Russian foreign office had officially rejected his approaches, even if Katkoff and the Irish had led him on. Perhaps he should settle for becoming 'a thorn in the side of Lord Dufferin'[1] and set himself up under French protection in Pondicherry, but then the president, M. Grévy, had not had the courtesy to reply to his request. Another plan was to establish himself as near as possible to the Indian frontier, where he could enter into communication with such potentially friendly princes as the maharajah of Kashmir, the nizam of Hyderabad, the Maharajah Holkar, the deposed King of Oudh, and the minister of Gwalior. Then again, he might get together with Ayub Khan, pretender to the Afghan throne, trouncer of General Burrows at Maiwand; Ayub Khan, beaten in his turn by General Roberts, was then licking his wounds on the Afghan frontier. In addition there were other recalcitrants under Russian protection who the Maharajah thought might be co-opted to his cause – French-Canadians, assorted Irish Nationalists, pro-Boers like Alfred Aylward, agents from Turkey, Egypt and the Sudan.

He finally decided he would go to Russia, where, with the help of Katkoff, he might influence official opinion in his favour. He planned to leave Paris on 17 March 1887 and take a ship from Marseilles via Constantinople to Odessa, but changed his mind when persuaded that this route laid him open to 'possible assassination through British intrigues'.[2] The British *were* in fact keeping an eye on him; 'We keep

through the Foreign Office the strictest watch on his movements in Paris,' Cross wrote to Dufferin in India, 'as we are
informed, he is to leave in company with a young girl for
Constantinople this morning.'[3] They were misinformed:
instead the Maharajah suddenly put out that he would pass
the winter shooting on the Caspian, and asked Katkoff to
obtain a letter of authority for his guns and ammunition to
be passed through Russia. Even the Caspian story turned out
to be a bluff – his latest intention was in fact to continue
through Persia to Merv, occupied by the Russians in 1884
and their furthest outpost, in the direction of Afghanistan and
India, or better still, to Sarakh, between Meshed and Herat,
where he could intrigue with Ayub Khan and encourage
Russian intervention via Persia. In the end he decided to
take the train to St Petersburg. At the last moment he realized
he needed a passport – the embassy would not provide one, so
Patrick Casey lent him his.

The Maharajah left Paris on 21 March, accompanied by
his mistress, now honorary maharani, and his servant Aroor
Singh, promoted to honorary ADC. Though equipped
with the passport of an Irish revolutionary, he cannot have
looked the part even if the events on Berlin railway station
were enacted in the appropriate spirit: while changing trains,
the Maharajah was parted from his portfolio, which, in
addition to his travel documents, contained £500 in notes,
498 sovereigns, and 3,000 French francs. The police were
summoned, and 'British detectives' were denounced by the
Maharajah as the culprits, though the guilty party was ultimately established as a professional pickpocket. The penniless, passportless Maharajah, alias Patrick Casey, sent urgent
messages to Katkoff, who used his influence with General
Bogdanovitch, a leading member of the military faction
favouring territorial expansion, to order the frontier police to
let him in. It was arranged for him to stay at the Hotel
Dussaux in Moscow.

The first real intimation the Maharajah had of the long
arm of the British government was a visit from August

Weber, the vice-consul in Moscow, who had been instructed
by the British embassy at St Petersburg to look out for him.
The Maharajah, who was under the erroneous impression
that he was being approached 'to propose to him to open
negotiations', curtly refused to see him. If that mission had
failed, Weber was soon pleased to report that he had seen
the Maharajah setting off from his hotel to Katkoff's house
at about nine o'clock at night 'in full Indian dress with the
"Star of India" on his breast and adorned with precious
stones', accompanied by Aroor Singh turbaned and in a 'black
dress'. Aroor Singh, described as 'loquacious', boasted to
Weber that their further stay in Moscow 'would entirely
depend on the movement of the Russians in Central Asia and
more especially so – on their movements towards Herat'.
Weber suggested to his superior that this information might
'justify any precautions that may in consequence be taken
to counterbalance that sort of game'.[4]

'Proper quarters' were quick to react to the diplomatically
embarrassing presence of a declared British rebel actively
engaged in political intrigue in the Russian arena at a time
of *détente*. What was the Maharajah doing in Moscow when
their foreign minister had asserted that he was unwelcome?
The British foreign secretary, Lord Salisbury, sent a sharp
note to his ambassador in St Petersburg, Sir Robert Morier,
instructing him to look into the matter. Morier, formerly
ambassador in Berlin, regarded himself as a diplomat of
some subtlety; he had personal talks with the Russian foreign
minister, who was probably better informed about the whole
affair than he pretended. Morier reported to Salisbury the
gist of his interviews with de Giers in a 'very secret' dispatch
dated 4 May 1887:

I saw H.E. ... & found him more than ever annoyed and per-
plexed at the anomalous position in which this extraordinary, I
might almost say grotesque, incident has placed him. He had
entirely failed to ascertain by whose assistance Dhuleep Singh had
crossed the frontier. I said I had heard that the culprit was Genl.
Bogdanovitch; and I asked whether he wd. have the sufficient

authority to enable a friend patronised by him to enter Russia without a passport – He said he probably would, because he had succeeded, strange to say, in getting himself attached to the Ministry of the Interior, as some sort of Inspector, and as such, if himself on the spot, he would be known to the police, both on the frontier and elsewhere. But the curious thing was that under any *circs* the case wd. have to be reported, which had certainly not been done, to S. Pbg. Genl. Crejeffski had only heard of it from himself (M. de Giers) two days before his resignation of the post of Chief of Gendarmerie, and had been beside himself at the breach of regulations & its results.

I saw M. de Giers again today and asked him what answer I was to give to Y.L.'s telegram. He had seen the Emperor, and would therefore I said, be in a position to give me a reply.

From what His Excellency said I gathered that there wd. have been no difficulty in obtaining the Emperor's authority for what I am convinced, though he did not explicitly say so, M. de Giers himself wished to do, namely to invite Dhuleep Singh to leave Russia. His Majesty appears to have been very angry at his police not having been aware of what had happened; and observed that it was odd that the British Ambassador should have a better police than himself in his own capital – an occasion wh. M. de Giers improved by remarking that a Nihilist might easily come in by similar means – where I am strongly inclined to believe M. de Giers met with opposition was from the Minister of the Interior: not that I for one moment believe that Ct. Tolstoy is aiding and abetting M. Katkoff in his intrigues with Dhuleep, but because he is an *obstinate* sort of man who never loses sight of the great grievance he considers Russia has against England, the harbouring of Nihilist refugees such as Hartman – It was clear that in his conversation with M. de Giers he had harped on the absence of reciprocity between the two countries in the exchange of dangerous individuals. But be this as it may, the upshot of my conversation with H.E. was that he declared the expulsion of the Maharajah wd. create great scandal: but that he cd. assure me that he wd. be watched, and that the necessary measures wd. be taken to render him harmless. . . . He however was extremely anxious that I should not represent him as having entered into any engagement with HMG to guarantee the innocuousness of Dhuleep Singh, for he said 'with the experience we have had, who can tell what might chance to happen.' I said that I fully realised the difficulty of his position, that I had recd. no instructions from HMG to ask for Dhuleep's expulsion, but had only been told to point out the impression which wd. certainly be produced by his travelling in the direction of Central Asia through Russian territory. I felt sure that H.E. wd. do all in his power to secure the innocuousness of the Maharajah: no one could do more...[5]

Certainly Katkoff, who referred to England as 'the concealer from time immemorial of all Russian political criminals',[6] was not the only man in Russia who objected to the harbouring in England of Russian terrorists such as Hartman. In 1881 the nihilist group 'People's Wing' had assassinated Tsar Alexander II, and Dimitri Tolstoy had been appointed minister of the interior with a mandate for stern repression. Sir Robert Morier, by now more sure of his ground, sent an account to London on a further meeting with de Giers on the 'harbouring' of the Maharajah and was now proud to report that he had been responsible for compromising General Bogdanovitch. The Tsar's first exclamation, de Giers had told him, on learning how his foreign minister had heard of the Maharajah's illicit entry had been: 'It is passing strange that the British Ambassador should have at his disposal at St. Petersburg a better police than I have.' Morier's dispatch continued:

In a word General Bogdanovitch, whose position is already undermined, had been caught in *flagrante delicto* doing a piece of Executive business behind the back of the Emperor, of H.M.'s Ministers and of H.M.'s Police officials. M. de Giers dropped the expression: *'C'etait un acte de trahison!'* I caught up the phrase as very strong for the occasion, and M. de Giers was proceeding to make some observation when he stopped himself & changed the conversation. From what he did say, however, I gathered clearly that the Maharajah's unlawful crossing of the frontier was only a link in the intrigue which there is no doubt M. Katkoff was carrying on through last winter in Paris and that his invitation to the Maharajah to come to Moscow was somehow or other connected with that intrigue.[7]

It was soon clear to the Maharajah, fretting in his seedy hotel, that, even with the support of Katkoff and the militarists led by Bogdanovitch, his personal cause was not likely to progress without the interest of the 'highest of the high'. He therefore applied for an interview with the Tsar and when he was told that under the circumstances such a meeting could not be considered 'desirable', addressed him a letter that effectively invited the Tsar to invade India on the Maharajah's behalf.

Before I take the liberty of placing before His Majesty's Government the request of the Princes and people of India for their deliverance from their oppressors, I wish to say that I seek no personal advantage for myself. I only desire the freedom of the 250,000,000 of my people from the British tyrants and thus also benefit the person who will free them. One thing alone I wish to have, when the people of India become free I wish to live in my own country in the Punjab from where the British expelled me. But I do not make this a condition. I desire to give the rest of my life to the interests of the Emperor whose loyal subject I earnestly wish to become.

Through my cousin Sirdar Thakur Singh (man known both in the Punjab and mostly all over India) I have been deputed by most of the powerful princes of India to come to Russia and pray the Imperial Government to take their cause in hand. These princes possess altogether some 300,000 soldiers in their service and are prepared to revolt should the Imperial Government think proper to make an advance upon the British provided that I, their representative, be permitted to accompany the Imperial Army so as to assure them of the generous and gracious intentions entertained towards them by the Emperor, for the English have taken good care to fill the minds of the people of India (who are extremely ignorant) with false reports as to the oppressive nature of the Russian Rule, though the British Government itself has broken solemn engagements whenever it suited its own purpose to do so, having broken two treaties with myself alone.

Among the many advantages that would acrue to the Imperial Government by invasion are the following:

The Princes of India when free, and if allowed to manage their affairs in their own way, would 'join' together and pay a large tribute annually into the Russian Treasury. Although I am authorised to name only £3,000,000 per annum yet in my opinion after the setting down of the country they could easily pay between £8,000,000 and £10,000,000. The British raise an annual revenue from the country of some £50,000,000 and £60,000,000 Sterling, out of which an army of 100,000 Europeans and Officers and English civilians (who receive very high salaries) are paid at least £25,000,000.

The rest is employed in the administration of the country and in the payment of interest upon capital advanced by England for the construction of rail, roads and upon the public debt of India and pensions to retired officials in England. Also, the import and export trade between England and India amounting to some £50,000,000 per annum each way would be secured by Russia. India is indeed a gold mine to England and most of her wealth has been and is derived from that source. I have been much struck already during my very short stay in Russia with the low value of things in the country from want (in my opinion) of suitable markets for their disposal. But could the same commodities be taken to India I feel persuaded that from 100 to 300 per cent over the prices they fetch here would be raised for them out there. The markets of Central Asia are not to be compared with that of India.

I guarantee an easy conquest of India. For besides the promised assistance of the Princes of India with their armies, it is in my power to raise the entire Punjab in revolt and cause the inhabitants to attack in their rear the British forces sent to oppose the Imperial Army.

My loyal subjects would also destroy all railway, telegraphic and other communications and blow up bridges and cut off all supplies while the Princes in revolt would harass the British troops left behind as a reserve. England is only strong at sea but she has no army. She has only some 100,000 Europeans and about the same number of native soldiers in her service in India. All these are loyal to me and will come over at once to the side of Russia (provided that I be permitted to accompany the Imperial Army of invasion) should they be sent to confront the Russian troops, or they will attack the opposing British forces in their rear, should these Sikhs be left behind.

Under these circumstances no British army could hold its own, however powerful it might be (which it is not), being attacked both in front and behind.

It may not, perhaps, be out of place with due modesty to state here why I have some power over my countrymen and can render such invaluable services to the Imperial Government in the way described above. In the first place I am the acknowledged head and sovereign of some 20,000,000 (of which about 8,000,000 are Sikhs) people of the entire Punjab, a country inhabited by the most warlike races of India and all loyal to me. Secondly the last teacher of the Sikhs prophesied somewhere about 1725 regarding myself and has mentioned me by name in his prophecy. He has besides other matters predicted also that a man bearing my name would, after becoming deposed (dispossessed) of all he had inherited and after residing alone in a foreign country for a long time, return, and with the aid of a European power, free the Sikhs from the cruel bondage that they would then be suffering under for their sins.

Therefore a great deal can be made out of the prophecy, if properly worked, as the predicted time of its fulfilment is near at hand and the people of my country are extremely ignorant as already stated.

At this moment, the whole of India is with me and as soon as the People of Hindoostan are assured of my arrival in Russia their joy will know no bounds at their coming deliverance. With all humility, I would endeavour to dissuade the Imperial Government from regarding complications in South West Europe for the present, because many powers are united to oppose the realisation of its wishes in that quarter but to turn its entire attention upon the conquest of India and upon crushing England. For by wrenching India out of the hands of England, the Imperial Government will acquire a source of great wealth, whereas I greatly doubt that so much will be gained by taking Constantinople.

Furthermore, if I may be permitted, I would venture to state that, should the invasion of India be entertained in the Imperial Councils, an army of not less than 200,000 men and 2,000 cannons be provided for the purpose. Not that this force is at all necessary for the conquest of India but to impress wavering Princes and people in that country of the greatness of the resources of Russia, and thus half the battle would be gained.

In having thus freely expressed my views, I pray that I may not be considered disrespectful towards the Imperial Government but as a loyal subject of the Emperor (which I already consider myself to be, though I have not yet received the right of naturalisation), I feel it my duty to say what I have to say without reserve.

The Imperial Government, whether it thinks it proper to invade India or not or to employ me or not, can please itself in the matter for it is no concern of mine. I have been deputed simply to make an appeal on behalf of 250,000,000 of my countrymen for deliverance from the cruel yoke of the British Rule and having done so my duty is ended and, if graciously permitted by the Emperor to enjoy both liberty and safety in His Majesty's dominions, I shall occupy myself in sport leaving the Almighty to bring about the deliverance of my unfortunate people in His own good time.

Should the Imperial Government, however, think proper to turn its attention towards the conquest of India and desire my services for that purpose, I would suggest then that 2 or 3 gentlemen speaking English well should be appointed both to further discuss the matter with me and to enquire into the truth of the assertions I have made with regard to India.[8]

That the Tsar took the dubious claims of the deceitful letter seriously is indicated from the notes he made on its margin: to the suggestion that the Maharajah was anxious to become his loyal subject he noted: 'It is desirable'; regarding the claim that the princes of India were all behind him, the Tsar, giving his first sign of perspicacity, wrote, 'It would be desirable to verify this fact', and to the suggestion that English-speaking gentlemen be appointed to 'discuss the matter', the Tsar noted, 'It can be done.'

The Tsar made no written observation on another letter that fell into the hands, perhaps intentionally, of his security police. It came from Paris and was addressed to the Maharajah:

Mon Prince, the hour has not yet sounded, but it is not distant. I know that in England the Government is convinced of the inevitability of an Anglo-Russian war and fears that France may take sides with the Muscovites. The two military parties of the Irish nationalists have drawn up a proposal for the establishment of an Irish military colony near the Indian frontier – 600 to 6,000 men engaging to attract to it 11,000 to 14,000 Irish deserters from the British army. The colony probably to be commanded by one of our most devoted friends, who will act as the Imperial Government of Russia may dictate, and it is suggested that, if necessary and expedient, it will be ready to march in the service of any deposed monarch and place him on the throne.[9]

The letter was signed 'C'. No doubt it was from Patrick Casey. The 'devoted friend', who was 'probably' to command the Irish legion, was a gentleman referred to in police reports as 'a former major in the British Army'.

The Maharajah seemed to be too absorbed in his intrigues to give much thought to the welfare of his family in England. Victor, about to leave Sandhurst, was establishing a pattern that was to become all too familiar, by getting into debt. The father's letter to an errant son promised little hope of immediate accommodation:

I am delighted to see your handwriting but what a fool you are, my son, to write such a letter. For I have repeatedly told that I have repudiated the treaty of the annexation, therefore how dare you tell me write and ask for the money said to belong to me at the India Office.

Whether the 'Tschar' helps me or not, I am quite independent of everybody, and perfectly happy and mean shortly to overthrow the British rule in India to which end I have dedicated the rest of my life. But take my advice, my child, and do not believe anything the newspapers write either in my favour or against me.

You will soon be of age and will consequently be able to settle your debts. Let the Trustees sell the pictures or the jewels if they please, for I cannot be bothered afresh with matters connected with England. All that is over as a dream and I have awakened to a new life and the destruction of the British power.

But if you wish to retain my affection for you, childie, do not mention again to me such matter, nor ask me to humble myself to my bitterest enemy. Look upon me as dead. But I will never swerve from my purpose or I would not be the son of the Lion of the Punjab whose name I dare not disgrace.

You will see, my childie, by and by. Let the English brag and boast; they will cease their high talk. They are utterly undone, believe me, my son.

P.S. I could see you starve and even would take your life to put an end to your misery, but will never return to England. I am entirely changed since you last saw me. I will freely shed my blood for the Emperor of Russia.[10]

A second letter, written a day or two later, was more relaxed in tone. If it sent love to Frederick, it gave no hint of concern for his wife, thought by Queen Victoria to be dying of a broken heart.

I cannot tell you how happy I am to be in Russia. There is plenty of grouse shooting and fine salmon fishing in the north of Russia, and if not better employed I mean to indulge myself in some first rate sport. The woodcock shooting on the coast of the Black Sea is very good and so is snipe and wild fowl shooting in the Crimea.

So you see, my dear old man, I have reached the sportsman's paradise. Besides money from India, in spite of the stupid British Government's forbidding, will flow to me like water now that I am in Russia. To once reach Russia was all that was necessary, and my loyal subjects required me to break off all relations with the British, and give them proof of my sincerity by entering the dominions of the Tsar before they would undertake to send me large sums of money.

I can imagine the rage that the India officials will be in at my success, though they will pretend to suppress me altogether, but which they will find impossible to do nevertheless. Yes! they have made a blunder the cost of which will be enormous to the British nation, though it may bring no good to me. But revenge for all the insults I have suffered will quite compensate me for all the inconvenience that I have had to undergo.

Write me a line, childie, about your health, though do not in it, or otherwise, mix yourself up in my affairs.

Send the two knives you and Fred have made for me to Purdey to pack up with my other things.

Send my love to Fred and blessing of the Guru of the Sikhs and with the same to yourself, my childie.

P.S. The joy of your cousins will know no bounds now! I telegraphed my arrival to them, so all India will know.[11]

The odd tendency in that letter to intersperse the mundane with the vainglorious gives some indication of the schizophrenic processes of the Maharajah's mind during this period. Old friends in England, who had not given him up for lost, would write kindly letters, really intended to 'bring him back to his sense'. 'I cannot subject myself to be placed between two stools,' he wrote to Lady Login, and begged to be left alone to go his own way – 'Think no more of the Duleep Singh you once knew, for he is dead, and another liveth in his place.' Lady Login received a number of letters which she described as 'extraordinary effusions, some of them madder than others, occasionally absurd in their recriminations and suggestions, but all of them bearing evidence of an unhinged mind, and in some cases written in the calligraphy and spelling of a small schoolboy!' She described how in the and spelling of a small schoolboy!' She described how in the same sentence he would speak of dying as a patriot in compassing the overthrow of British rule in India and his anticipation of some good pheasant-shooting in Russia. mockery on my part to address you as "My dear Lady Login" and sign myself "Your affectionate", simply because I would shoot down on the battlefield any of your relations without the slightest hesitation, as I would any other Englishman.' Lady Login thought it evident that 'he most bitterly resented any reference to his former loyalty and devotion to Her Majesty, and to her kindness to him, and, like a naughty child took a kind of impish glee in putting his own actions in the worst light and ... trying to make out that from his boyhood he had been a perfect little monster of duplicity, and had set himself to deceive all the good folk concerned with his upbringing'.[12]

In that vein he wrote to his playmate from Futteghur days, Frank Boileau: 'My brave Colonel ... I wonder if you and I will one day meet on the battlefield, for generally the unexpected happens. Poor Sir John Login! Had he come to life now he would be in his grave the next instant again!... Oh, for a general European war! ... Would you believe it that I am endeavouring to land in India at the head of a small European volunteer army of my own? Does it not seem ridiculous on my part? With kind regards, that is if a proud rebel is permitted to send them ...'[13]

In one letter he asked for Bamba's riding saddle, presumably for Ada's use, to be forwarded to Kieff. 'I am setting aside all political affairs for some time to come,' he confided. 'I am going to indulge in some splendid sport in the Caucasus, "The Sportsman's Paradise".'[14] But there was no word for Queen Victoria, though perhaps the Maharajah's odd communication to her daughter Vicky, Crown Princess of Prussia, was meant for her eyes also, for it was sent to Osborne when the addressee was in fact in Germany. The crown princess immediately sent the letter on to her mother, asking for advice as to how to reply.

My beloved Mama, To my great surprise – I today received the enclosed! I hope you will tell me *whether* I am to send an answer or not, & if so – in what terms! I cannot help feeling *sorry* for him & regretting that he has fallen into such bad hands, & become *so soured* and an enemy to England!

I was told the Maharajah was still very grateful to *you* for the kindness you showed him personally. – Perhaps there might be some means of bringing him to his senses & back to the right road. He may have *some real* grievances too.

Why he should write to *me* I am sure I don't know, – perhaps because the German Govt. & Court make such professions of friendship to Russia which I may be supposed to share....[15]

The Maharajah had enclosed for the crown princess the text of a letter he had sent to the *Daily Telegraph* which, though he complained they had not, they had in fact published. It contained a lengthy reiteration of his grievances and ended: 'Yes, I prefer being the puppet of Mr Katkoff, and a Russian subject, to being the dupe of Great Britain, a nation which professes to be guided by a high code of Christian morality, though practising not even the rudimentary justice towards her weak victims.' The Maharajah's letter to the crown princess read:

Madame, Thinking it might interest Your Imperial Highness to read the reply I have written to an article which *The Times* published against me some time back but which the Editor of *The Daily Telegraph* has not produced – so much therefore for the vaunted use of fair-play by the English – I do myself the honour to forward a copy.

Little did I dream when shortly after my arrival in England from India, now some thirty years ago, I had the honour of being presented at Osborne to your Imperial Highness who was then very young and who used to admire my Oriental costume that I should ever become the proud reble [*sic*] and Patriot that I am this day against the government of your Illustrious Mother: but the injustice, the cruel opposition, and the humiliation which have been inflicted upon me by England have opened my eyes as to what that Power really is, though professing a high Code of Christian Morality. I am convinced in my own mind that, if there be a God in the Universe, the British Empire of India which is founded upon swindle and fraud will come to an ignominious end eventually.

The account of the manner in which I was robbed at Berlin while travelling as 'Patrick Casey' must have afforded some little amusement to Your Imperial Highness.[16]

Before sending the Maharajah's letter on to Lord Cross, for advice, the queen showed it to Ponsonby, whose memorandum on the subject indicated the limited effect his rebellious activities seemed to be having in official circles: 'General Sir Henry Ponsonby begs leave to thank Your Majesty for allowing him to see this extraordinary letter from Maharajah Duleep Singh. He supposes that the India Office do not allow him any of his money? His proclamations are dated from the Irish Secret Press in Paris. Mr Balfour said he did not care about these proclamations which would have no effect, but if he supplied the Irish rebels in Paris with funds he might become dangerous.'[17]

On 18 September 1887, before the queen had time to advise her daughter how to reply, a telegram was delivered at Balmoral: 'Regret inform you Maharanee died of collapse suddenly this morning with renal complications following chill on Friday. Sir William Gull's representative Dr Acland

2 x

was in attendance. Prince Victor is here. Mother unconscious twelve hours before death. Family wish buried at Elveden. Am arranging accordingly. Everything very quiet. Arthur Oliphant.'[18]

The queen noted in her journal for that day: 'The unfortunate M. D.S. has published a most violent, crazy letter, speaking of being "the lawful Sovereign of the Sikhs" and "England's implacable foe"! Heard this evening that his poor abandoned wife, the M'ee Bamba, had died quite suddenly yesterday. How terrible for the poor children, who are quite fatherless & motherless!'

On hearing the news the Maharajah telegraphed to Victor: 'Heart-broken – can't realize – will write next week.'[19] Queen Victoria sent a message of condolence to the Maharajah, as did the Prince of Wales. The queen had no acknowledgement, but the prince showed her his reply which could hardly be considered gracious. 'Bertie came & sat with me when I came home,' she entered in the journal on 7 October, '& showed me a really monstrous letter from the Maharajah D.S. to Sir Dighton Probyn, who in spite of all the M's violent rebellious letters & publications, had written in Bertie's name, to console him on the death of his wife. He surely must be off his head.' The letter read:

Sir Dighton Probyn's letter conveying to me Your Royal Highness' sympathy in my late bereavement has been forwarded to me from England – Under other circumstances I should have felt most grateful for Your Royal Highness's condescension, but in the present circumstances, while your illustrious Mother proclaims Herself the Sovereign of a throne and an Empire both of which have been acquired by fraud by Pious Christian England, and of which Your Royal Highness also hopes one day to become the Emperor, these empty conventional words addressed to me amount to an insult. For Your Royal Highness's sympathy can only be expressed by one friend towards another – but which cannot ever exist between enemies.

signed Duleep Singh
Sovereign of the Sikh Nation and proud implacable foe of England.[20]

The secretary of state, Lord Cross, had advised that the crown princess's reply to the Maharajah's letter might reasonably contain condolences on the death of his wife and remind him that his children were fatherless as well as motherless. But when shown his letter to the Prince of Wales, Cross advised that she would do best not to reply at all. The queen informed her daughter accordingly:

I was just going to write to you to send the dreadful answer wh. the demented Maharajah gave Bertie & wh. I enclose, when I read your 2 of the 7th & 9th from charming Villa Clara at Baveno, – where I like to think you are living – I at once Cyphered to Ld. Cross (who left yesterday) to ask him whether your letter shld. be sent after this dreadful letter to Bertie – And I got his answer that it shld. certainly not be sent. The reports one hears of D.S.'s conduct politically & morally is as bad as possible. It is most sad & grieves me very much. – Many mistakes have been made – but he shld. not be so ungrateful for all the gt. kindness shown him....[21]

Lord Cross had some gossip for Lord Dufferin: 'The Prince of Wales had written his private condolences to him on his wife's death, and received in return a most insulting letter, which he showed to me and which made him very angry. I believe he will send it to the Emperor.'[22]

In July 1887 the Maharajah's patron and protagonist, Katkoff, fell ill. 'M. Katkoff's serious and dangerous illness is causing me great uneasiness,' he wrote to his Russian friend, Count Cheremetoff. 'For were he to die, I would be left without anyone to protect me and might be turned out of Russia through some intrigue at the "High Quarters".'[23] In general his projects could not be said to be advancing beyond the plotting stages. Despite letters and messengers, no money was coming in from India to support his cause; indeed several of his so-called princely allies were even then in London celebrating Queen Victoria's Golden Jubilee and whatever money the impoverished Thakur Singh might have collected he was probably keeping to himself. The Maharajah had a plan to enter the Punjab in disguise, suddenly throw it off, and declare himself the awaited Guru and their rightful king; the Russian military party pretended to approve and promised any number of officers to lead his men in revolt against the British. There was another plan to go to Meshed and Merv, but his movement towards Asia was still discouraged by the foreign minister. He was heard to complain 'all is to be wretched peace'.[24]

Ada had become a positive block to his mobility. She was heavily pregnant and would not let him out of her sight, damping his enthusiasm and initiatives with feminine reservations; sometimes he thought she might be a British spy and would not let her read his mail from India. Following the report of Bamba's death in the Russian press, the word soon went round that she was not the real maharani as had been supposed and her position in Moscow society was compromised. Morale did not improve when lack of funds forced them to move to the cheaper Hotel Billow.

To make matters worse, Katkoff died that August. 'Katkoff's death is indeed a very heavy blow to me,' he wrote to Count Cheremetoff, a copy of which letter ended up in the hands of the Security Police, 'and I am now left without a protector alone in a strange land and the Imperial Foreign Office I fear against me; but trusting in God I take courage and am ready to meet all difficulties.'[25]

On the day after Christmas Ada gave birth to a daughter, Paulina Alexandra, at a time when money was so short that the Maharajah was even offering his rich Indian clothes for sale. He wrote to his lawyer settling what was left of his property on his illegitimate child.[26]

Even if Katkoff was dead, the Maharajah had a few powerful friends with whom to conspire. The newspaper proprietor had asked General Kuhlberg, head of the boundary commission, to befriend him, but there was little help he could give at that time. Katkoff's son-in-law, who was a member of the imperial council, and his friends, assured the Maharajah that as soon as railway communications were established to the Afghan frontier the Russians would drive the British out of India. Their government would, they promised, make India over to him as they had more land than they could possibly rule already; Russia's sole object, they claimed, was to weaken the British in Europe. But all these grand plans, it seemed, were put forward to humour him. 'Dalip is now living in a fool's paradise – himself as Sovereign of the Sikhs, the Cockney girl as an Empress of India,'[27] a spy reported. The Maharajah had also quarrelled with Jamul-ud-Din, a Persian renegade whom he had hoped would help him on the Afghan frontier. Jamul-ud-Din, another Katkoff protégé, had made a better impression on Muscovite society and this rankled with the Maharajah. When de Giers had questioned the Persian about the Maharajah's influence in India, he replied, 'there was not a dog in India with him and the new generation knew nothing about him'.[28] Nobody seemed to be taking him seriously.

The main hope lay in the outcome of the activities of his ADC Aroor Singh, who had been sent off to India to obtain money from the native prices and, if possible, to get written assurances of their support. These would be shown to the Russians, who would then send out an officer to verify them. He was also to obtain money for the purpose of bribing 'high Russian officials', and to visit influential Sikhs and work out a plan to cut railway lines and telegraph wires when a Russian force should appear at the frontier. Aroor Singh had been ordered by the Maharajah to contact the sender of an unsigned letter he had received from India offering to help his cause in any possible way. Introducing his servant to this unknown well-wisher, the Maharajah had written:

My unknown friend, I received your letter without signature which made me happy, but you must be careful in writing to me for your own sake. Your letter appeared to me to have been opened. I pray to God that your second, giving your name, may not fall into the hands of the British Government. I think the best way to communicate important news would be to send a special messenger to me. The expenses would not be very great, and he could come from Calcutta by a French boat to Port Said, and from there to Constantinople, and via Odessa. A French passport would be better than an English one. The bearer of this will give you news by word of mouth. Please help him in every way.[29]

Aroor Singh, bearing this message, had duly proceeded to India by a complicated route designed to outwit British spies. Secreted on his person was his master's appeal to his 'Brother Princes of Hindustan':

We send our faithful and trusted Aroor Singh from here to announce to you our arrival in Russia and to inform you that we shall soon come to India to your assistance. Therefore, believe no reports to the contrary whether they be published by the British Government or by the newspapers. We shall give our life to free you from the English yoke, and only ask you to be prepared for your deliverance, for by the aid of the Almighty we shall succeed. But as it is necessary that we should report to the Emperor of Russia who among you are for His Imperial Majesty and who for the continuance of the British rule, therefore, we request you to inform by word of mouth only our trusted Ambassador on which side you mean to take part in the coming struggle.

If you should decide on serving the Emperor then confirm your fidelity to His Imperial Majesty by sending some kind of token, in order that you might not lose the reward for your preferred loyalty on the day of the defeat of the accursed British.

Look to the efficiency of your armies and get them in order.

The above is our address should you wish to communicate direct with us, but we advise you not to write to us for fear of your letters falling into the hands of the British Government.

Dalip Singh,
Sovereign of the Punjab.[30]

Another letter for delivery was to the ex-king of Oudh, then living in some comfort and contentment on a pension considerably larger than Duleep Singh's, in Calcutta:

With great joy I announce to you that I have reached Russia and hope through the mercy of God and with the aid of the Emperor of Russia soon to come to India and deliver your Majesty from the hands of the accursed English and to replace you on your throne.

You and I though placed in similar circumstances by the same wicked hand, yet I have reached this great Empire, while you are still in the hands of your enemies, therefore, I advise you to be very careful.

Many Princes of India have written to say that they will assist me both with their armies and money. Also some 45,000 Sikhs in the British army in India are with the entire Punjab loyal to me, but as I desire your Majesty to join us also, I therefore address you on the subject.

Please do not write, but send me some token that I may be assured of your goodwill also to the glorious cause of liberating our mother country from the hateful yoke of the accursed English rule ...[31]

Aroor Singh had not been long enough in India to fulfil any part of his mission when he called, as instructed, on the writer of the friendly letter to Moscow. The man turned out to be a Bengali and the two were soon entering into a conspiratorial conversation concerning the Maharajah's great plans. Invited for a drive by his new friend, their horse-drawn conveyance drove straight into the police compound where Aroor Singh was promptly arrested. The amiable Bengali was in fact a police inspector who had written a dummy letter to the Maharajah which had completely taken him in. Aroor Singh's compromising papers were confiscated and interrogation began. Triumphant British police officers considered him 'a man of no great intelligence' and it was suggested that he might be a 'plant' from the other side.[32] But his interrogators had some difficulty in extracting information. According to Colonel Henderson of the Police Department: 'His story is that he was sent by Dalip Singh for the sole object of raising money in India and was told not to show his face again unless he returned with a large sum. Aroor Singh is a dull, heavy man and to all appearances about as bad a messenger as Dalip Singh could have chosen.'[33] His captors were undecided about the way he should be treated: 'The prisoner having asked me for some ice, brandy, claret and Vichy water, I propose to supply him at present with such stimulants as the medical officer may recommend, and I would request instructions if he can have ice or Vichy water,'[34] the commandant of the Chunar prison wrote to his superior. But Aroor Singh appeared to have had no inhibitions in his conversations with the secret agent who had brought about his arrest. This intelligence was incorporated in a report to Mortimer Durand, the Indian Government foreign secretary:

Plan of Campaign: As soon as the Russians have completed the Railway they are making through Central Asia (which is expected to be in about a year and a half), a Russian army accompanied by Dalip Singh is to invade India, the native soldiers who will be sent to the front with the British army on reaching the neighbourhood of the Russians, are to desert and place themselves under the command of Dalip Singh, whilst the native soldiers on their way to the front are suddenly to mutiny, loot the stores and attack the British regiments; at the same time arrangements will be made to destroy railway and telegraph wires all over the country; and to enable the people, in certain places, to rise against British rule the native states are at this time to declare themselves for Dalip Singh and to attack the British with their armies.

After Plans: When the British have been turned out of India, Russia is to be recompensed by receiving double the amount incurred by her for the expenses of the war ... a yearly tribute is also to be paid to Russia. Dalip Singh is to be installed as ruler of India, and is to be helped by a Supreme Council, the country to be governed on liberal principles and the people to be allowed to have local self-government and freedom of speech.

For correspondence, a crude and cumbersome cypher is used, in which each letter of the alphabet is represented by a number of dots corresponding with its numerical position.[35]

The police in India, with memories of the mutiny, were keeping a close eye on the situation and their spies were successfully infiltrating the Duleep Singh plotters. Thakur Singh, supposedly out of their clutches in French Pondicherry, was under surveillance. He was in bad health and short of money, but there was reason to believe that he had successfully suborned a senior officer and a number of Sikh

soldiers who had slipped into Pondicherry to enlist in the
Maharajah's name.

Thakur Singh was soon to die, and it was rumoured in the
bazaars that he had been poisoned by British agents. With
Aroor Singh in gaol, the Maharajah's only effective ally was
now the mysterious Kashmiri Abdul Rasul, now styled
'private secretary', who had come over from Paris to join him.
Abdul Rasul, who spoke fluent English, Persian, Turkish,
Arabic, Hindustani and Kashmiri, had settled in London after
the Russo-Turkish war and started an anti-British newspaper
in Persian. His description, according to the police file, was
unprepossessing: 'Age about 47: height 5' 6"; fair complexion, medium build, true type of Kashmiri in appearance
with a very quick nervous expression: marked strongly from
small pox, has a scarlike deep burn on his left cheek or chin,
dividing a closely cropped grisly beard. The hair does not
grow on this scar.' [36]

In 1884 he had joined Wolseley's Nile expedition as interpreter, but had been suspected of carrying on intrigues with
the Mahdi. He had been put on trial but had been released
on lack of evidence, though he subsequently admitted to the
Maharajah that in fact he had been an enemy agent. Abdul
Rasul was a man of parts and had useful contacts throughout the Mediterranean, including Zobair Pasha, Gordon's
former colleague in the Sudan. That disenchanted ex-slaver
could hardly be likely to love the British: he himself had been
imprisoned in Gibraltar, his money had been confiscated,
and his son had been shot for continuing the slave trade. But
even the wily professional Abdul Rasul was no match for
the British. A native agent of the police, referred to in reports
only by the initials 'A.S.', and to the conspirators as 'The
Father of the Turban' on account of his large floppy head-
gear, gained Abdul Rasul's complete confidence, travelling
with him on his mission to the Mediterranean and sending
reports to his masters in India covering every aspect of the
great intrigue, which included the closing of the Suez Canal
and causing uprisings in the Sudan.

The crafty 'Father of the Turban' even got to see the great Zobair in Cairo and duly reported his encounter to the Indian authorities:

I saw Zobair Pasha today and A.R. [Abdul Rasul] explained in Arabic that I am a fellow countryman of the Maharajah. When I took leave Zobair said (in Arabic translated by A.R.) that being of the same complexion, he had a great regard for the people of Hindustan and was ready to assist the Maharajah with person, wealth and men; he could not publish his plans but would do everything. He regretted that of the 50 crores of people in India nothing can be done against the English. He said that he always understood the Sikhs are brave but unfortunately had no hopes from them; his own people though few in number are ready to fight.

I represented that the Sikhs are unarmed but he replied this was the case of the Sudanese but they possessed themselves of the arms of the Englishmen. He told me to give Salam to the Raja of Faridkot and Bawa Khem Singh, and bid them to raise a revolt in the Punjab when he gave a signal by a hostile attack on the English.

A.R. told me afterwards that Zobair's plan is to close the Suez Canal and that until this is done, the English power in India cannot be shaken. The Sultan's ministers who are favourable to the English are not concerned in this plan but only some of them who are favourable to Russia and also to Dalip Singh. The plan will be carried out soon and the Canal will be entirely closed.[37]

But all this was mere plotting. Nothing was actually happening to make the Maharajah feel that he was striking a positive blow at his enemies. He seemed to be losing his nerve: sometimes he would be in tears, bewailing the day he had ever listened to Thakur Singh who had led him into such treacherous depths, cursing the Indians for their infirmity of purpose and lack of generosity, and the Russians for not taking him seriously.

Indications of his moods and activities filtered back to London through the reports of the British vice-consul in Moscow:

25th February 1888

I hasten to report to you that the Maharaja Dalip Singh told a friend of mine the other day that as soon as the Maharani, who is very ill after accouchement, is sufficiently recovered to enable her to bear the fatigues of the journey, he will leave Russia for good and return to France, for, he said, 'I find I can do no good here.'

Judging from the visits he has had of late, the rumours that have reached me, I have reason to believe that the authorities here have had instructions to request the Maharaja to leave the country. In a few days I expect to be able to report to you more fully and definitely on the subject.

27th February 1888

I beg to inform you that the Maharaja Dalip Singh has left Hotel Billow for a kind of private hotel or boarding house, called Paris, for sake of economy.

He also told his bankers that he intends staying in Moscow until next winter when he proposes leaving for the south of Russia, that he knows he is under espionage and that it will go hard with any spy that gets into their clutches.

It appears that Dalip Singh is a very talkative man, always full of threats as to what he can and will do.[38]

At the beginning of May the Maharajah, Ada and the baby moved down to Kieff and established themselves at the Hotel de France. A further report was received in July from an English traveller passing through the city:

Another person of whom I heard something at Kieff was Dalip Singh. He is living at a villa near Bojarka about 13 miles south-west of Kieff and within the last six weeks has been twice officially visited there by General Dentelin.

The English girl with whom he lives, and who last winter had a child by him, is apparently recognised as his wife and he himself is known in Kieff as the 'Indian Prince'. He has a Russian German somewhat vaguely attached to him as a kind of Secretary, interpreter and general factotum and his financial affairs would appear to have improved.

I may add while on the subject that one of my Panslavist acquaintances, a Russian official, who had seen Jamul-ud-din during his visit to this country, seemed much impressed by the prospect which that imposter had held out of a general rising in India, whenever the Russians chose to give the signal.[39]

As he could hardly return to his estate in England, the Maharajah had the idea of buying one in Russia and becoming a Russian citizen. He had 'taken refuge' in a village in the neighbourhood of Kieff, where there was good shooting. But money was short and plans were developing with depressing slowness. Lord Cross, who was then staying at Balmoral, had some recent intelligence to impart to Lord Dufferin: 'So far as I can learn Duleep Singh begins to see that he has failed in a dangerous game, and talks of going to Algiers or Italy; but he is a dangerous and crafty fellow, and for anything I know all this may be put forward as a blind; but I believe that as far as Russia is concerned, for some reason or other she is not inclined to take him up, and wishes, for the present at all events, to act in a conciliatory manner towards England.'[40]

The British Foreign Office was under the impression that the Maharajah planned to move on to the Crimea and thence to Tiflis. In fact he had decided to return to Paris for a time, to raise money by the sale of jewellery he had deposited with his agent, and from there carry on the struggle in any way that presented itself. He was again in a hopeful mood – he had just completed his fiftieth year and according to the Guru's prophecy 'in the first battle he would be defeated and he would take refuge in a little village where the spirit would fall upon him and he would know himself. Thenceforward his career would be triumphant.'[41]

CHAPTER 16

'Apologizing All Round'

THE Maharajah was back in Paris at the beginning of November 1888. Though his rebellious plans had been foiled by the political climate, his pride would not allow him to admit defeat even if a part of him wanted a reconciliation with his imagined persecutors. He maintained that ninety per cent of the Indian princes were behind him and that as soon as the Russians had finished building their railway, they would move towards India. He claimed to have forty thousand Sikh troops on whom he could count absolutely and volunteers from Ireland, Hungary, Austria, France and Germany ready on his command to proceed to the Indian frontier without pay. That he needed £4 million to train and equip his army, he admitted, and if it did not seem to be forthcoming from his brother princes, that was because it would be difficult for them to send it without incurring British suspicions. That was the story he gave to the Paris correspondent of *The Standard*. He closed the interview in typical Maharajah style: 'You will see. I shall make my appearance in India. I do not care a jot for my life, and I am certain of being supported by my people. I may be beaten, but I do not believe it, and at least I shall either die or be victorious.'[1] To another journalist he described the British as 'a thieving, hypocritical Christian nation, grabbing at what does not belong to them all over the world'. He continued in top form:

Let them wait a bit. In less than three years – in less than two perhaps – I and my 250,000,000 fellow-countrymen will have driven them out of India. I am working quietly, secretly, but none the less surely, and in the long run we shall see who will pre-vail. I am the proud and implacable foe of England. Individually I do not hate Englishmen, from whom, during the course of my thirty-two years' residence in their country, I received much kindness. But as a nation I hate them. I am laying my plans for a grand *coup*. I intend to consolidate the natives of India against the common enemy. No compromise with the British Govern-ment is possible now. I would not even accept from it the indemnity I originally asked. It is war to the knife. Wait and see!'

He was still playing the role of the sovereign of the Sikhs, and planned to revive an order of chivalry created by Runjit Singh for distribution in Russia and elsewhere to worthy adherents. To the people of India he addressed another of his proclamations: 'Countrymen, be brave!' he exhorted them. 'Be great and noble, like your ancestors! Remember that only in unity can strength be found against our enemies.'[3] Once again he opened up a correspondence with the queen, boldly asking her not so much for the return of his dominion, which he said was not hers to bestow, but for his family jewel, the Koh-i-noor or at least its value in cash from her own pocket:

Madam, While residing in England, I appealed both to your Majesty and to England's Prime Minister the Marquis of Salisbury, for justice. I asked that a competent Court of Law Lords of the House of Peers pronounce judgement upon the conduct of your Indian Administration towards me, your unfortunate Ward, be appointed: but I suppose as your Majesty is a Constitutional Sovereign, justice was refused me. And for the same reasons, it will be useless for me to demand the restoration of my Kingdom, swindled from me by your Christian Government, but which I hope shortly, by the aid of Providence, to retake from my robbers.

But my diamond, the Koh-i-noor, I understand, is entirely at your own personal disposal. Therefore, believing your Majesty to be 'the most religious lady' that your subjects pray for every Sunday, I do not hesitate to ask that this gem be restored to me, or else that a fair price be paid for it to me out of your privy purse.

By such an act of justice, your Majesty would acquire a clear conscience before God, before whom all of us, whether Christians,

Mahommedans or Sikhs, must render an account of deeds done in the body and fulfil the law of Christ, thus washing your hands of at least one of the black works of your Majesty's righteous Government.

Remember that the tenets of Christianity teach every true believer to defraud no man and to do to others as you would wish that they should do unto you.

The Treaty of the annexation of the Punjab was extorted from me, when I was a mere infant of some eleven years of age by my Christian Guardian, for his own benefit, and by that illegal instrument he confiscated both my diamond and my dominions.

But as that Treaty was abrogated by the arbitrary interpretation of its stipulations by your Government, in its own favour, I demand and reclaim the restoration of my jewel and of my sovereign rights, of which I was defrauded by the perfidious representative of England.

I pray your Majesty to forgive any apparent expression of disrespect that may appear in my letter. It is unintentional. I would not willingly be discourteous to any Sovereign, and far less to your Majesty, who is not only a lady, but who personally showed to me the kindness of a Mother during my long sojourn in England and exile from my native land.

I have the honour to subscribe myself, Your Most Gracious Majesty, The deeply wronged legitimate Sovereign of the Sikhs,

Duleep Singh, Maharajah.[4]

He sent a copy of his letter to the queen to his neighbour in Norfolk, Lord Walsingham. 'I doubt that you will approve of it,' he wrote, 'but my object is to try to make the B. Govt. to explain before Christendom why it was that I have been dispossessed of my kingdom by Christian England.' He ended with a request that must have seemed oddly juxtaposed with its impertinent enclosure: 'I had definitely arranged to return to Russia in July next. If any of your friends have a pup or two (setters or pointers) that they have no use for themselves would you mind *asking for two for me* and send them to Elveden from where they will be forwarded to *me*. I ask this favour for the sake of old times.'[5]

Victor was angry and embarrassed when Walsingham

showed him his father's letter. He had returned to England from Canada, where he had been sent as ADC to Sir John Ross so that he might be kept away from what Cross called 'evil influences',[6] to discuss the possible sale of Elveden. The Maharajah, when pressed to sell by his friends in order to provide for his family, had declared 'it must rest on my son's wishes'.[7] It was quite clear to the son that if his father continued on his present course there was no hope at all of retaining it. Victor could see that his father's proclamations and vengeful outbursts were damaging the family interests and wrote imploring him to give up his 'mad schemes'[8] and to come back to them as a father. Arthur Oliphant, at that time, suggested to Ponsonby that Victor might personally influence affairs: 'I should be very glad to hear,' he wrote, 'that it is deemed expedient for Victor to visit his father, for, in my opinion, such a meeting could not result in harm to the son – and might do good to the father.'[9]

In the same letter Oliphant indicated that the other children hoped that Elveden might be retained: 'Princess Bamba has a most difficult disposition – & we think it is very probable that she would be more inclined to accept the situation in which the family is now placed if the old home at Elveden were finally disposed of. I believe there is a constant hope on her part that somehow or other they will be able to get back there. I know Prince Victor also entertains a similar empty hope. Princess Catherine shares Bamba's views on the subject; the two little ones only are content as they are ... Prince Frederick, whenever he can get away from Cambridge, spends some days at farmhouses on the estate.' Certainly Frederick wanted to keep the place going; like his father he was a first-class shot and he used to bring over from Cambridge his fellow undergraduate, the future Lord Rothschild, for a day's shooting, for which he charged £10.

A week after Oliphant suggested that Victor might go over and see his father, a celebration took place in Paris to which he was not invited. None of the children of the first marriage were to attend the legalization of the second; all they knew of the event was what they read in the *Daily Telegraph* for 21 May 1889:

This afternoon took place the civil marriage of his Highness the Maharajah Dhuleep Singh with a young English lady – Miss Ada Douglas Wetherill – in the Mayor's office of the Eighth arrondissement, or 'Quartier de la Madeleine'. The ceremony was strictly private, and was only attended by one or two of the Paris friends of the bride and bridegroom. In the register the latter was described as 'Maharajah Dhuleep Singh, Sovereign of the Sikh Nation, living at No. 24, Rue Marbeuf, Paris, and formerly in the Faubourg Saint-Germain. Profession Rajah, and widower of Bamba Muller, who died in London.' The bride, a young and good-looking lady who wore a lavender-coloured travelling costume and orange-blossoms, was registered as 'the daughter of B.D. Wetherill, deceased, and Sarah, his wife, both of Hampshire, England'. When the nuptial knot had been duly tied in the prompt and business-like manner peculiar to civil ceremonies, the Mayor, girt with his tricolour scarf of office, addressed a brief hymeneal homily to the bride and bridegroom, and the proceedings were then explained in English to the Maharajah. After this the Mayor read a kind of address to the bridegroom, and in which his Worship showed that he was evidently suffering from a mild form of Anglophobia. He saluted in the Maharajah the last of the Kings of Lahore, and spoke of him having been despoiled of his territories and finding hospitality in France. Next followed a few references to the former greatness of the dethroned Prince, and Monsieur le Maire finally wound up by hoping that the Royal union would be propitious. The ceremony was then terminated, and the bride and bridegroom received the congratulations of their friends. The Maharajah and his bride will shortly leave Paris for Russia.

Ada, four months pregnant with her second child, was an 'honest woman' at last!

The newly wedded Maharajah still had financial problems, despite the sale of his remaining jewels. Arthur Oliphant, who did not disclose his source, passed the information on to the palace: 'The Queen will be interested to learn that ... I have most trustworthy information that he (the M.R.)

expressed during the last few days the following: "That if he does not obtain from India the pecuniary aid which he expects, he might find himself in extreme poverty, in which case he thought the Government would show its magnanimity by giving him back his rejected stipend on his returning here 'and apologising all round': His mental condition is a curious study." [10]

'Apologising all round' might have been an effective way out of an ambivalent situation in early editions of *The Boys' Own Book*, but Lord Cross, to whom Oliphant's information was forwarded, responded in a manner that implied the Maharajah was hardly 'playing the game': 'Viscount Cross ... is quite aware that the Maharajah, who has sold his jewels, is becoming poorer every day, and that at the present moment he is increasing his endeavours to do mischief, especially through his agents in Pondicherry.' [11]

It may have been true that dissident Sikhs were still turning up in French Pondicherry, but now that Thakur Singh was dead there was not much to be hoped for from that quarter. Nor had the Maharajah's latest plea to the Sikhs, issued from Geneva on 25 June 1889, as yet brought in any of the funds it so earnestly requested:

Beloved Fellow-Countrymen, It is with feelings of deep gratitude and sincere pride that we thank you for the offer of your lives to the sacred cause of Freedom of which we are the champion.

But as you say that you have no money to give, it becomes necessary for us to explain how small a sacrifice is asked of you to enable us to enter India with a European army and deliver you from the accursed British Raj.

Beloved fellow countrymen, you number in all India some 250,000,000 souls, and if each of you would subscribe only one pice during eight or nine months, the required sum would be raised and surely this is within the means of us all.

Believe not that this money is for our personal use.

Our personal necessities are provided for from our own slender resources and you must bear in mind that all contributions will be receipted for with tokens, by authorized agents appointed by us conjointly with the committee of organization and that upon our return among you those tokens will be redeemed by us with the addition of their annual interest of 50 per cent.

Sri Khalsa Ji, for you, our cause is not only national but also religious. You number about 8,000,000 in the Punjab and we believe that to none of you will it be a great hardship to lay by, in the name of Sri Guru Govind Singh Ji, one anna each month during eight months' time.

And above all things, do we desire that those who contribute should send on delegates to the Committee, to take part in the deliberations and superintend the expenditure of the funds which are subscribed for the purchase of arms and ammunition ...

The moment is fast approaching when you must choose between independence and eternal slavery. The great Emperor of Russia has spoken words which show that the hour of conflict is near. In that conflict England must be arrayed against our friends and it will be your own fault, if these friends do not come to our assistance.

And in the provisions for the future, we decree that from the date of this our present Royal proclamation:

1st. Cow killing is absolutely prohibited throughout all Hindustan and as compensation to the Mohammadans who have hitherto enjoyed this privilege, they will receive from the Hindus a pecuniary indemnity which shall be paid upon our arrival in India.

2nd. The payment of all taxes to the British Government is forbidden and the population is hereby commanded to refuse compliance with every order for their collection, all who disobey this decree will be properly punished later and in the meantime should be put out of caste immediately by ourselves.

3rd. The Public debt of India is hereby repudiated and all Railway and telegraph lines are confiscated. But such natives as may have held stock in either of the above, for a period of at least three years prior to the publication of this our sovereign decree, shall be secured against all loss.

This exception applies to natives only and only to those who by their acts shall prove themselves to be genuine practical patriots.

4th. All debts upon which the interest exceeds 5 per cent per annum are abolished, except where the lender can prove that he has contributed liberally to the success of our mission.

5th. All persons imprisoned by the British authorities shall be released from confinement and their places in jails shall be occupied by those who, having means at their disposal, have refused to subscribe to the fund for the liberation of their native country.

6th. All persons who have suffered from the tyranny and injustice of the accursed British Government will be reinstated as far as practicable upon their thrones and in their rights after a scrupulous investigation of their grievances.

7th. As soon after our return to India as circumstances will permit a plebiscite will be held in every province, not under the rule of any Native Prince, and the people called upon to select the government of its choice. For example Bengal will be permitted to try the virtues of the Republic.

8th. All Hindus, Sikhs, Mohammadans and Christians are invited to offer up prayers to God for our triumph, and upon furnishing evidence that they have so done, all shall be rewarded, according to the well known liberality of our ancestors, as soon as by the aid of the Almighty and the material support of Russia, we will appear again among you as a conqueror.

As circumstances may oblige us to be scrupulously prudent, it may so happen that we might be prevented direct future communication with our beloved fellow countrymen, who in that case are invited to attach to all proclamations issued by the Executive Committee the same importance as if they have our royal signature.

Dalip Singh,

Sovereign of the Sikh Nation and Implacable Foe of the British Government.[12]

A first-hand report on the 'implacable foe' came from Arthur Oliphant in mid-September:

Last week I went to Paris ... for a few days. While there I saw the Maharajah more than once. His Highness introduced me to 'his young wife', as he termed her, & she is young, (only a year older than the eldest daughter Princess Bamba). She is a pleasant mannered person, and speaks English well, but with an accent. The Maharajah was exceedingly pleasant to me – and thanked me heartily for my care of his children. He had my father's picture in his apartment and said he is never without it. He is full of plans for *revenge*, – and raved in loud tones, from time to time, calling upon God to come out of his hiding and enable him to crush his enemies, the British power. At times he had all the appearance of being raving mad. He told me he that he intends remaining in Paris for two months more, (during which time his wife's confinement may be expected ...) and then going for a little shooting to Algiers. He did not say if he intends returning to Russia.[13]

At the beginning of 1890 an untoward event took place that undermined whatever might have remained of the Maharajah's fighting spirit. Alone in his small hotel bedroom he had a stroke. Uncertain of the nature of this sudden affliction, he had staggered out into the street and taken a cab to his doctor. The doctor was out and he had then driven all round Paris looking for another. Thus the seriousness of the attack had been aggravated and the final result had been paralysis in his left leg and side and the left half of his face.

Victor, who had seen a report of the occurrence in the papers, got leave from his regiment and hurried to Paris. He himself was in a gloomy mood. While serving with the army in Canada he had got into debt and a writ had been served by a money-lender. Going to New York to look for a rich wife he had fallen in love with a girl who was penniless. He had then transferred his affections to the daughter of a banker, described by him as 'most charming and beautiful',[14] but her father had refused to allow the match. The situation for Victor was critical: his father might die without his status as a rebel being reviewed. Victor's own financial future depended on his inheritance and he had his brothers and sisters to consider also. He had no wish to identify himself in any way with India and his father's cause in the Punjab, only to settle down in England and become as much of an Englishman as possible. In his talks with his father Victor used all his powers of persuasion to make him give up his 'mad schemes'[15] and accept his responsibilities towards his family. It was not too difficult to make him agree that the best thing for everybody was for him to ask the queen for a pardon. The ailing Maharajah was pleased to leave it to Victor to be the 'go-between for a reconciliation'.[16]

On 2 April, Cross wrote to Lord Lansdowne, the new viceroy: 'I fancy he [the Maharajah] is in a bad way and getting worse both morally and bodily. His eldest son has been over to Paris once or twice, I am sorry to say. They will not do each other any good. The son has committed an act of bankruptcy; I cannot pay his debts again, but I mean to keep him in the army if I can. He is, however, a thorough oriental in extravagance.'[17] Like his father's, Victor's money troubles were to be a continuing source of worry to the queen.

It was not until the middle of July that plans to ask for a pardon began to mature. Ponsonby had news of them from the ever-informative Oliphant:

I write these lines to say that I have heard from P. Victor Duleep Singh just now ... to inform me that his father is no worse, altho' he seems very much weaker. P. Victor also says that his father is going to write the Queen for pardon – and leave to return to England. P. Frederick is also there by his father's request helping his brother & his father's wife to nurse the Maharajah – Victor has written to a Doctor to send a man-nurse at once; & has begged me to write to his sisters, who are at Cassel, to tell them that their father is ill, that the two brothers are with him, & that there is no danger, & I am to suggest that they will be so pleased to hear of their father's desire to return.

P.S. Since receiving P. Victor's note I went to Lincoln's Inn & saw Mr Burrell of Farrer & Co., the MR's solicitors – Mr Burrell went to Paris on Sunday night by Maharajah's desire – & Mr Burrell says that the left leg & side are paralized [sic] – & the left side of the face is drawn – but that the M.R. can move his left hand. He said that the Doctor was of the opinion that he should be moved out of Paris speedily. Mr Burrell said the Maharajah was calm – & he was not surprised to hear from me of the intention to ask for pardon – Mr Burrell appears to think that the M.R. will never walk again – & that another stroke may possibly follow soon. If the poor deluded M.R. only returned to England to die, it would be a matter of consolation to the children to know that the Queen had forgiven him. I shall be pleased if I can be of any service.'[18]

Lady Login was also anxious to be of service: the Maharajah had written to tell her that he had asked for pardon, and in a letter to Ponsonby she claimed some credit for her part in the affair: 'I hope I may not be deemed too presumptuous but I should be most deeply grateful if you can tell me that the Queen has granted the pardon sought. I think you understand my motive in asking this. I told you that I have more than once urged this step on the Maharajah, but he was then too mad to yield, God however is omnipotent and has opened his eyes.'[19]

On 22 July the Maharajah had a surprise visitor. It was his friend from earlier days, Ronald Leslie-Melville, now Lord Leven, who 'happened' to be in Paris and had decided to pay a call. The Maharajah had been moved into a larger, more airy room.

He was a pitiable sight [Leven wrote to Ponsonby]. All his left side paralysed, he held out a trembling right hand, drew me towards him, & with floods of tears thanked me for coming – over & over again. He wished to be at peace with everybody, he said: and repeatedly expressed the utmost contrition for all he had done. It seemed indeed as if his deep religious fervour (and in his youth he was the most truly conscientious Boy I ever knew) had returned – and I trust it has. He spoke of the disgraceful way he had behaved towards Her Majesty, & told me he had written, or rather dictated, a letter, in the hope that she might graciously be pleased to forgive him – He also wrote an abject apology to the Prince of Wales ... He expressed frequently his deep satisfaction to the Almighty for having struck him down, & thus brought him to a sense of his wrong doing – but he was not always coherent, and I think now, as I have long thought, that he is hardly responsible for his actions. His doctor, who attended him years ago, tells me the M. was even then suffering from diabetes, & that he does not doubt his brain and liver are all affected – as is often the case with that disease.[20]

But despite his shocking state of health the Maharajah appeared not to have lost all his old spirit. He talked 'openly' to Ronald Leven about his recent adventures in Russia and told him that 'they could do nothing now, but when they go to war with us *then* they would arrange matters with him',[21] an attitude that did not seem to relate to the humility he expressed in the letter just written to the queen and which he now showed to Leven:

May it please Your Majesty, My son Victor is writing this letter from my dictation – I have been struck down by the hand of God and am in consequence quite unable to write myself – I have been disappointed in everyone in whom I had been led to believe and now my one desire is to die at peace with all men – I therefore pray Your Majesty to pardon me for all I have done against You and Your Government and I throw myself entirely on Your clemency.

It seems to me that it is the will of God that I should suffer injustice at the hands of Your people.

I can find no one to curse Great Britain and in spite of all her faults and her injustices God blesses her and makes her great and when I look at her, I feel that in fighting against Your country I have been fighting against God – I would return to England were I assured of Your free pardon. I am Your Majesty's obedient servant . . .[22]

On his return to England Leven hastened to consult that other friend and supporter of the Maharajah, the Duke of Grafton. Grafton had already pressed the matter of a pardon with Ponsonby: 'I feel that something ought to be done to *save* him from himself, his greatest enemy,' he had recently written. 'Is there any hope of the Queen accepting his regrets and allowing him to return . . . With all his faults he is not alone to blame, the Government have behaved worse & they are the real cause of the whole case.' As a near neighbour, the duke was also concerned with the situation at Elveden – the house denuded of furniture and the shooting going to the dogs: 'If he does not come it is high time his Estate is put in order for it is a disgrace to the Country that such mismanagement shd. be carried out by Trustees appointed by the Government. 16,000 acres without a labourer employed except under keepers who are a disgrace to the place, also men temporarily employed without homes & living where they can, game live & dead, eggs sold and all around poached for them.'[23]

Leven showed Grafton a copy of the Maharajah's letter and produced it again to the third member of the 'Maharajah committee', Lord Henniker. Henniker, who had already had a word with the secretary of state for India, Lord Cross, on the subject, considered that 'the effect on India must be the chief consideration',[24] in which case it must have been clear to them both that a pardon might be the most effective way to muzzle the Maharajah for all time by publishing his submission and demonstrating clemency. Henniker took up the matter with Ponsonby, commenting on the letter's odd composition: 'It shows to my mind most distinctly that the writer is off his head. The end of it is laughable, were it not sad to think of his being in such a state.' Henniker went on to say that he was not very keen on the idea of the Maharajah coming to England: as their guardian his main concern was the welfare of the children who, under Oliphant's paternal care, were beginning to settle down, even if the latter found it 'impossible to gain any confidence in the Princess Bamba, who rules the others'.[25] Henniker continued:

We have the children in hand, at last now; and if he came back, he must take charge of them. He is surrounded by all sorts of people who will cling to him if he has money to give them. He is, evidently, not responsible for his actions, & I think Lord Leven's suggestion a good one – that he should, if he is pardoned, have a certain income given to him under trust, the residue of his stipend to be accumulated for the benefit of his children. If he had £5,000 a year & we were to go on with the children as we do now, he would have enough to live on, but not enough to encourage those who get money out of him ... The Maharajah would like to live in Italy. Might not this be better than his return to this country – for the present at all events. The question is a *most* difficult one.[26]

Queen Victoria did not see why she should not have her chastened Maharajah back, even if Lord Salisbury was set against his returning. '[I] cannot agree with Ld. S's objection to this poor unfortunate Maharajah's return to England as he wd. be far safer here,' she cyphered Lord Cross. 'I believe many feel with me that the former Govt. are very gtly to blame for what has happened & therefore we shd. be merciful.'[27]

In Paris, the Maharajah, and in particular his family, anxiously awaited a reply to his request for pardon. The reaction from the palace simply indicated that the matter was not to be settled there, but that it would be necessary to apply through the correct channel, in this case the secretary of state. Accordingly he wrote to the despised department, though obliquely soliciting the indulgence of the queen rather than Cross, her minister: 'My Lord, I write to express my great regret for my past conduct towards Her Majesty the Queen-Empress of India. I humbly ask Her Majesty to pardon me, and I trust entirely to the clemency of the Queen.'[28] If the Maharajah had indeed chosen his words carefully so as to avoid prostration before the India Office, Lord Cross's reply made it perfectly clear that it was the government to whom the petitioner's *ultimate* obedience was required: '... I am now commanded to inform you that, on the understanding that henceforward your Highness will remain obedient to the Queen-Empress of India, and will regulate your movements in conformity with instructions that may be issued to you by Her Government, Her Majesty, by the advice of Her Ministers, has been graciously pleased to accord you the pardon you have sought.'[29] The Maharajah chose not to reply, getting Victor to acknowledge and say that his father was too ill to write.[30]

The Maharajah did in fact have a 'slight relapse' at the beginning of August, and Victor considered himself in duty bound to stay with him. The colonel of his regiment 'flatly refused'[31] to give him any more leave and it was finally agreed that he should leave the army where his performance had not in any case shown great promise. But by the middle of the month his father was apparently well enough to contemplate a visit to England, which would indulge his restless wife, give him some sea air and allow him to see his children. Victor informed Ponsonby of the impending visit: 'I hope to bring my father over to England on Tuesday next the 26th and I have taken No. 6 Clifton Gardens, Folkestone, for him for one month. Although he is rapidly recovering his strength and can now walk a little by himself, his head is not quite clear yet and he has been therefore compelled to postpone writing to the Queen himself as he has so much wished.'[32]

The Maharajah arrived in England on the date arranged and settled into the small house with Victor and Frederick, Ada and her two little children. Oliphant, who had been holidaying with the younger children in Lowestoft, had sent eleven-year-old Edward and thirteen-year-old Sophia to visit their father and meet for the first time their stepmother and half-sisters. There was no room for them in the house, so they and their nurse stayed at an hotel nearby. Bamba and Catherine were still at Dresden with their governess Miss Schäfer, but they saw their father when they returned in September on their way to Oxford where they had entered Somerville Hall. 'The Maharajah was delighted with the children,' wrote Arthur Oliphant, 'and was profuse in his thanks for our care of them.'[33] Lord Cross, even if it did not seem to be any of his business, wrote to Ponsonby 'I do not want these young ladies to go to D. Singh. They are much better off at Oxford. At the same time if their father insists upon it I am not quite sure that I can prevent it.' The queen wrote in the margin 'think we cd. *urge* strongly agst. it.'[34]

Financial arrangements for the Maharajah's future had not yet been settled, though Grafton and Henniker were still trying to have their plan agreed to by all parties. 'Pray say nothing about it,' the latter had counselled Ponsonby the day before the Maharajah's arrival in England, 'as the whole thing is very difficult to arrange at present, with a man who is partially mad, & an Indian Council not at all on his side. The Queen will understand this, and will know that I do my best. I propose to let the M.R. settle down at Folkestone & then go there to see him. Perhaps I ought to go to meet him but I think not, and I decide to leave him alone for a short while.'[35]

An account of activities at Folkestone duly reached the queen via Oliphant in his regular letter to her private secretary:

I think I saw that you were to be at Windsor today so I write you a line to say that I went down to Folkestone yesterday and lunched with the Maharajah – I found him very feeble – very humble – very penitent – poor fellow – but in a better condition than I had expected. He complained a good deal of a heavy & dizzy sort of feeling in the head – I recommended massage for the muscles at the back of the neck, & he appeared to think well of the idea.... It is very nice to see the thorough understanding between the Father and Prince Victor who has been quite a nurse and mother & sister to his Father. – I hope that this episode may be for Victor's lasting benefit. The MR talks of going to Aix-la-Chapelle for baths – and then to winter in Paris.[36]

While the Maharajah was taking the waters at Aix-la-Chapelle a plot had been hatched by Henniker and Ponsonby for him to meet the queen during one of her trips to the Continent. She was to be in France in March of 1891 and Victor and Frederick were to arrange for their father to be on hand. Thus the Maharajah, who had expressed his wish to see her, was at Nice when she duly arrived at nearby Grasse and installed herself and her small retinue at the Grand Hôtel. The queen had registered on this occasion as the Countess of Balmoral and her informal programme on the morning of the thirty-first had been a drive in a donkey cart round Miss Alice de Rothschild's beautiful garden to admire her red and mauve anemones which were then looking their best. After luncheon at the hotel she received, in the 'small drawing room below', 'the poor misguided Maharajah'.[37]

She described the meeting in her journal, but with more emotion in a letter to her daughter Vicky:

The poor Maharajah Duleep Singh came to see me yesterday having driven over from Nice with his 2nd son Frederic. He is quite bald & vy. grey but has the same pleasant manner as ever. When I came in I gave him my hand wh. he kissed, and said: 'Pardon my not kneeling' for his left arm and leg are paralysed tho' he can stand and walk a little. I asked him to sit down – & almost directly he burst out into a most terrible & violent fit of crying almost screaming (just as my poor *fat* Indian servant Muhammed did when he lost his child) – and I stroked & held his hand, & he became calm & said: 'Pray excuse me & forgive my faults' & I answered 'They are forgotten & forgiven.' He said: 'I am a poor broken down man' & dwelt on the loss of the use of his left arm as a gt. trial. – I soon took leave & he seemed pleased with the interview – but it was vy. sad –; still I am so glad that we met again & I cld. say I forgave him. His 2nd son came with him ...[38]

Correspondence reveals that the Maharajah was put out by the fact that the queen had not seen fit to receive his wife, for he wrote to complain about it to the Prince of Wales, who seemed to have had no such inhibitions when he met the lady in Paris some time previously. The prince asked Ponsonby for advice as to how to deal with the delicate question:

I cannot do otherwise than send you the extraordinary letter fr. the Maharajah Duleep Singh. When I called upon him at Paris I made the acquaintance of his wife – who was pretty – but appeared to me '*de la bourgeoisie*'. Beyond being English I never heard who she was, but have been told she was an actress. Probably Ld Henniker may know about her antecedents. You must advise me what answer to make & I must say that the last part of his letter is most impertinent – but he is decidedly rather 'crushed' still & not answerable for what he does. I fear if he comes to London this summer he will be troublesome. I have no idea if his wife was received in Parisian Society – but Ld Lytton may know.[39]

In his reply to the prince's letter, Ponsonby implied that the queen had nothing at all to do with the arrangements made for her to meet the Maharajah, adding his first written reference to 'Miss Ashsted', otherwise the Maharajah's former mistress Polly Ash of the Alhambra, and her allowance of £3,000 a year, which may have been common gossip at the India Office all along.

Sir Henry Ponsonby with his humble duty thinks the best answer the Prince of Wales can give the Maharajah is that he knows nothing of the arrangements for his visit here as they were made by Prince Victor and Lord Henniker.

Prince Victor, who was at Aachen, wrote 3 times and telegraphed twice to settle it for his father and said his brother would come with the Maharajah.

Mr. Oliphant told Sir Henry Ponsonby that he did not think there was anything against the Maharani's character though she was of low origin. There was another – a Miss Ashsted (?) who he gave 3,000 a year to during his first wife's life.[40]

The Prince of Wales, who probably knew all about Miss 'Ash', replied: 'Thanks for your letter of 9th. I am not at all keen about entering into a correspondence with the Maharajah with reference to the non-reception of the Maharanee by the Queen – & why on earth he wrote to me I don't know. He ought of course to have written to *you*! but I suppose poor Henniker will have to supply the "broad shoulders" on this occasion.'[41]

A note by the queen on the draft of Ponsonby's letter indicated that it was not because of her former profession that she would not receive the new maharani, but because she disapproved of the fact that she had lived with the Maharajah during his first wife's lifetime. As she expressed it: '. . . the Queen has the strong impression that this Maharani has not been correct. Her being an actress wd. not raise any objections.'

The next news of the Maharajah to arrive at the palace came in a letter from Henniker to Ponsonby, dated 8 May:

I hear from Victor Duleep Singh that his father is taking rooms for the Maharani in Paris, and proposes to take a house near Paris for the summer. I think this is the best solution of the present difficulty. I hope the Queen will think I am right. To have the Maharajah over here just now would not be convenient: but I told Victor that I hoped his father would understand that he was not prevented from coming to England – only that it seemed expedient he should not do so just now.... He – Victor – told me that the Maharajah was quite well in his mind on all ordinary topics, but went off at random when speaking of his troubles, and on serious business.[42]

From Oliphant came the usual comprehensive report on his young charges:

Princess Catherine passed her first examination at Somerville Hall, but her elder sister Princess Bamba failed in French prose and translation, tho' she succeeded in grammar. After they came down from Oxford they, with Miss Schäfer, spent a few days in London with Mrs Oliphant and me; & saw pictures – went to the opera & concerts – & they much enjoyed it – after that they went to Essen where they spent a few days with their aunt, a daughter of old Mr Muller (their grandfather) who is married to the financial manager of Krupp's works, then to Wilhelm (which is close to Miss Schäfer's home) and on to Bayreuth – which they very much enjoyed.

Then they went to Basle where I sent the younger sister & little Edward to meet them, and they are now altogether very happy at Hotel Axenstein, Lake of Lucerne ... I think Her Majesty will see that improvement has taken place in Princess Bamba's mind, – the letter (enclosed) from Bayreuth being quite chatty, and showing how much they have been interested there.

I shall be very sorry for them if they have to return to their father's house, but, if he insists, I don't know that there is any course for us to pursue than that of yielding to his wish.

There was additional news about the father: 'I was in Paris a fortnight ago and saw the Maharajah. He is still very weak and unable to walk much. I did not like the appearance of his face – he looked bloated and unhealthy. In speech he was very humble and grateful for all God's mercies; but he did not touch on the subject of his children, tho' he was pleased to hear from me of their well doing.'

Oliphant added a postscript which contained more positive information of the Maharajah's movements: 'The Maharajah had contemplated visiting Rome just now with his son Frederick, but I hear from the latter that he has deferred his visit until after the Autumn – The Maharajah's wife is at Ostend with her children – Prince Frederick is at Carlsbad and Prince Victor is with his father at St. Cloud.'[43]

The younger children spent the summer on the Continent, chaperoned by the excellent Miss Schäfer. In Switzerland Bamba played the part of the queen of Sheba in a *tableau vivant* and looked, according to her governess, 'extremely well' in her oriental costume. There was an adventure at Grindelwald when the Bear Hotel, where they were staying, caught fire and some of their belongings were burned. The Maharajah, meanwhile, was taking the waters at Royan, near Bordeaux. He was drinking excessively and his health was by no means good – 'very indifferent', according to Oliphant – 'he is, I fear, a miserable being.'[44]

The Maharajah wintered in Algiers, where Victor and Frederick joined him; Ada's younger daughter was christened Ada Irene Helen Beryl in the English church there. Early in 1893 there was bad news from Oliphant: it seemed that thirteen-year-old Edward had returned from his preparatory school at Cobham and developed pleuro-pneumonia; the doctors feared the worst. The Maharajah commissioned Oliphant to send a daily telegram reporting on his son's health.[45] Although Edward showed some improvement, the doctor said there was no question of going to Eton, as he was supposed to do in April. In that month the boy's condition was worse: the tubercular swellings in his stomach would not subside. 'The little boy is on a *water bed*,' wrote the ever-solicitous Oliphant to Ponsonby for the benefit of the queen, '– and life is sustained by *Brandy, Champagne, Brands Essence, Valentine and nutrient enemas of egg, milk, etc.*' Oliphant feared that it was 'only a question of time as to the wearing out of the delicate little frame'.[46] Bamba was showing what Oliphant described as 'the imperious side of her nature' – she did not believe in doctors and nurses and resented their strict régime. Victor travelled from Paris several times to visit his brother; the Maharajah announced that he too planned to come over, though Oliphant did not think the visit at all likely to take place as the poor man had recently had two heart attacks.[47]

Nevertheless the Maharajah did manage the journey, staying at a Hastings hotel for the weekend of 24 April. Oliphant reported that he was 'very much overcome on seeing his little son, and wept bitterly and loudly – when Prince Victor told him he must not do so, he was quiet. He told his little boy he had come a long way to see him, and hoped his visit would do him good.' Before leaving the Maharajah wrote on a sheet of paper 'The Lord is my Shepherd' and gave it to his son.[48]

Queen Victoria had been following Edward's illness with concern. There was bad news on 29 April. Oliphant's last *communiqué* read: 'I write to inform Her Majesty with the greatest regret that the little prince is rapidly failing.'[49] A week after the Maharajah's return to Paris, the news came of his youngest son's death. He was not well enough to be present at the burial at Elveden.

The Maharajah fretted in the close confinement of his Paris lodging, missing his sport and his old friends, assailed by feelings of melancholy and self-pity. Oliphant reported that he was 'in a most critical condition, kidney trouble – dropsical symptoms – intense irritability of temper'.[50] At times he would be his amiable old self, at others he would fulminate against the India Office and concoct wild plans to get even with them; sometimes he would express regret for his ingratitude to 'his only real friend' – the queen. He seemed to have given up altogether his aspirations to saintly Sikhdom – Abdul Rasul, back in Paris after release from imprisonment in India, was suing him for breach of contract. Lord Dufferin, his old antagonist, who was just then Ambassador in Paris, reported back to the queen that Baron Texter de

Ravisi, a Paris friend of the Maharajah, had told him he had talked a great deal about religion and the Bible and had 'expressed his wish to die with his hand upon that Book'.[51]

Victor, despite his admirable patience and sense of duty as his father's eldest son, was having a difficult time. The poor Maharajah must have realized that he was being a burden to his family and, perhaps because his second wife was not showing him the dedication he felt was his due, said he would go to Egypt for the winter, and would go alone. No doubt he wished to make his peace with the American missionaries in Cairo who must have felt uncomfortable at the outcome of a marriage they had encouraged. It was, of course, not practical for him to travel alone, so Victor said he would accompany him and made all the arrangements for the journey, but no sooner had he done so than his father changed his mind, declaring that he had thought better of the idea and would re-visit Algiers. It could be imagined that he had a hankering for the temperate Mediterranean, but despite any ideas he may have had in this direction he was finally persuaded that they would take a small house in London for the winter, and accordingly in October, Frederick went to look for one with his stepmother, glad to escape from the difficult domestic atmosphere. Victor hurried off to Berlin to be with his best friend, Lord Carnarvon, who had been taken ill there.[52]

It was the first time in two years that his wife had left him without her, but there were his two little girls, Paulina and Ada, to keep him company. He had them visit him every day and enjoyed their simple prattle. Five-year-old Paulina reported that she had had a letter from 'Mammy' and that she was planning a reply. Her father told her to send his love and to ask when she was coming back. He would let the children play with his silver hawk bells, retained since boyhood, a treat they invariably demanded. On Saturday, 21 October, he sent for them three times during the course of the day and on the last occasion, in a spirit they did not then understand, made them a present of the precious mementos of his sporting youth.[53]

That night the Maharajah had what was described as an apoplectic fit. He died on the evening of the following day, never having regained consciousness.

The queen heard the sad news even before the family. Lord Dufferin telegraphed: 'The Maharajah Duleep Singh has died here suddenly in the absence of any of his family who will not arrive till this evening – I have recommended to sanction the body being embalmed.'[54] The following day the Prince of Wales telegraphed his mother from Newmarket: 'I was much shocked at poor Duleep Singh's death having known him so long and saw him in Paris three years ago.'[55]

To Victor, now returned to Paris, and very distressed at having been absent at the critical time, the queen wrote her condolences:

My dear Victor Duleep Singh, It is with sincere concern that I heard of the death of your father which was telegraphed to me by Lord Dufferin & of which I was afterwards informed by your kind letter for which I thank you very much. I need hardly say how I like to *dwell* on former years when I knew your dear Father so well, and saw him so often, & we were all so fond of him. He was so handsome & so charming! But I will *not* dwell on the few years which followed & which were so painful. It is however a great comfort & satisfaction to me that I saw the Maharajah Duleep Singh two years ago at Grasse, & that all was made up between us. I know that this was much owing to your, & your brother Frederick's good influence. I have desired my Lord in Waiting, Lord Camoys, to attend your Father's funeral on my behalf, & to place a wreath on his coffin. Pray accept the expression of my warmest sympathy in your heavy loss, & to convey the same to your brothers & sisters. Be assured that I shall always take the deepest interest in the welfare & happiness of yourself and your Brother & Sisters – & Believe me always your affectionate friend & Godmother. Victoria R.I.[56]

It is not on record if the bereaved maharani was in any way put out by the queen's continuing lack of recognition.

The funeral took place on 29 October in the little church opposite the house at Elveden. The Maharajah's coffin stood on low pine trestles in the simple chancel, flanked on each side by family pews. Long before half-past twelve, when the service was scheduled to begin, the church was quite filled by estate workers and people from neighbouring villages, many of whom discreetly withdrew into the churchyard on the arrival of the 'gentry' come up from London by special train. To the accompaniment of appropriately gloomy chords from the organ, Ada entered the church led by Victor, followed by Frederick, Bamba, Catherine and Sophia. Lord Camoys made a stately stand-in for the queen. Lord Kimberley also sent a representative. Sir Owen Burne attended in person. After the service the coffin was carried on the shoulders of burly tenants to the open grave and deposited in a small stone vault. Wreaths from old friends lay round about: the maharani's was a star of lilies and camellias with ADA worked in violets in the middle; there were remembrances from the Walsinghams, the Hennikers, Ronald Leven, Mitchell Henry MP, the Logins' son, and many other friends from France and England. The Prince of Wales sent a wreath inscribed 'For old Lang Syne'. Another, made of immortelles, simply said 'From Queen Victoria'.[57] The plate on the coffin lid told a brief story of birth and death – 'Duleep Singh, Maharajah of Lahore, GHCSI. Born 4th September 1838. Died 22 October 1893.'

Postscript

❧

THE Maharajah's second wife, Ada, died in 1930.

Of the Maharajah's children by his first marriage, Victor married Lady Anne Coventry in 1892 and died without issue in 1918. Frederick died unmarried in 1928; he was a popular Norfolk squire and an enthusiastic local historian. He lived at Blo Norton Hall. Bamba married Dr Sutherland, who was at one time in charge of the Lahore Medical School. Bamba died in Lahore, without issue, in 1957. Of Catherine and Sophia, little information can be found, except that neither had children, and Sophia died in 1948.

As for the children of the second marriage: Ada married M. Villement and died without issue in 1926, having committed suicide. Paulina married Lieut. Terry and was also childless.

Thus, so far as the record shows, there are no living direct descendants of the Maharajah Duleep Singh.

Elveden was sold by the Maharajah's trustees at the India Office to the 1st Earl of Iveagh in 1894 for £159,000. The estate is owned today by the present Lord Iveagh.

In 1966 Thakur Singh's grandson was paid 5,000 rupees by the Government of the Punjab as payment of 'symbolic compensation of land confiscated during the British regime', and in recognition of the part he played in Duleep Singh's 'struggle against the British Government in India'.

Reference Notes

LIST OF ABBREVIATIONS

RA   The Royal Archives, Windsor Castle.
Vic. Add. Victorian additional manuscripts under above reference.
PRO   Public Record Office.
FO   Foreign Office document under above reference.
IOR   India Office Records.
GS   Document published in *Maharajah Duleep Singh Correspondence* ed. Ganda Singh. Dept. of Punjab Historical Studies, Punjabi University, Patiala, 1972.

CHAPTER I

1 Punjab Papers, ed. Bikrama Jit Hasrat (Hoshiapur, 1970).
2 Queen Victoria's Journal, 6 July 1854 (RA).
3 H. Edwardes, *Indian Policy* (London 1868).
4 GS (33) Hardinge to Lawrence, 23 Oct. 1847.
5 Broughton Mss, Hardinge to Hobhouse, 14 Aug. 1847.
6 Ed. J. Mahajan, *The Private Corresp. of Sir Frederick Currie* (New Delhi 1947). Hardinge to Currie, 14 Dec. 1847.
7 Broughton Mss, Hardinge to Lawrence, 14 Aug. 1847.
8 Sir H.Lawrence, *Lahore Political Diaries* (Allahabad 1909). Extract dated 21 Aug. 1847.
9 GS (25), Rani Jindan to J.Lawrence, undated. Translated from the Punjabi.
10 GS (26), Rani Jindan to J.Lawrence, undated. Translated from the Punjabi.
11 GS (27), Rani Jindan to J.Lawrence, 30 Aug. 1847. Translated from the Punjabi.
12 GS (32), Hardinge to Eliot, 27 Aug. 1847.
13 Sir H.Lawrence, op. cit., extract dated 4 Dec. 1847.
14 Ibid., 24 Nov. 1847.
15 Ibid., 10 July 1847.
16 Punjab Papers, op. cit.
17 Ibid.
18 Ibid.
19 Ibid.
20 G.Meredith, 'Chillianwallah', *Chambers' Edinburgh Journal*, 7 July 1849.
21 Treaty of Bhyrowal, 29 Mar. 1849.
22 Broughton Mss, Dalhousie to Hobhouse, 22 Dec. 1848.

23 Ibid., Dalhousie to Hobhouse, 4 April 1849.
24 L.Login, *Sir John Login and Duleep Singh* (London 1890). Report by H.M.Eliot, 29 March 1849.
25 Ibid., Login to Mrs Login, 29 April 1849.
26 Ibid., Login to Mrs Login, 10 April 1849.
27 Ibid., Login to Lawrence, 31 Aug. 1849.
28 Ibid., Login to Mrs Login, 5 Sept. 1849.
29 Helen C.Mackenzie, *Life in the Mission, the Camp and the Zanana.* (London 1853).
30 Ed. J.Baird, *Private Letters of the Marquess of Dalhousie* (Edinburgh 1910). Dalhousie to Couper, 15 Dec. 1854.
31 RA 09/3, Dalhousie to Queen Victoria, 20 Jan. 1851. Copy.
32 RA 09/2, Dalhousie to Queen Victoria, 6 Feb. 1850.
33 L.Login, op. cit., Login to Mrs Login, 29 April 1849.
34 IOR Eur. Mss F85/322/381, Hodson to Lawrence, 20 July 1849.
35. L.Login, op. cit., Login to Mrs Login, 5 Sept. 1849.

CHAPTER 2

1 L.Login, op. cit., Burn to Login, 11 Dec. 1849.
2 Ibid., Eliot to Login, 11 Dec. 1849.
3 Ibid., Login to Mrs Login, 16 July 1850.
4 Ibid., Login to Mrs Login, 21 Feb. 1850.
5 Ibid., Login to Mrs Login, 15 Feb. 1850.
6 Ibid., Login to Mrs Login, 6 March 1850.
7 Ibid., Login to Mrs Login, 21 April 1850.
8 Ibid., Login to Mrs Login, 10 July 1850.
9 Ed. E. Dalhousie Login, *Lady Login's Recollections* (London 1916).
10 RA 09/22, Dalhousie to Queen Victoria, 2 Oct. 1854.
11 L.Login, op. cit., undated.
12 Ibid., Login to Dalhousie, 4 April 1850.
13 Ibid., Duleep Singh to Login, 2 Dec. 1850.
14 Ibid., Duleep Singh to Login, 9 Dec. 1850.
15 Ibid., Dalhousie to Login, undated.
16 Ibid., Login to Mrs Login, undated.
17 Ibid., Report to Governor General, 27 Jan. 1851.
18 Ibid., Bhajun Lal's Report, 17 Jan. 1851.
19 J.Baird, op. cit., Dalhousie to Couper, 3 March 1851.
20 L.Login, op. cit., Dalhousie to Login, 23 July 1851.
21 E.Dalhousie Login, op. cit.
22 L.Login, op. cit., Dalhousie to Login, 7 June 1852.
23 Ibid., Dalhousie to Duleep Singh, 17 July 1852.
24 Ibid., Dalhousie to Login, 24 Sept. 1852.
25 Ibid., Login to Dalhousie, 10 May 1852.
26 Ibid., Dalhousie to Duleep Singh, 16 Nov. 1853.
27 J.Baird, op. cit., Dalhousie to Couper, 12 March 1853.
28 E.Dalhousie Login, op. cit.
29 London Missionary Society Archives, Jay to Montgomery, 8 March 1853.
30 L.Login, op. cit., Dalhousie to Login, 4 Aug. 1852.

31 J.Baird, op. cit., Dalhousie to Couper, 12 March 1853.

32 L.Login, op. cit., Dalhousie to Duleep Singh, 31 Jan. 1854.

33 Ibid., Dalhousie to Login, 31 Jan. 1854.

34 Ibid., Dalhousie to Login, undated.

35 Ibid., Dalhousie to Login, 25 Feb. 1854.

36 Ibid. Dalhousie to Login, 3 April 1854.

37 Ibid., Sleeman to Login, 17 March 1854.

38 E.Dalhousie Login, op. cit.

39 J.Baird, op. cit., Dalhousie to Couper, 5 April 1854.

40 L.Login, op. cit., Dalhousie to Duleep Singh, 18 April 1854.

CHAPTER 3

1 Queen Victoria's Journal, 6 July 1854 (RA).

2 RA N14/74, Queen Victoria to Dalhousie, 26 July 1854.

3 RA O9/22, Dalhousie to Queen Victoria, 2 Oct. 1854.

4 Queen Victoria's Journal, 10 July 1854 (RA).

5 Ibid., 11 July 1854.

6 Ibid., 13 July 1854.

7 E.Dalhousie Login, op. cit.

8 J.Baird, op. cit., Dalhousie to Couper, 26 Aug. 1854.

9 Queen Victoria's Journal, 23 Oct. 1851 (RA).

10 J.Lord, The Maharajahs (London 1972).

11 Queen Victoria's Journal, 10 July 1854.

12 Ibid., 21, 22 Aug. 1854.

13 RA O9/20, Queen Victoria Memo 23 Aug. 1854.

14 Queen Victoria's Journal, 23, 24 Aug. 1854 (RA).

15 J.Baird, op. cit., Dalhousie to Couper, 11 Oct. 1854.

16 RA A23/123, Aberdeen to Queen Victoria, 31 July 1854.

17 RA A23/141, Aberdeen to Queen Victoria, 26 Aug. 1854.

18 RA A23/142, Queen Victoria Memo, 27 Aug. 1854.

19 Queen Victoria's Journal, 21 Nov. 1854 (RA).

20 IOR L/P&S/18 D17, Lord Dalhousie Minute, 15 Feb. 1856.

21 L.Login, op. cit., Login to Dalhousie, 22 Nov. 1854.

22 E.Dalhousie Login, op. cit.

23 RA S26/55, Queen Victoria to Clarendon, 26 Dec. 1855.

24 L.Login, op. cit., Dalhousie to Login, 22 Sept. 1854.

25 RA O9/19, Login to Phipps, 10 Aug. 1854.

26 Queen Victoria's Journal, 13 July 1854 (RA).

27 L.Login, op. cit., Login to Dalhousie, 9 April 1855.

28 E.Dalhousie Login, op. cit.

CHAPTER 4

1 E.Dalhousie Login, op. cit., Phipps to Login, 5 Sept. 1854.

2 Ibid.

3 RA Vic. Add. N14/77, Queen Victoria to Dalhousie, 24 Nov. 1854.

4 RA Vic. Add. N14/6, Dalhousie to Queen Victoria, 14 March 1856.

5 Queen Victoria's Journal, 14 Dec. 1856 (RA).

6 RA O9/23, Queen Victoria Memo to Stanley, 15 Dec. 1856.

7 RA 09/259, Stanley to Queen Victoria, 30 Oct. 1856.

8 E.Dalhousie Login, op. cit.

9 RA Vic. Add. N15/82, Clarendon to Queen Victoria, 20 Sept. 1857.

10 RA N15/83, Queen Victoria to Clarendon, 23 Sept. 1857.

11 RA N15/90, Queen Victoria to Clarendon, 28 Sept. 1857.

12 RA 09/24, Login to Phipps, 30 Sept. 1857.

13 L.Login, op. cit., Phipps to Login, 9 Feb. 1858.

14 Queen Victoria's Journal, 18 Feb. 1858 (RA).

15 L.Login, op. cit., Duleep Singh to Lady Login, 3 March 1858.

16 Ibid., Duleep Singh to Lady Login, 3 May 1858.

17 Ibid., Duleep Singh to Lady Login, 3 Sept. 1858.

18 Queen Victoria's Journal, 11 Nov. 1858 (RA).

19 RA 09/26, Queen Victoria to Stanley, 12 Nov. 1858.

20 RA 09/27, Stanley to Queen Victoria, 13 Nov. 1858.

21 RA Vic. Add. N20/140, Queen Victoria to Canning, 2 Dec. 1858.

22 Norfolk County Record Office, Baker to Wharncliffe, 30 March 1859.

23 Ibid.

24 Ibid. Baker to his sister Min., 4 Feb. 1859.

25 E.Dalhousie Login, op. cit.

26 RA Vic. Add. N3/205, Lady Login to Phipps, 26 Feb. 1859.

27 E.Dalhousie Login, op. cit., Lady Login to Queen Victoria, 31 March 1859.

28 RA Vic. Add. N3/206, Lady Login to Phipps, 25 April 1859.

29 E.Dalhousie Login, op. cit.

30 Ibid.

31 Ibid., Phipps to Lady Login, 8 April 1859.

32 RA Vic. Add. N3/24, Queen Victoria to Prince of Wales, 16 April 1859.

33 E.Dalhousie Login, op. cit.

34 RA Vic. Add. N3/286, Lady Login to Phipps, 25 April 1859.

35 RA 010/1, Stanley to Duleep Singh, 20 May 1859.

36 RA PP3396, Wood to Phipps, 1 Feb. 1860.

37 RA 010/4, Phipps to Duleep Singh, 23 June 1859.

38 Queen Victoria's Journal, 31 March 1855 (RA).

39 L.Login, op. cit., Duleep Singh to Lady Login, 9 July 1859.

40 Duleep Singh to Login, Nov. 1859.

41 Normanby Archives, Lady Normanby to Lord Mulgrave, 22 Sept. 1859.

42 Ibid., Lady Normanby to Lord Mulgrave, 3 Oct. 1859.

43 RA Vic. Add. N3/270, Harcourt to Phipps, 20 Dec. 1859.

44 RA Vic. Add. N3/262, Queen Victoria to Prince of Wales, 15 Dec. 1859.

45 RA Vic. Add. N3/252, Prince Consort to Phipps.

46 RA Vic. Add. N3/299, Phipps to Hogg, 25 May 1860.

CHAPTER 5

1 L.Login, op. cit., Ramsay to Login, 28 Nov. 1860.

2 RA Y21/56, Duleep Singh to Queen Victoria, 19 Dec. 1860.

3 RA N24/80, Canning to Wood, 3 March 1861.

4 Ibid.

5 Ibid.

6 L.Login, op. cit., Login to Duleep Singh, 18 Jan. 1861.

7 Ibid., Duleep Singh to Login, undated Feb. 1861.

8 Ibid., Duleep Singh to Login, un-dated Feb. 1861.
9 E.Dalhousie Login, op. cit.
10 Queen Victoria's Journal, 2 July 1861 (RA).
11 E.Dalhousie Login, op. cit., Duleep Singh to Lady Login, 30 Sept. 1861.
12 Normanby Archives, Lady Normanby to Lord Mulgrave, 2 July 1861.
13 RA PP9877, Login to Phipps, 30 Dec. 1861.
14 L.Login, op. cit., Duleep Singh to Login, undated (July 1861).
15 E.Dalhousie Login, op. cit., Duleep Singh to Login, undated (1861).

16 Queen Victoria's Journals, 1 Nov. 1860.
17 L.Login, op. sit., Phipps to Login, 4 Jan. 1862.
18 Ibid., Duleep Singh to Login, un-dated June 1862.
19 Ibid., Lawrence to Login, 8 June 1862.
20 Ibid., Phipps to Login, 16 June 1862.
21 W.P.Frith, My Autobiography and Reminiscences (London 1887).
22 E.Dalhousie Login, op. cit.
23 Ibid.
24 A.Watson, The American Mission in Egypt (Pittsburgh 1898).

CHAPTER 6

1 A.Watson, op. cit.
2 Ibid.
3 Ibid.
4 Ibid.
5 E.Dalhousie Login, op. cit.
6 A.Watson, op. cit.
7 RA PP17340, Colquhoun to Palmerston, 28 April 1864.
8 RA 010/15, Oliphant to Phipps, 1 May 1864.
9 RA PP17340, Duleep Singh to Phipps, 10 May 1864.

10 RA 010/14, Lady Login to Phipps, undated (1864).
11 RA PP 5413, Oliphant to Phipps, 28 June 1869.
12 The Times of India (Calcutta), 30 June 1864.
13 RA PP 17340, Oliphant to Phipps, 26 July 1864.
14 E.Dalhousie Login, op. cit., Lady Leven to Lady Login, 29 July 1864.
15 RA PP 17736, Oliphant to Phipps, 20 Aug. 1864.

CHAPTER 7

1 The Builder (London), 18 Nov. 1871.
2 H.Gladstone, Record Bags and Shooting Records (London 1930).
3 T.W.Turner, Memoirs of a Gamekeeper (London 1954).
4 E.Dalhousie Login, op. cit., Lady Leven to Lady Login, 28 Dec. 1865.
5 'One of the Old Brigade', London in the Sixties (London 1908).

6 Queen Victoria's Journal, 20 March 1867 (RA).
7 Ibid., 16 March 1868.
8 IOR L/P&S/18 D25 (72), Argyll to Duleep Singh 4 July 1870.
9 IOR L/P&S/18 D25 (75), Duleep Singh to Argyll, 8 July 1870.
10 Ibid., Argyll to Duleep Singh, 21 July 1870.
11 'One of the Old Brigade', op. cit.
12 Anon. (J.F.Osgood), Uncensored Recollections (London 1924).

13 *The Times of India* (Calcutta), 6 May 1873.
14 Queen Victoria's Journal, 30 Aug. 1873 (RA).
15 RA 010/19, Biddulph to Oliphant.

16 *Vanity Fair* (London), 26 Jan. 1878.
17 Princess Bamba Singh, Introduction in *Portraits in Norfolk Houses*, ed. E.Farrar (Norwich 1928).

CHAPTER 8

1 RA 09/32, Queen Victoria to Maharani Bamba Duleep Singh, undated Jan. 1878. Draft.
2 RA 09/34, Messrs Coutts and Co. to Duleep Singh, 9 Jan. 1878. Copy.
3 RA 010/22, Duleep Singh to Salisbury, undated (Jan. 1978). Copy.
4 RA 09/36, Salisbury to Queen Victoria, 4 March 1878.
5 IOR L/P&S/18 D25 (83), Minutes of Political Committee, 10, 28 March 1878.
6 Ibid. (85), Salisbury to Duleep Singh, 2 April 1878.
7 RA 09/39, Duleep Singh to Salisbury, 8 April 1878.
8 IOR L/P&S/18 D25 (87), Mallet to Sackville-West, 24 May 1876.
9 Ibid. (89), Duleep Singh to Cranbrook, 13 May 1878.
10 Ibid. (92), Cranbrook to Duleep Singh, 31 May 1878.
11 RA Vic. Add. N2/11, Duleep Singh to Queen Victoria, 4 Oct. 1880.
12 IOR L/P&S/18 D25 (95), Report by Colonel the Hon. W.Sackville-West, 12 Aug. 1878.
13 Ibid. (93), Duleep Singh to Cranbrook, 2 Aug. 1878.
14 RA 09/43, Duleep Singh to Queen Victoria, 3 Aug. 1878.
15 RA 09/46, Queen Victoria to Duleep Singh, 12 Aug. 1878. Copy.
16 RA 09/45 Queen Victoria to Cranbrook, 9 Aug. 1878.
17 Hertford Archives, Duleep Singh to Hertford, undated.

18 RA 010/23, Hertford to Biddulph, 1 Aug. 1878.
19 Sir O.T.Burne, *Memories* (London 1907).
20 IOR L/P&S/18 D25 (110), Hartington to Duleep Singh, 20 Aug. 1878. Enclosure.
21 Ibid. (95), Sec. of State to Govt. of India, 6 March 1879.
22 Ibid. (98), Govt. of India to Sec. of State, 7 July 1879.
23 Ibid. (100), Cranbrook to Duleep Singh, 20 Aug. 1879.
24 Ibid. (101), Duleep Singh to Cranbrook, 25 Aug. 1879.
25 RA Vic. Add. N2/2, Duleep Singh to Queen Victoria, 25 Aug. 1879.
26 IOR L/P&S/18 D25 (102), Duleep Singh to Cranbrook, 18 Feb. 1880.
27 Ibid. (106), Cranbrook to Duleep Singh, 10 March 1880.
28 Ibid. (107), Duleep Singh to Cranbrook, 12 March 1880.
29 Ed. M.V.Brett, *Journals and Letters* (London 1934). Esher to Stead, 22 April 1880.
30 IOR L/P&S/18 D25 (110), Hartington to Duleep Singh, 20 Aug. 1880.
31 Ibid. (112), Duleep Singh to Hartington, 24 Aug. 1880.
32 RA Vic. Add. N2/65, Duleep Singh to Queen Victoria, 13 Sept. 1880.
33 RA Vic. Add. N2/8, Queen Victoria to Duleep Singh, 18 Sept. 1880.
34 RA Vic. Add. N2/6, Queen Victoria to Hartington, 16 Sept. 1880.

35 RA Vic. Add. N2/11, Duleep Singh to Queen Victoria, 4 Oct. 1880.

36 RA Vic. Add. N2/17, Queen Victoria to Duleep Singh, 5 Nov. 1880.

37 RA Vic. Add. N2/19, Duleep Singh to Queen Victoria, 10 Nov. 1880.

CHAPTER 9

1 IOR L/P&S/18 D25 (118), Duleep Singh to Hartington, 3 Feb 1881.

2 RA 010/35, Duleep Singh to Hartington, 1 April 1882.

3 RA 010/36, Hartington to Ponsonby, 7 Sept. 1881.

4 RA 010/37, Queen Victoria Memo, 4 Sept. 1881.

5 IOR L/P&S/18 D25 (121), Duleep Singh to Hartington, 27 March 1882.

6 Ibid. (124), Duleep Singh to Hartington, 1 April 1882.

7 Ibid. (125), Hartington to Duleep Singh, 4 April 1882.

8 Ibid. (127), Duleep Singh to Hartington, 16 April 1882.

9 Ibid. (128), Duleep Singh to Hartington, 26 June 1882.

10 RA Vic. Add. N2/22, Duleep Singh to Hartington, 21 July 1882. Copy.

11 RA Vic. Add. N2/22b, Vaughan Hawkins Opinion, 10 Aug. 1882.

12 RA Vic. Add. N2/20, Duleep Singh to Queen Victoria, 15 Aug. 1882.

13 *The Times* (London), 31 Aug. 1882.

14 Evans Bell, *The English in India* (London 1859).

15 Evans Bell, *The Annexation of the Punjab and the Maharajah Duleep Singh* (London 1882).

< RA Vic. Add. N2/29, Burne to Ponsonby, 2 Nov. 1882.

17 RA Vic. Add. N2/26, Duleep Singh to Queen Victoria, 27 Sept. 1882.

18 RA Vic. Add. N2/29, Burne to Ponsonby, 2 Nov. 1882.

19 RA Vic. Add. N2/30, Queen Victoria Memo to Ponsonby, undated Nov. 1882.

20 RA Vic. Add. N2/32, Queen Victoria to Duleep Singh, 5 Nov. 1882.

CHAPTER 10

1 RA Vic. Add. N2/37, Duleep Singh to Kimberley, 1 March 1883.

2 RA Vic. Add. N2/39, Kimberley to Duleep Singh, 21 March 1883.

3 RA Vic. Add. N2/40, Queen Victoria Memo to Ponsonby, undated March 1883.

4 RA Vic. Add. N2/42, Burne to Ponsonby, 22 April 1883.

5 RA Vic. Add. N2/51, Hertford to Ponsonby, 28 June 1883.

6 RA Vic. Add. N2/57, Queen Victoria Memo to Ponsonby, 2 Aug. 1883.

7 *Hansard Parliamentary Debates*, vol. cclxxxii (London 1883).

8 RA Vic. Add. N2/43, Duleep Singh Petition, undated.

9 Ibid., Duleep Singh to Ponsonby, 19 July 1883.

10 RA Vic. Add. N2/61, Queen Victoria to Duleep Singh, 3 Aug. 1883.

11 RA Vic. Add. N2/83, Hertford to Ponsonby, 25 Aug. 1883.

12 GS (161), Lord Ripon and six others to Kimberley, 17 Aug. 1883.

13 RA Vic. Add. N2/98, Leslie-Melville to Ponsonby, 3 Sept. 1883.

14 RA Vic. Add. N2/107, Hertford to Ponsonby, 15 Sept. 1883.

15 RA Vic. Add. N2/85, Queen

Victoria to Kimberley, 26 Aug. 1883. Draft by Ponsonby.

16 RA Vic. Add. N2/73, Gladstone to Queen Victoria, 11 Aug. 1883.

17 RA Vic. Add. N2/129, Kimberley to Ponsonby, 4 Dec. 1883.

18 RA Vic. Add. N2/80, Duleep Singh to Ponsonby, 21 Aug. 1883.

19 RA Vic. Add. N2/145, Duleep Singh to Palace, Memo, 15 Dec. 1883.

20 RA Vic. Add. N2/174, Duleep Singh to Ponsonby, 15 Dec. 1883.

21 RA Vic. Add. N2/162, Duleep Singh to Ponsonby, 19 Jan. 1884.

22 RA Vic. Add. N2/167, Duleep Singh to Ponsonby, 15 July 1884.

23 RA Vic. Add. N2/183, Knollys to Ponsonby, 16 Aug. 1884.

24 RA Vic. Add. N2/173, Queen Victoria to Duleep Singh, 12 Sept. 1884.

25 RA Vic. Add. N2/176, Duleep Singh to Queen Victoria, 16 Sept. 1884.

26 RA Vic. Add. N2/165, Note by Queen Victoria on Duleep Singh's letter.

27 RA Vic. Add. N2/180, Queen Victoria to Duleep Singh, 29 Sept. 1884.

28 RA Vic. Add. N2/114, Duleep Singh to Queen Victoria, 4 Oct. 1884.

29 RA Vic. Add. N2/196, Duleep Singh to Ponsonby, 18 March 1885.

30 RA Vic. Add. N2/202, Duleep Singh to Ponsonby, 9 April 1885.

31 RA Vic. Add. N2/203, Ponsonby to Duleep Singh, 13 April 1885.

32 RA Vic. Add. N2/210, Ponsonby Memo, undated.

33 IOR L/P&S/18 D25, Kimberley to Dufferin, 15 April 1885.

34 Ibid., Dufferin to Kimberley, 16 April 1885.

35 RA Vic. Add. N2/205, Duleep Singh to Kimberley, 21 April 1885.

36 RA Vic. Add. N2/209, Dufferin to Kimberley, 1 May 1885.

37 Ibid.

CHAPTER II

1 GS (209), Tupper to Durand, 12 Dec. 1885.

2 GS (117), Thakur Singh to Duleep Singh, 9 Nov. 1883.

3 IOR Home 101, Memo, 4 Dec. 1885.

4 RA Vic. Add. N2/215, Duleep Singh to Ponsonby, 12 May 1885.

5 RA Vic. Add. N2/242, Ponsonby Memo to Queen Victoria, 14 Aug. 1885.

6 RA Vic. Add. N2/243, Ponsonby to Churchill, 15 April 1885.

7 RA Vic. Add. N2/245, Churchill to Ponsonby, 17 Aug. 1885.

8 RA Vic. Add. N2/260, Henniker to Ponsonby, 25 Aug. 1885.

9 RA Vic. Add. N2/249, Moore to Ponsonby, 17 Aug. 1885.

10 RA Vic. Add. N2/272, Grafton to Ponsonby, 25 Aug. 1885.

11 RA Vic. Add. N2/262, St George Walker, Rector of Elveden, to Under-Sec. of State, 11 Sept. 1885.

12 RA Vic. Add. N2/265, Duleep Singh to Queen Victoria, 17 Sept. 1885.

13 Ibid.

14 RA Vic. Add. N2/278, Duleep Singh to Churchill, 2 Nov. 1885.

15 RA Vic. Add. N2/290, Duleep Singh to Churchill, 2 Dec. 1885.

16 RA Vic. Add. N2/288, Queen Vic-

toria's note attached to Duleep Singh's letter. See note 14 above.

17 RA Vic. Add. N2/293, Letter from Duke of Grafton and Lord Henniker, accompanying Petition on behalf of Maharajah Duleep Singh, to Queen Victoria, 8 Dec. 1885.

CHAPTER 12

1 RA Vic. Add. N2/306, Ponsonby to Queen Victoria, 21 Jan. 1886.
2 RA Vic. Add. N2/317, Grafton to Ponsonby, 17 Feb. 1886.
3 IOR L/P&S/18 D25, Duleep Singh to Kimberley, 10 Feb. 1886.
4 RA Vic. Add. N2/309, Henniker to Ponsonby, 24 Jan. 1886.
5 RA Vic. Add. N2/314, Grafton to Ponsonby, 30 Jan. 1886.
6 Ibid.
7 RA Vic. Add. N2/321, Kimberley to Ponsonby, 30 Jan. 1886.
8 RA Vic. Add. N2/322, Gladstone to Ponsonby, 25 Feb. 1886.
9 IOR L/P&&S/18 D25 (187), Dufferin to Churchill, 16 Jan. 1886.
10 GS (216), Memorandum of Conversation between Sir Owen Burne and Maharajah Duleep Singh, 29 Jan. 1886.
11 GS (218), Kimberley to Dufferin, 2 Feb. 1886.
12 IOR L/P&S/18 D25 (194), Record of Interview between Lord Kimberley and Maharajah Duleep Singh, 8 Feb. 1886.
13 Ibid.
14 Ibid. (201), Dufferin to Kimberley, 18 March 1886.
15 Ibid. (202), Kimberley to Dufferin, 18 March 1886.
16 Ibid. (203), Dufferin to Kimberley, 20 March 1886.
17 Ibid. (206), Sir Owen Burne Memo, 24 March 1886.
18 Ibid. (207), Duleep Singh to Burne, 24 March 1886.
19 The Standard (London), 25 March 1886.
20 The Pioneer (Lahore), 16 April 1886.
21 GS (254), Duleep Singh to Burne, 30 March 1886.
22 Queen Victoria's Journal, 30 April 1886 (RA).
23 RA Vic. Add. N2/328, Duleep Singh to Queen Victoria, 31 March 1886.
24 GS (293), Forbes to Young, 19 April 1886.

CHAPTER 13

1 GS (435), Col. Hennessy's Opinion, 10 Feb. 1886.
GS (237), Abstract of Political Intel-
2 ligence, Punjab Police, 20 March 1886.
3 IOR L/P&S/18 D25 (214), Kimberley to Dufferin, 31 March 1886.
4 GS (265), Macpherson to Forbes, 6 April 1886.
5 GS (280), Private Sec. Lieut. Gov. Punjab to Foreign Secretary (India), 16 April 1886.
6 IOR L/P&S/18 D25 (215), Dufferin to the Res., Aden, 3 March 1886.
7 Ibid. (216), Dufferin to Kimberley, 15 April 1886.
8 The Pioneer (Lahore), 16 April 1886.
9 GS (288), Ilbert, Memo, 20 April 1886.
10 IOR L/P&S/18 D25 (217), Dufferin to Kimberley, 16 April 1886.
11 RA Vic. Add. N2/329, Kimberley to Ponsonby, 20 April 1886.

12 GS (331), Abstract of Political Intelligence, Punjab Police, 8 May 1886.

13 *The Tribune* (Lahore), 1 May 1886.

14 GS (276), Viceroy to Res., Aden, 15 April 1886.

15 GS (328), Res., Aden, to Dufferin, 5 May 1886.

16 GS (300), Duleep Singh to Dufferin, 22 April 1886.

17 GS (301), Dufferin to Duleep Singh, 22 April 1886.

18 RA Vic. Add. N2/341, Baring to Dufferin, 30 April 1886. Copy.

19 GS (316), Duleep Singh to Dufferin, 29 April 1886.

20 IOR L/P&S/18 D25 (222), Dufferin to Duleep Singh, 30 April 1886.

21 GS (373), Res. Aden to Viceroy, 1 May 1886.

22 IOR L/P&S/18 D25 (222), Duleep Singh to Dufferin, 1 May 1886.

23 GS (311), Duleep Singh to Dufferin, 27 April 1886.

24 RA 09/50/51, Dufferin to Queen Victoria, 14 May 1886.

25 RA 09/52, Queen Victoria to Dufferin, 10 June 1886.

26 GS (341), Duleep Singh to Dufferin, 12 May 1886.

27 GS (342), Lieut. Gov., Lahore, to Foreign Sec., Simla, 14 May 1886.

28 IOR L/P&S/18 D25 (222), Dufferin to Res., Aden, 15 May 1886.

29 Ibid. (225), Res., Aden to Dufferin, 25 May 1886.

30 *Hansard Parliamentary Debates*, vol. cccvi (London 1886).

31 GS (395), *Shamsher Akhbar* (Madras), 24 May 1886.

32 IOR L/PAS/18 D25 (225), Duleep Singh to Dufferin, 28 May 1886.

33 GS (372), Durand to Burne, 28 May 1886.

34 IOR L/P&S/18 D25, Durand to Dufferin, 1 June 1886.

35 Ibid., Dufferin to Duleep Singh, 1 June 1886.

36 RA Vic. Add. N2/346, Duleep Singh to Queen Victoria, 1 June 1886.

37 RA Vic. Add. N2/347, Queen Victoria to Duleep Singh, 2 June 1886.

38 RA Vic. Add. N2/348, Duleep Singh to Queen Victoria, 2 June 1886.

39 RA Vic. Add. N2/356, Kimberley to Ponsonby, 3 June 1886.

40 IOR L/P&S/18 D25 (225), Dufferin to Res., Aden, 30 May 1886.

41 Ibid., Duleep Singh to Dufferin, 1 June 1886.

42 RA Vic. Add. N2/346, Duleep Singh to Ponsonby, 1 June 1886.

43 RA Vic. Add. N2/358, Queen Victoria Memo, 4 June 1886.

44 RA Vic. Add. N2/365, Queen Victoria Note, 3 July 1886.

45 *The Times of India* (Calcutta), 6 July 1886.

CHAPTER 14

1 RA Vic. Add. N2/359, Ponsonby to Queen Victoria, 7 June 1886.

2 GS (432), Duleep Singh to Montgomery, 17 June 1886.

3 RA Vic. Add. N2/360, Duleep Singh to Grafton, 26 June 1886. Copy.

4 A.C. Benson and Viscount Esher (ed.), *Letters of Queen Victoria* (London 1908). Queen Victoria to Salisbury, 22 Aug. 1886.

5 RA Vic. Add. N2/368, Queen Victoria to Duleep Singh, 6 July 1886.

6 RA Vic. Add. N2/370, Grafton to Ponsonby, 8 July 1886.
7 RAO 10/39, Duleep Singh to Queen Victoria, 10 July 1886.
8 K.S.Thapar, op. cit., Kotzbue to de Giers, July 1886.
9 Ibid.
10 Ibid., Kotzbue to Duleep Singh'
11 RA Vic. Add. N2/383, Grafton to Ponsonby, 12 Aug. 1886.
12 Ibid., Enclosure to above.
13 RA Vic. Add. N2/388, Dufferin to Queen Victoria, 17 Aug. 1886.
14 RA Vic. Add. N2/398, Grafton to Ponsonby, 31 Aug. 1886.
15 RA Vic. Add. N2/406, Duleep Singh to Grafton, 7 Sept. 1886.
16 RA Vic. Add. N2/402, Henniker to Ponsonby, 7 Sept. 1886.
17 RA Vic. Add. N2/416, Ponsonby to Queen Victoria, 10 Oct. 1886.
18 RA Vic. Add. N2/404a, Grafton to Ponsonby, 8 Sept. 1886.
19 Thapar, op. cit., Kotzbue to de Giers, Sept. 1886.
20 RA Vic. Add. N2/415, Duleep Singh to Henniker, 10 Oct. 1886. Copy.
21 RA Vic. Add. N2/417, Ponsonby to Henniker, 18 Oct. 1886. Copy.
22 GS (404), Duleep Singh to Watson, 7 Dec. 1886.
23 Ibid.
24 Ibid.
25 Ibid. (405), Watson to Duleep Singh, 9 Dec. 1886.
26 Ibid. (406), Watson to Queen Victoria, 9 Dec. 1886.
27 Ibid. (408), Duleep Singh to Watson, 27 Dec. 1886.
28 Ibid. (412), Watson to Cross, 12 Jan. 1887.
29 Ibid. (415), Cross to Watson, Jan. 1887.
30 Ibid. (416), Duleep Singh to Montgomery, 28 Jan. 1887.
31 Queen Victoria's Journal, 20 Aug. 1886.
32 RA 09/53, Dufferin to Queen Victoria, 8 July 1886.
33 RA Vic. Add. N2/433, Henniker to Ponsonby, 27 Dec. 1887.
34 RA Vic. Add. N2/363, Ponsonby Memo, 3 July 1886.
35 RA Vic. Add. N2/369, Kimberley to Ponsonby, 7 July 1886.
36 RA Vic. Add. N2/428, Oliphant to Ponsonby, 3 Oct. 1887.
37 Ibid.
38 IOR Eur. 243/17 (Cross Papers) Dufferin to Cross. Enclosure 10 Oct. 1887.

CHAPTER 15

1 See Chapter 14, p. 229.
2 RA Vic. Add. Duleep Singh to Duke of Grafton, 26 June 1887.
3 IOR Eur. 243, Cross to Dufferin, 2 June 1887.
4 PRO/FO/181/683/2 X/M 02713, Weber to Cooke, 3 May 1887.
5 Ibid., Morier to Salisbury, 4 May 1887.
6 GS (429), 'St Petersburskia Viedmosti', 21 April 1870. Translation enclosed with Morier despatch.
7 PRO/FO/181/683/2 X/M 02713, Morier to Salisbury, 6 July 1887.
8 GS (428), Duleep Singh to the Tsar, 10 May 1887.
9 GS (450), 'C' to Duleep Singh, undated.
10 GS (430), Duleep Singh to Prince Victor Duleep Singh, 26 May 1887.
11 GS (431), Duleep Singh to Prince Victor Duleep Singh, 26 May 1887.
12 E.Dalhousie Login, op. cit.
13 Ibid.

14 RA Vic. Add. N2/428, Duleep Singh to Prince Victor quoted in Oliphant to Ponsonby, 3 Oct. 1887.

15 RA 010/45, Empress of Prussia to Queen Victoria, 11 Sept. 1887.

16 RA010/44, Duleep Singh to the Empress of Prussia, 25 Aug. 1887.

17 Ibid., Ponsonby Memo to Queen Victoria, Sept. 1887.

18 RA Vic. Add. N2/428, Oliphant to Ponsonby, 18 Sept. 1887.

19 Telegram, Duleep Singh to Prince Victor Duleep Singh, undated.

20 RA Vic. Add. U32/476, Duleep Singh to the Prince of Wales, 1 Oct. 1887.

21 RA Vic. Add. U32/, Queen Victoria to Princess Royal Empress of Prussia), 12 Oct. 1887.

22 IOR Eur. 243/17 (Cross Papers), Cross to Dufferin, 13 Oct. 1887.

23 K.S.Thapar, op. cit., Duleep Singh to Cheremetoff, 6 July 1887.

24 IOR Eur. 243/17 (Cross Papers), Cross to Dufferin, 13 Oct. 1887.

25 K.S.Thapar, op. cit., Duleep Singh to Cheremetoff, 2 Aug. 1887.

26 RA Vic. Add. N2/423, Burne to Ponsonby, 3 Jan. 1888.

27 IOR Eur. 243/17 (Cross Papers), Munshi Azis-ud-Din to Foreign Sec., 2 April 1888.

28 K.S.Thapar, op. cit.

29 GS (450), Duleep Singh to anonymous correspondent, undated.

30 Ibid., Duleep Singh to Indian Princess, undated.

31 Ibid., Duleep Singh to ex-King of Oudh, undated.

32 GS (454), Durand to Bradford, 19 Aug. 1887.

33 GS (460), Henderson to Durand, 22 Aug. 1887.

34 GS (474), Burnby to Durand, 8 Sept. 1887.

35 GS (484), Edgar to Durand, 11 Sept. 1887.

36 IOR Foreign. (Secret 1), 'A.S.' to Foreign Dept., 23 May 1888.

37 GS (543), Letter from 'A.S.' (translated), 23 May 1888.

38 PRO/FO/181 683/2 Hornstedt to Michell, 27 Feb. 1888.

39 GS (563), Report by Hardinge to Foreign Office, 29 July 1888.

40 IOR Eur. 243/17 (Cross Papers), Cross to Dufferin, 30 May 1888.

41 See Chapter 11, p. 194.

CHAPTER 16

1 The Standard (London), 12 Nov. 1888.

2 RA Vic. Add. N2/472, Press cutting (paper not named), 14 Nov. 1888.

3 RA 010/83, Press cutting (The Standard), 13 Feb. 1889.

4 Norfolk Record Office, WLSLY 84, Duleep Singh to Queen Victoria, 23 Feb. 1889.

5 Ibid., Duleep Singh to Walsingham, 20 March 1889.

6 RA Vic. Add. N2/482, Oliphant to Ponsonby, 4 May 1889.

7 Ibid.

8 Ibid.

9 Ibid.

10 RA 010/87, Oliphant to Bigge, 2 Oct. 1889.

11 RA 010/88, Cross to Queen Victoria, 5 Oct. 1889.

12 GS (624), Govt. of India to Sec. of State, 9 Aug. 1889.

13 RA Vic. Add. N2/496, Oliphant to Ponsonby, 16 Sept. 1889.

14 RA Vic. Add. N2/510, Cross to Ponsonby, 14 Nov. 1889.

15 RA Vic. Add. N2/482, Oliphant to Ponsonby, 4 May 1889.
16 RA Vic. Add. N2/522, Oliphant to Ponsonby, 5 Feb. 1890.
17 IOR Eur. 243/17, Cross to Lansdowne, 2 April 1890.
18 RA Vic. Add. N2/548, Oliphant to Ponsonby, 18 July 1890.
19 RA Vic. Add. N2/553, Lady Login to Ponsonby, 22 July 1890.
20 RA Vic. Add. N2/532, Leven to Ponsonby, 22 July 1890.
21 RA Vic. Add. N2/557, Grafton to Ponsonby, 21 July 1890.
22 RA 010/94, Duleep Singh to Queen Victoria, 18 July 1890.
23 RA Vic. Add. N2/557, Grafton to Ponsonby, 21 July 1890.
24 RA Vic. Add. N2/556, Henniker to Ponsonby, 23 July 1890.
25 RA Vic. Add. N2/522, Oliphant to Ponsonby, 5 Feb. 1890.
26 RA Vic. Add. N2/556, Henniker to Ponsonby, 23 July 1890.
27 RA 010/97, Queen Victoria to Cross, undated.
28 RA 010/99, Duleep Singh to Cross, 27 July 1890.
29 RA 010/102, Cross to Duleep Singh, 1 Aug. 1890.
30 RA 010/103, Victor Duleep Singh to Queen Victoria, 3 Aug. 1890.
31 RA Vic. Add. N2/567, Henniker to Ponsonby, 3 Aug. 1890.
32 RA Vic. Add. N2/570, Victor Duleep Singh to Ponsonby, 23 Aug. 1890.
33 Ibid.
34 RA Vic. Add. N2/574, Cross to Ponsonby, 12 Dec. 1890.
35 RA Vic. Add. N2/571, Henniker to Ponsonby, 25 Aug. 1890.
36 RA Vic. Add. N2/573, Oliphant to Ponsonby, 20 Sept. 1890.
37 Queen Victoria's Journal, 31 March 1891.
38 RA Vic. Add., U32, Queen Victoria to Princess Royal, 1 April, 1891.
39 RA Vic. Add., A/12/1768, Prince of Wales to Ponsonby, 4 April, 1891.
40 RA Vic. Add. A/12/1770, Ponsonby to Prince of Wales, 9 April 1891.
41 RA Vic. Add. A/12/1773, Prince of Wales to Ponsonby, 12 April 1891.
42 RA Vic. Add. N2/586, Henniker to Ponsonby, 8 May 1891.
43 RA Vic. Add. N2/587, Oliphant to Ponsonby, 9 Aug. 1891.
44 RA Vic. Add. N2/589, Oliphant to Ponsonby, 17 Oct. 1892.
45 RA Vic. Add. N2/591, Oliphant to Ponsonby, 1 Feb. 1893.
46 RA 010/108, Oliphant to Ponsonby, 29 April 1893.
47 RA Vic. Add. N2/592, Oliphant to Ponsonby, 18 April 1893.
48 RA 010/108, Oliphant to Ponsonby, 29 April 1893.
49 Ibid.
50 RA Vic. Add. N2/594, Oliphant to Ponsonby, 15 July 1893.
51 RA J89/25, Dufferin to Queen Victoria, 15 Oct. 1893.
52 RA 010/121, Oliphant to Ponsonby, 29 Oct. 1893.
53 RA Vic. Add. N2/608, Oliphant to Ponsonby, 29 Oct. 1893.
54 RA 010/116, Dufferin to Rosebery. Telegram, 23 Oct. 1893.
55 RA Z457/170, Prince of Wales to Queen Victoria, 24 Oct. 1893.
56 RA 010/119, Queen Victoria to Victor Duleep Singh, 28 Oct. 1893.
57 The Standard (London), 30 Oct. 1893.

Index

Duleep Singh—*contd.*

marries Bamba Müller, 98–9,
  100–1, 102–9
to Scotland and Egypt with
  Bamba, 109
return to India projected by
  (*see also* ruler/guru *above*),
  115, 148, 169, 174–5, 176,
  178–9, 180, 182–4, 187–9,
  190, 192–5, 199, 203–9,
  210–12, 226–7, 237–9, 247–8
his morals, 116–17, 169, 191
and politics, 117–19, 164–5
a peerage proposed, 118–20
studies Sikh history, 120
composes an opera, 121
a whist player, 130
rank and title to be
  relinquished?, 144–5, 146
jewels etc. sold by, 169–72, 207
a justice of the peace, 174
rejects Christianity for the
  Sikh religion, 178, 179,
  180–2, 187–8, 201–2, 206,
  221–2
and Russia, 178–9, 211,
  228–33, 236–7, 250–76
  passim, 288
offers to join Indian Army,
  184–6
embarks for India, 209
arrested at Aden, 212–26
sails for France, 226
in Paris, 228
his proclamations to the Sikhs,
  233–6, 239–45, 248, 278,
  282–5
official plans for his family,
  248–50, 289, 291
and Fenians, 250–1
meets Ada Wetherill, 251
writes to Victor, 261–3
writes to friends, 263–5
and death of Bamba, 266–7

his children by Ada, 268, 296,
  301
returns to Paris, 277
marries Ada, 281
paralysed by a stroke, 285
negotiates reconciliation,
  285–93
returns to England, 291
in Aix, Nice, Paris and
  Algiers, 292–8
his death, 298
his funeral, 300

Duleep Singh, Ada (*née*
  Wetherill)
to Russia with D., 251, 253
pregnant, 268
her daughter Paulina, 268,
  298, 301
marries, D., pregnant again,
  281
meets Arthur Oliphant, 284
to Folkestone with D., 291
not received by Queen
  Victoria, 293–4
her daughter Ada, 296, 301
at D.'s funeral, 300
her death, 301

Duleep Singh, Ada Irene Helen
  Beryl, 296, 301

Duleep Singh, Bamba (*née*
  Müller), 23
meets D. while at Cairo
  mission school, 100–1
plans for marriage, 100–1,
  102–5, 108–9
her appearance and character,
  103, 105, 106–7
marries D., 105–6
to Scotland and Egypt with
  D., 109
received by Queen Victoria,
  113
her children, 114; *see also
  individual names*

Queen Victoria bestows
  'Crown of India', 122
depressed, ill, 187, 249, 249–50
allowance made to, 248
said to be heartbroken, 262
her death, 265–7
Duleep Singh, Bamba Sofia
  Jindan, 27
  born, 114
  and Elveden, 280
  her disposition, mentality, 280,
    295, 296–7
  at Dresden and Oxford, 291,
    295
  in Switzerland, 296
  at D.'s funeral, 300
  her marriage and death, 301
Duleep Singh, Catherine Hilda,
  114, 280, 291, 295, 300, 27
Duleep Singh, Edward Albert
  Alexander, 114, 291, 296–7,
  27
Duleep Singh, Frederick Victor,
  25
  born, 114
  to Aden with D., 214
  official plans for, 248–9
  and Elveden, 280
  at Folkestone with D., 291
  in Algiers with D., 296
  seeks house for D. in London,
    298
  at D.'s funeral, 300
  his death, 301
Duleep Singh, Paulina
  Alexandra, 268, 298, 301
Duleep Singh, Sophia
  Alexandra, 114, 291, 300, 27
Duleep Singh, Victor Albert Jay,
  26, 28
  born and christened, 114
  Queen Victoria requests
    portrait, 129
  to Aden with D., 214–15

official plans for, 248–9
his debts, 261, 286
opposes D.'s 'mad schemes',
  279–80, 285–6
and Elveden, 280
with D. in Paris and England,
  290–1
in Algiers with D., 296
difficulties with D., 298
at D.'s funeral, 300
his marriage and death, 301
Durand, Henry Mortimer, 223,
  272

East India Company, 1, 66, 71
Edward, Prince (Prince of
  Wales)
  makes friends with D. at
    Osborne, 53
  and Princess Gouramma, 77,
    85
  his marriage, 96
  at Elveden, 111, 24
  and death of Bamba, 266–7
  and D.'s second wife, 293–4
  and death of D., 299, 300
  mentioned, 81
Edwardes, Sir Herbert, 6, 151
Egypt
  D. meets first wife in, 98,
    100–1
  D.'s projected visit to, from
    Aden, 215, 217
Eliot, Henry, 11–12, 13
Ellenborough, Lord, 3
Elliott, Sergeant, 68–9
Elveden, rector of, 192
Elveden Hall, 20, 21, 24
  D.'s purchase of, mortgage on,
    97, 110, 114
  refurbished by D., 110–11,
    159, 162
  game, shooting, at, 111–13,
    186

321

Jamul-ud-Din, 269
Jay, Osborne, 119–20
Jay, Rev. William, 38, 114
Jewahir Singh, 4, 44
Jindan Kour, Rani, 2, 2, 17
  and power struggles in
    Punjab, 3–5
  and British in Punjab, 6–8, 10,
    21
  in Nepal, 19, 87
  D. 'protected' from, 24–5
  D.'s visit to, in India, 86, 87,
    89–90
  to England with D., 91–5, 96
  death of, 97
  cremated, 101
Jung Bahadur, 19, 33, 87
Jutes, 40–1, 56

Kashmir, 5
Katkoff, Mikhail Nikiforovich,
  251, 253, 256, 267, 268
Keppel, Admiral (first Earl of
  Albemarle), 110
Khalsa, 188
Kimberley, Lord,
  and D.'s financial affairs,
    167–8, 175, 176, 197, 198,
    202–4
  and D.'s visit to India, 174,
    176, 185–6, 208, 211–12
  and D.'s arrest at Aden, 241
  sends representative to D.'s
    funeral, 300
  mentioned, 226
Knollys, Sir Francis, 179
Koh-i-noor, 15
  given to Queen Victoria, 12,
    13, 15
  shown to D. by Queen
    Victoria, 46–9
  D.'s claim to, 94, 136, 145,
    178, 278–9
Kotzbue, Wilhelm, 232–3

Kour, Jindan, see Jindan Kour
Kuhlberg, General, 268

Lahore, Treaty of, 5
Lansdowne, Lord, 286
Lawrence, (Sir) Henry, 6–9, 11,
  14, 16, 68, 5, 8
Lawrence, Sir John, 95
Lawson, Dr, 249
Le Blanc, Léonide, 116
Leicester, Lord, 111, 191, 24
Leopold, Prince, 53, 179
Leslie-Melville, Ronald (later
  Lord Leven)
  makes friends with D. in
    Scotland, 61
  on the Continent with D., 67,
    68
  and D.'s marriage, 103
  D. to enter politics?, 117
  and D.'s visit to India, 174–5
  visits D. in Paris, 287–8
  and pardon for D., 288, 289
  and D.'s funeral, 300
  mentioned, 107, 130, 135
Leven, Lady, 107–8, 113
Leven, Lord (half-brother of
  Ronald Leslie-Melville,
  q.v.), 107
Lind, Jenny (Mme
  Goldschmidt), 108
Login, Edwy, 107, 300
Login, Dr (later Sir) John, 9
  appointed D.'s
    'superintendent', 14
  with D. in India, 14–17,
    19–20, 21–7, 32–3, 35–40
  on Rani Jindan, 19, 24–5
  Queen Victoria on, 45, 46
  with D. in England, 55–6,
    59–61
  knighted, 57
  house at Kew, 59
  with D. to the Continent, 67